I0813548

The Art of Gluten-Free Bread

Country White Cheese Bread (left) and Country White Sourdough Bread

The Art of Gluten-Free Bread

Groundbreaking Recipes for Artisanal Breads and Pastries

Aran Goyoaga

ARTISAN / NEW YORK

—

Library of Congress Control Number: 2025933483

ISBN 978-1-64829-202-6 (hardcover)
ISBN 978-1-64829-549-2 (ebook)

—

Design by Amanda Jane Jones

Published by Artisan,
an imprint of Workman Publishing,
a division of Hachette Book Group, Inc.
1290 Avenue of the Americas
New York, NY 10104
artisanbooks.com

Printed in China (APO) on responsibly sourced paper

10 9 8 7 6 5 4 3

This book is dedicated to my family and all of you who have supported my work and have bought my books through the years.

I couldn't have made this book without you.

Sourdough Salted Miso Baguett

Contents

Sourdough Focaccia

Introduction

Welcome, dear reader, to a journey that's close to my heart—the art of gluten-free bread baking. As a former pastry chef, I started my career carrying fifty pounds of wheat flour on my shoulders, breathing and living gluten. My transition to gluten-free baking was both a challenge and a revelation. When I embarked on this path nearly two decades ago, after developing debilitating health issues, I yearned for the crusty loaves and tender crumb of the breads of my childhood. I missed the satisfying chew of a rustic country loaf, the delicate layers of a croissant, the comforting softness of a dinner roll. I spent years recipe testing, learning about gluten-free flours, experimenting, and developing new techniques. I soon realized that I could bake gluten-free breads that had all those textures that I had missed and discovered a whole new world of flavors along the way.

In this book, I am excited to share with you the magic that happens when we make breads with alternative grains and flours—how the nuttiness of teff, the subtle sweetness of sorghum, or the earthy notes of buckwheat can create breads with depth and character that rival, and often surpass, their wheat-based counterparts. In these pages, I will teach you how to grow a gluten-free sourdough starter to infuse bread with the complex, developed flavors that come from slow fermentation. I will teach you to craft a loaf with tender and moist crumb and to achieve the coveted crackle of a well-baked crust. There are also recipes using baker's yeast for the times when you need to get a bread on the table quickly. I have drawn inspiration for the breads from my heritage as well as my travels and other global bread traditions: from the golden brioche of my childhood, the olive-studded fougasses and croissants of France, the crispy fermented dosa of India, sourdough pizza and focaccia of Italy, to the soft and tender challah from Israel and sesame-studded Jerusalem bagels. This book is a celebration of possibility, of the beauty that emerges when we embrace new ingredients and techniques. It's about creating breads that are not just good for gluten-free eaters but are also perfect for anyone who loves *good* bread. These are breads that stand on their own—nourishing, delicious, and deeply satisfying—no matter your dietary preferences.

MY JOURNEY

The nostalgic bread memories from my childhood were inextricably linked to another major influence—my family's deep roots in the pastry tradition. I grew up immersed in flour, butter, and sugar, as my grandparents, Angel Ayarza and Miren Gaztelu, operated our renowned family pastry shop, Pastelería Ayarza, in the heart of Amorebieta (in Basque Country in Northern Spain) since 1949. My grandparents lived in the flat right above the shop, which we lovingly called "upstairs," with the pastelería being "downstairs." The entire family pitched in—my parents, aunts, uncles, cousins, and I were the built-in cheap labor force, my mother would joke. Weekends meant delivering pastries around town on foot, while after-school hours were spent doing homework amid the aromas of our famous bollos de mantequilla (brioche buns filled with buttercream), tartas de arroz (custard tarts), palmeras (palmiers), and shortbread assortments. I vividly recall helping my grandmother meticulously chop day-old bollos for Napoleon tarts, spreading jam on shortbread cookies, or peeling the almonds she had just blanched. Despite all this, bread remained distinctly separate from our pastry domain back then. Bakers made bread and pastry chefs made pastry. While both traded in viennoiserie like brioche and croissants, a pastry chef's versions were refined, delicate works of art compared to the rustic, bread-like incarnations from the bakers. Those childhood experiences cemented baking's irreplaceable role in my life from an early age. Little did I know that, decades later, baking would become the catalyst for profound personal transformation.

Bread was an enigma that eluded me for most of my life. While my grandfather occasionally baked for our family, the loaves were unremarkable—bread was something we bought, not made. It wasn't until culinary school, under the tutelage of German master baker Manfred Schmidtke, that I finally unraveled the mysteries of bread during an entire quarter dedicated to its craft. Later, as a pastry cook at the Ritz-Carlton Palm Beach, I had the privilege of observing Chef Johann Willar's bread team at work. Though our shifts barely overlapped, I watched, inquired, and tried to absorb as much as I could, yet never actively made bread there—a regret that lingers to this day.

It was when I left the professional kitchen to raise my children, burned out and directionless, that I faced a pivotal health crisis. "You have genetic gluten and casein intolerance," the doctor's words echoed, providing relief in finally identifying one of the root causes of my autoimmune disorders. In an instant, those warm bread memories came to the forefront. How could I re-create the comforting aromas, the chewy interiors, the crackly crusts, without gluten? In hindsight, this moment ignited a new purpose within me—a drive to make an impact by teaching others how to cook and bake without gluten.

What followed was an arduous journey of experimentation in my home kitchen, born from an urgent need to heal, as well as a deep-rooted passion for bread's craft. Early attempts were disheartening—cake-like batters, dry pucks, and gummy loaves. I persisted, motivated by romantic recollections of past breads and my unwavering belief that pleasure and nutrition need not be mutually exclusive for those who cannot consume gluten. I tweaked, researched, and innovated gluten-free recipes until, finally, I found my way back to the bread I loved—loaves with the promised "lift," the faint tang of sourdough cultures, crispy scored tops, flaky croissants, and ineffable comfort in every tender bite. This book is the culmination of that quest. Each recipe is a testament to the transformative power of time, patience, and passion. Making bread is a ritual; a space of meditation and creativity.

How to Use This Book

The book is divided into eight chapters, covering everything from sourdough breads, breads using baker's yeast, enriched breads, and flatbreads to holiday bakes. There is also an entire chapter where you will find recipes that use up sourdough discard, as well as another on sandwiches, soups, dips, salads, and more.

The recipes on these pages are completely gluten- and dairy-free, although I do include dairy options since I realize some of you tolerate dairy proteins without issue and likely prefer it that way. I started creating the recipes with the intention of also making them completely egg-free and vegan-friendly, but I had to make some compromises and use eggs occasionally. Nearly all the breads, except the enriched ones, such as those using Danish Dough (page 222) or Quickest Buttery Brioche (page 208), are eggless as written. The Vegan Brioche (page 220) can be used in place of the egg-containing one; it is not as fluffy and soft without the eggs, but it's a good one. Please read How to Replace Eggs (page 26) for more details.

Too often, gluten-free breads rely on a heavy amount of starches and gums to provide elasticity and softness. I am hyperaware of this dilemma. I want my recipes to be as wholesome and nutrient-rich as possible. Breads such as the starch-free Nordic-Style Seed Bread (page 66), Flourless Fermented Buckwheat and Red Lentil Bread (page 79), or Seeded Whole-Grain Teff Sourdough Boule (page 61) are examples of this. On the other hand, I also want to offer recipes that need starches and sugar to achieve their best texture and lift. A gluten-free croissant is the one recipe I have been asked for most frequently, and I am happy to offer it in this book (see page 234). Recipes like Chocolatines (page 239), Tahini-Marzipan Challah (page 342), and Pain de Mie (page 159), where a lighter and softer crumb is desired, require starch. Hopefully you will find a wide array of recipes you enjoy.

Before you start making any recipe in this book, I encourage you to read How to Be a Successful Gluten-Free Bread Baker (page 14). There is a lot of important information in there that will set you up for success, especially when it comes to different ingredients and techniques. If there is one ingredient that will make or break your bread recipes, it is psyllium. Pay special attention to it (see page 24) and purchase the best quality you are able to.

Whether you're newly diagnosed with celiac disease, have a gluten sensitivity, or simply want to learn about new ingredients and techniques, this book will empower you to fill your kitchen with the irresistible aroma and taste of freshly baked bread. Get ready to rediscover the joy of breaking bread with family and friends, and to create loaves that are so delicious, no one will believe they're gluten-free.

Sourdough Brioche

How to Be a Successful Gluten-Free Bread Baker

Bread baking requires equal parts precision and intuition; weigh your ingredients, understand the purpose and characteristics of each ingredient, follow the steps as written, and eventually, through repetition, you will develop an intuition about your doughs that will let you make your own adjustments. The following lists present a breakdown of the tools, ingredients, and bread-baking steps in more detail.

EQUIPMENT AND BAKING TOOLS

Bench knife and bowl scraper. A bench knife is a rectangle or square metal scraper, usually with a wooden handle, that is perfect for cutting dough and scraping any remnants of dough from your work surface. It is the perfect cleanup tool and really versatile in the kitchen beyond bread baking. A bowl scraper is similar but more flexible, and usually does not have a handle. It is made out of plastic and it's perfect for handling dough as well as shaping.

Bread knife. Don't let your bread knife be an afterthought. It is an important tool, and getting a good one will avoid wrecking the beautiful freshly baked loaf you made. Look for an offset serrated bread knife with a relatively thin blade. This allows you to apply pressure from the top without bumping into the loaf.

Combo cooker. A combo cooker is a cast-iron skillet with a shallow pot that fits tightly on top, both with handles. The dough is inverted from the proofing basket into the skillet, and the pot is set on top and acts as a lid. The combo cooker is easier to use than a Dutch oven, the depth of which makes getting dough in and out awkward and leaves the baker at risk of burning themselves. My favorite combo cooker is from Lodge (see Resources, page 390); it's inexpensive and will last years with proper care.

Digital scale. You will need a digital scale to make the breads in this book because no volume measures are provided for flours and other key ingredients. I cannot emphasize enough the importance of weighing ingredients in baking, particularly in gluten-free baking where there is such inconsistency of milling across flour brands. I have weighed 1 cup of brown rice flour from different manufacturers to find variance in the weight amounts. Weighing gives you accuracy and control. It is also less messy. You place your bowl on your scale and add ingredients directly into it without making a mess on your counter or having to clean measuring cups. I prefer a heavy-duty metal scale with a lifted platform, but a flat one will work as well.

Digital thermometer. You can bake bread without a digital thermometer, but it is very useful to measure water temperature when mixing dough and also the internal bread temperature after baking. Compact folding thermometers are inexpensive and take little space in your tool drawer.

Dutch oven. A Dutch oven is a deep cast-iron pot with a lid. They are heavy and will last you years with proper care. They are often enamel-coated, but for bread-baking purposes, I prefer one that isn't. My favorite Dutch oven is a 5.5-quart (5.2 L) Lodge that is similar to a combo cooker but without long handles. In a traditional Dutch oven, you have to lower the dough into the bottom of the pot, which can be tricky and can lead to burns, which is why a combo cooker is the best option for bread.

Lame or razor blade. Lame (pronounced "lahm") is the French word for blade. It is a handheld tool that holds a double-edged razor blade. It is used to score the top of bread dough to create decorative designs but also, more importantly, to allow the bread to expand properly while baking and not crack in unwanted places. Lames come in various shapes, but my favorites are a wooden circular one that holds the blade in a straight position on one end and a wooden handle with a metal top where a flexible razor blade is inserted, creating a curve. I use the straight razor blade for detailed decorative work and the curved blade for baguettes or when I want to score deeply. I highly recommend scoring your bread with a lame rather than a knife as the cuts will be much sharper, thinner, and more precise.

Loaf pans. The recipes in this book call for a loaf pan that is 8 ½ by 4½ inches (22 by 11 cm) or alternatively a 9-by-4-inch (23 by 10 cm)

Pullman loaf pan. The difference between the two is that Pullman pans have straight sides compared to the slightly slanted sides of loaf pans. I bake in Pullman pans especially because the narrower sides offer a bit more support for gluten-free dough while it rises. I also prefer the look of the narrow and tall loaf of bread that the Pullman pan creates. Invest in heavy-duty metal pans, such as Chicago Metal or USA Pan. They should feel sturdy and have some weight to them. Do not use glass or silicone pans for bread baking.

Oven. Your oven will have a big impact on your bread. In general, I don't like gas ovens for bread baking as they don't heat as evenly as electric ones. Fan ovens or convection ovens tend to dry out baked goods, so I would recommend avoiding baking in convection when possible. I have a Miele (see Resources, page 390) dual-fuel range, meaning it has a gas stovetop and an electric oven. It is 36 inches (91 cm) wide, which means I can fit a standard half-sheet pan in there next to a quarter-sheet pan (but not a full sheet, as is used in professional ovens). It has a steam-injection function, which yields beautiful breads when I am baking directly on sheet pans and not in a Dutch oven. All the recipes in this book were tested in this Miele oven on a conventional setting.

Oven gloves. Regular oven gloves are not thick enough to withstand holding flaming-hot Dutch ovens. Invest in a pair of heat-resistant, rubberized, forearm-length oven gloves rated to 500°F (260°C) for best protection. You will thank me.

Oven thermometer. You shouldn't blindly trust your oven's temperature setting. I have had instances where my oven said it was preheated to 450°F (230°C), but I could tell as soon as I opened the door that it was not really that hot in there. I recommend having an oven thermometer inside to make sure you know exactly *how* hot it is and *when* your oven has reached the desired temperature. You might have to set your oven to a slightly higher or lower temperature if your oven is not properly calibrated. Let the oven heat for at least 15 minutes to the set temperature before transferring anything to it to make sure the oven walls are truly heated and retain the heat even after you open the door to place a pan inside.

Proofing basket or banneton. A banneton is a basket, usually made from bamboo or rattan, used to proof dough. It usually comes with a linen cloth that lines the inside, but in general, I prefer to dust the inside of the basket with some bench flour (generally rice flour) and place the dough directly in it. Because gluten-free dough tends to expand sideways more than it does upward, I like baskets that are as narrow as possible to give the dough a taller appearance. I use 7- and 8-inch (18 cm and 20 cm) round baskets to make a boule (round) and a 9-inch (23 cm) oval to make a batard. After each use, I scrape the inside of the basket with a stiff dusting brush and knock out excess flour. Because many of the breads in this book are high-moisture doughs, it's important to let the basket dry out well so mold doesn't grow on it.

Silicone mat. This is definitely an optional item but one that I have been using for enriched doughs. A large silicone mat will help you roll sticky enriched doughs. Mine is 26 by 16 inches (66 by 41 cm) and has ruler markings in both inches and centimeters on the edges of the mat, which really help when rolling out doughs.

Stand mixer. You don't necessarily need a stand mixer to mix your dough, but it does help get it smoother more quickly, especially with enriched breads that have eggs and butter. I have a 6-quart (5.6 L) refurbished KitchenAid stand mixer (see Resources, page 390) that is twenty years old and has never given me any trouble. They truly are an investment that will last you years.

INGREDIENTS AND PANTRY STAPLES

This list includes the ingredients you will find throughout the book. Once you learn the protein content and water-absorption properties of different flours, you can easily switch up one flour for another.

FLOURS

There are many gluten-free flours in the world, and deciding which ones to purchase to stock your pantry can be overwhelming. The flours listed here are the ones you will see used in these recipes and they tend to be my go-tos.

I divide gluten-free flours into two categories: whole-grain flours and starchy flours. The real magic in gluten-free baking comes from having the right balance of whole-grain and starchy flours to yield the right structure, elasticity, airy crumb, and moisture specific to each recipe. The higher the whole-grain flour content the more flavorful and dense your bread will be. Adding some starch to your recipe will create bread that is airy, open, and a crumb that "pulls" a bit more. However, use too much starch and your bread will be gummy and inedible. Every bread recipe in this book has been written and tweaked so that the whole-grain flour and starch ratio is adequate for the final texture and structure I envisioned. In broad terms, I find that a recipe using about 70% whole-grain flour and 30% starch flour yields bread that has great structure, flavor, and open crumb, although this will vary depending on the recipe. In these pages, you'll find a whole array of breads from dense and textural like the Seeded Whole-Grain Teff Sourdough Boule (page 61) or Mini Whole-Grain Walnut Baguettes (page 172) to something airy with an open crumb like the Sourdough Ciabatta Rolls (page 93) or Rosemary Focaccia (page 266).

WHOLE-GRAIN FLOURS

Whole-grain flours provide protein, elasticity, and flavor. The protein content will never compare to that of gluten, of course, but there is still protein in whole-grain flours. There is also a variance in how elastic the different whole-grain flours can be. You can subdivide them into two categories: flours that add elasticity and chew to your bread, such as buckwheat, teff, and oat, and those flours that dry out and set your crumb, such as brown rice. Sorghum, millet, and chestnut are somewhere in the middle. Whole-grain flours absorb more water than starch flours (see chart, page 23). There are also some flours listed that are technically not grains (buckwheat, cassava, and chestnut), but I added them in this category for simplicity. I encourage you to stick to the flours I list in each recipe, but if you must replace one for some reason, check the chart and substitute flours in a similar category of protein content and water absorption. For example, you may replace sorghum with millet, but you will likely have a dough that is somewhat moister. In that case, reduce the water amount by 10% and add more if needed while you are mixing the dough.

Milling your grains at home is always ideal since freshly milled flour will have the freshest natural oils, enzymes, and minerals, but for practical purposes and to replicate the results of most home bakers, I wrote the recipes in this book using store-bought milled flour. Flours that are triple-milled and labeled as superfine will always work best because they hydrate much better, resulting in better crumb and crust.

Brown rice flour. The recipes in this book call for superfine brown rice flour. It is not imperative you use superfine brown rice flour, but it will greatly improve the texture of your bread if you do. Brown rice is a hard grain to mill finely, and you will not be able to take stone-ground brown rice flour and make it superfine by running it in your blender. You might be able to get it to a fine texture by triple-milling it in a high-quality grain mill and sifting it in between. The finer this flour is, the better results you will achieve. Brown rice flour has a mild, slightly sweet flavor that works very well in bread recipes. It is also the base of my most-used sourdough starter, the Whole-Grain Brown Rice–Teff Sourdough Starter (page 48). It is not a very elastic flour, so I wouldn't use it on its own, but it works very well in combination with more elastic flours, such as buckwheat and oat.

Buckwheat flour. Despite its name, buckwheat is not a grain and is therefore suitable for grain-free baking. It's a fruit seed with an earthy flavor. In the United States, some of the most widely available buckwheat flours tend to have extra hull in them, making them darker in color, denser, and with an overpowering earthiness. I prefer lighter buckwheat flour, which is a light beige color (with a tinge of green) and a slightly less pronounced earthy flavor. If you want to make your own buckwheat flour without a mill, raw hulled buckwheat groats (not toasted ones or kasha) are very soft and easy to grind in a high-powered blender.

Cassava flour. Cassava flour is also a grain-free flour. It is made by peeling, drying, and grinding the entire yuca root. It is light in color; look for flours that are very finely milled (unfortunately cassava flour is also one that can be very inconsistent across flour brands). Its mild taste reminds me slightly of wheat. It is elastic and starchier than the rest of the whole-grain flours in this list. Cassava flour adds tenderness to bread. It also absorbs a lot of moisture and if you use using too much of it in bread, it could make it gummy.

Chestnut flour. Chestnut, which is a nut, not a grain, is made into flour by milling dried and roasted sweet chestnuts. It lends a nutty, slightly sweet, and earthy flavor to anything it is added to, and it is

How to Make Chestnut Flour at Home

Preheat the oven to 350°F (180°C). Carefully cut whole chestnuts in half (no need to peel outer shell) with a large kitchen knife and arrange on a sheet pan cut-side up. Bake for 35 minutes. Let the chestnuts cool completely, then peel off the shells and papery inner skins. Working in small batches, grind the chestnuts in a high-powered blender until you have a coarse meal. Spread the chestnut meal on sheet pans and dry in a low oven at 125°F (50°C), turning every hour or so, until completely dried. Again pulverize the meal in a high-powered blender, or ideally a grain mill, until you have a fine flour. Store the chestnut flour in a tightly sealed container for up to 6 months.

great for grain-free baking. It can usually be found in specialty food markets and can be a bit pricey, but you can also make your own.

Millet flour. Millet flour is a mildly sweet flour with a creamy yellow color. It pairs well with flours that have an earthier flavor like buckwheat or teff. I tend to use sorghum more commonly than millet, but I give it as an option here because it is a flour extensively used in some parts of the world, especially Eastern Europe.

Oat flour. Oat flour is a sweet, high-protein, high-elasticity whole-grain flour that makes excellent bread. In the US, it is easy to find certified gluten-free oat flour, but in certain parts of the world, oat flour is not considered suitable for those with celiac disease and those with gluten intolerance. It is also possible to be allergic to avenin (the protein in oats) even in certified gluten-free oats. If you cannot have oats, substitute with light buckwheat flour. The flavor profile is different, but buckwheat provides similar elasticity.

Sorghum flour. This slightly sweet, wheat-y tasting, and light yellow flour is high in protein and works well with other whole-grain flours. It is original to Africa. It grows well in the US, but it seems to be harder to find in parts of Europe. You can use millet in its place, although millet absorbs somewhat less water.

Teff flour. Teff is a nutrient-dense flour that originates in Ethiopia. It is the flour used in traditional Ethiopian injera. Its flavor is earthy and sour, making it a great addition to your sourdough starter and sourdough breads. Teff flour is high in protein and fairly elastic. You can find ivory or brown teff flours in the market; all the recipes in this book were created with the ivory variety.

STARCHY FLOURS

Starchy flours have a low protein content and very fine particles that can improve the dough, creating a fluffy, tender, and airy crumb. There are multiple starchy flours; here are the ones I use the most.

Potato starch. Potato starch, not to be confused with potato flour, provides a soft and tender crumb. It is a very finely milled and dense flour. If you cannot have potatoes, substitute the amount the recipe calls for with cornstarch. If you cannot have cornstarch, replace potato starch with half tapioca starch and half whatever other whole-grain flour is in the recipe. The final texture will not be the same, but the bread will come together.

Sweet white rice flour. Sweet white rice flour or glutinous flour is made from grinding short-grain rice. Just like brown rice flour, it is a hard grain to mill, so seek out the brands that say superfine on their label. The final texture will be much less gritty and your dough will hydrate better. It is very stretchy and elastic like tapioca starch and can also make breads gummy if used in excess.

Tapioca starch. Tapioca starch is extracted from the yuca root. It helps bind and create a crisp thin crust in your bread. Tapioca starch becomes very stretchy when mixed with water and too much of it in a recipe will result in a gummy crumb. Cornstarch and arrowroot are good substitutes for tapioca (although somewhat less stretchy).

Importance of Finely Milled Flours and Milling Your Own Flour

One of the most frustrating things about writing gluten-free baking recipes is the inconsistencies among flour brands when it comes to milling. Because my favorite brands won't necessarily be available in your location, as much as possible, I encourage you to shop for flours labeled as fine or superfine. Stone-ground flours have larger flour particles that don't hydrate the same way, resulting in less elasticity and coarser crust and crumb texture. You will likely have to order some flours online (see Resources, page 390) and they are going be a bit more expensive, but they are worth it.

Milling your own flour allows you to have control over the quality of the grains, making it more nutritious and fresher than flour that has been sitting in a bag for a while. However, for this book, I used packaged flour due to potential inconsistencies when testing and writing recipes. If you have a mill at home, make sure that you triple-mill and sift your harder grains, especially rice (both white and brown). Rolled oats and buckwheat groats are the softest and easiest to mill at home.

Storing Flours and Dry Goods

I store all my flours in large glass jars (anywhere between 8 ounces/225 ml and 2 quarts/1.9 L) in a dry and cool place away from direct sunlight. As soon as I bring the flour home, I take it out of the package and transfer it into the jars. I do the same with grains, nuts and seeds, dried fruit, and anything that will go in the dry goods pantry. The jars are labeled with the ingredient name. This allows me to see clearly all the ingredients I have and how much I have of them. I understand the efficiency of buying flours in bulk, but I rarely do because I cannot quite trust the freshness.

BINDERS

Gluten-free bread would simply not rise without binders. Along with the starches, the binders listed here provide elasticity, which helps dough expand when the gases that are released during fermentation are trapped.

Flaxseed meal. Flaxseed meal is made by finely milling flaxseeds. It provides additional elasticity to the dough without making it gummy and that is why I use it in combination with psyllium in many recipes. However, it doesn't have the strength and water-absorption capacity of psyllium, so you cannot simply replace the same quantity of psyllium with flaxseed. Just like with psyllium, make sure your

Whole-Grain Flour and Starch Characteristics

Gluten-Free Flour or Starch	Protein Content	Hydration Capacity	Flavor Profile
BROWN RICE FLOUR	Medium	Medium-high	Mildly sweet
BUCKWHEAT FLOUR	Medium-high	Medium-high	Earthy, nutty, bitter
CASSAVA FLOUR	Low	High	Mildly sweet
CHESTNUT FLOUR	Low	Medium	Sweet, nutty
MILLET FLOUR	Medium-high	Medium	Mildly sweet
OAT FLOUR	High	High	Mildly sweet, nutty, milky
SORGHUM FLOUR	Medium-high	Medium-high	Mildly sweet, slightly earthy
TEFF FLOUR	High	High	Earthy, molasses-like
POTATO STARCH	Low	Low	Mild
SWEET WHITE RICE FLOUR	Low	Medium	Mildly sweet
TAPIOCA STARCH	Low	Low	Mild

flaxseed meal is finely milled so it completely absorbs the liquid in the recipe.

Psyllium husk powder. Undoubtedly, psyllium is the star of gluten-free bread baking. It can absorb large quantities of water (much more than xanthan gum), which in turn creates an open and airy crumb, as well as a chewy crust. Psyllium creates a dough that feels like traditional bread—it can be kneaded, shaped, is bouncy, and spongy. As soon as psyllium touches water, it will immediately begin gelling, which is why it's very important to whisk your psyllium into your liquid right away (the warmer your liquid, the faster it will gel). In most of my recipes, the psyllium is whisked into water or milk to create a gel before adding it to the dry ingredients. For some of the recipes, the psyllium is whisked into the sponge. Only in a couple of recipes is the psyllium added straight into the dry ingredients without creating a gel first. This has mostly to do with how much water there is in the recipe. Psyllium needs about ten times its weight in water to able to create a gel without it becoming a solid mess that sets too fast. If you don't have enough water, the psyllium will be hard to break down, leaving you with chunks that are difficult to incorporate into the dough. It is very hard to replace psyllium in a recipe without having to adjust the water content. If you are allergic to psyllium, you can use a combination of xanthan gum and ground chia seeds, but you will definitely need to tweak the liquid in the recipe.

VERY IMPORTANT ---->

Make sure that you are using psyllium husk powder and not whole husks, and shop for brands that are ideal for baking and are lighter in color. Much of the psyllium you find at supermarkets is sold for digestive issues, is usually not very pure, and tints the dough with a beige-purple color. If your psyllium is not very pure, it will not absorb all the water in the recipe and your dough will end up being wet and not bouncy. If you are unsure how pure your psyllium husk powder is, reduce the amount of water in the recipe by 10% and then add more as you need it. Finally, note that too much psyllium can make your bread gummy.

Xanthan gum. Xanthan gum also binds dough together, but it works slightly differently than psyllium. Xanthan gum works best for recipes where you don't need a lot of liquid, and it's best suited for lamination or when you are looking to create a flaky texture. For example, you need xanthan gum (in addition to psyllium) for Danish pastry, where the dough will be stretched, rolled, and laminated. In general terms, the binding power of 1 teaspoon of xanthan gum is about equivalent to 2 tablespoons of psyllium husk powder, but remember that you will have to adjust the liquid amount in your recipe. As a final note, xanthan gum has a bit of a bad reputation in the health and nutrition world. It can be difficult to digest and it's just not as natural as fibers like psyllium and flax. I try to avoid xanthan gum as much as possible, but there are some instances where I use it because it does help create structure and elasticity. You can omit it from a recipe if I list it as optional; otherwise, keep it in or your recipe will not come together.

BAKER'S YEAST

Yeasts are single-celled microorganisms that are part of the fungus world. *Saccharomyces cerevisiae* is the species used commonly in bread baking. Commercial baker's yeast is cultivated under a controlled environment to create a consistent and fast-fermenting product.

I use active dry yeast in all the recipes that call for baker's yeast because it's the most widely available in the US. Active dry yeast consists of live yeast cells that are surrounded by some dead yeast cells. It needs to be proofed in warm liquid to remove the outer dead cells and to activate the live ones. Never heat your liquid higher than 115°F (46°C) or you could kill your yeast. Mixing a small amount of sugar in with the yeast and water allows for the yeast to activate faster, but know that you can activate yeast without sugar. Make sure that your yeast is not expired before using it. You could always test it to see how fresh it is by mixing a small amount in some warm water and making sure it is bubbly and that it does actually proof.

There is also instant yeast, which has finer granules than active dry yeast and can be added directly into the dry ingredients without having to proof it in warm liquid. Instant yeast is also about 20 percent more potent than active dry yeast, so you need 20 percent less (by weight) of it. Since instant yeast doesn't need to be dissolved in warm liquid, your dough temperature will be lower and that might slow down fermentation times slightly.

Fresh yeast or cake yeast is what I grew up using, but I have never seen it in any supermarket in the US. I absolutely love its smell and it immediately takes me back to my family's pastry shop in Spain. It is sold as a crumbly and soft block that needs to be refrigerated at all times. It is made of 100 percent living cells and must be dissolved with a little bit of warm liquid. If you can find it, use it in these recipes, but be sure to use double the amount (by weight) listed for active dry yeast.

DAIRY AND DAIRY ALTERNATIVES

Butter. For enriched doughs, and especially for laminated doughs such as Danish Dough (page 222), I prefer European-style butters, as they are higher in fat and have more elasticity.

Vegan butter. There is a wide variety of vegan butters on the market. Use butters that come specifically formulated for baking and not spreads that come in tubs, as these have higher water content. Not all vegan butters perform the same, so you might have to experiment with a few brands to see what you like best.

Oat milk. The recipes in this book have been tested using both whole cow's milk and oat milk (Oatly is my go-to). If you cannot tolerate oats or cow's milk, replace with nut milk, but make sure it contains no extra sweeteners or gums.

SALT

I use both sea salt and kosher salt in my bread recipes—both fine and slightly coarser. My preferred brand of kosher salt is Diamond Crystal. Different salts offer different degrees of minerality and

How to Replace Eggs

Many of the recipes in the book are egg-free as written or offer a substitute in the headnote. For enriched breads that use Sourdough Brioche (page 198) or Quickest Buttery Brioche (page 208), simply use the recipe for Vegan Brioche (page 220). For other enriched doughs using Danish Dough (page 222) or the Buckwheat and Cardamom Buns (page 307), you can replace the eggs with flax egg (see below). Unfortunately, the final lift and layering won't be as distinct and perfect as when using eggs, but the dough should come together. For a recipe like Sourdough Yorkshire Puddings or Popovers (page 149) or Pastry Cream (page 215), there is no substitute, as eggs are the absolute glue of it all.

Flax egg: To create 1 flax egg, which can substitute for 1 chicken egg, in a small bowl, whisk together 7 grams very finely ground flaxseed meal with 30 grams warm water until smooth. Let the mixture gel for 5 minutes, then add to your recipe.

flavor. Don't treat salt as an afterthought. Invest in great-quality, small-batch salt; you will notice the difference.

BAKER'S PERCENTAGE

Baker's percentage expresses a ratio, in percentages, of each ingredient's weight in relation to the total flour weight in the recipe. For example, if your recipe has 100 grams of flour (as a sum of all the gluten-free flours and starches in the recipe), 200 grams of milk, 50 grams of sugar, and 4 grams of yeast, the baker's percentages would be expressed as flour 100%, milk 200%, sugar 50%, and yeast 4%. This is how most professional bread bakers adapt recipes to accommodate larger yields, and it's an easy way to create variations. When I am creating recipes, I use baker's percentages, but I didn't include them in these recipes because they can seem overwhelming for the home baker. Break down a recipe to its baker's percentage so you can see the ratios of flour, water, and binder; use these ratios as a base for your formulations and experiments.

MIXING AND KNEADING

I mix my doughs in a stand mixer with the dough hook attachment, but these recipes can easily be mixed by hand. To do so, add the dry ingredients to a large bowl, make a well in the center, and pour the wet ingredients into it. Use your fingers to incorporate the wet ingredients into the dry slowly by grabbing some of the flour that is close to it, mixing, then adding some more. Eventually you will end up with a shaggy mass. Transfer this to a work surface and keep kneading until it comes together into a smooth dough. When you knead, you are not really developing gluten like in traditional bread baking (since there isn't any), but kneading does allow for the flour particles to hydrate and build some stretch. Depending on the flour and psyllium you are using, or how the flours were milled, your dough might need more or less water. It is easier to add water than to take it away. If you are unsure, hold back on 10% of the water listed in the recipe; make sure you allow for a couple of minutes of mixing and kneading, then finally add more water if needed.

TO AUTOLYZE OR NOT AUTOLYZE IN GLUTEN-FREE BREAD BAKING

Autolyze, also known as autolyse or autolysis, is a technique used in bread making that entails combining only the flour and water, then allowing for a rest period before adding yeast, salt, starters, or other ingredients. This is a technique used mainly in gluten-containing recipes because during the autolyze stage the enzymes in flour are activated, creating gluten bonds that result in a smoother and stronger dough. But is this step necessary in gluten-free bread recipes since there is no gluten to develop? I personally haven't seen an overall improvement in my bread results (in either crumb or crust) by adding an autolyze to the recipe steps. My sourdough bread recipes, even many using baker's yeast, start by creating a sponge. This is not technically an autolyze since we are introducing a starter or yeast, but it helps flour to hydrate well during that first stage, and a well-hydrated dough will yield a more open crumb. There is only one recipe in the book where I include an autolyze step and that is the Whole-Grain Sourdough Cinnamon-Raisin Loaf (page 96), but you could experiment with doing this in other recipes. Make your sponge and, before mixing all the dough ingredients, mix the whole-grain flours listed in the dough portion with part of the water, let them sit for at least an hour, and then mix with the remaining ingredients.

SHAPING AND ROLLING

You know those social media videos you see where highly hydrated, gluten-containing doughs are folded, laminated, and tucked a multitude of times? That will really not be possible with gluten-free doughs as there isn't the rubber-band effect that gluten creates. However, shaping your dough into a neat and tight ball is still important and I reference it in every recipe. If there are creases on the surface of your dough, those will open up while baking, creating cracks and uneven texture. Texture can be desirable in crusty-style breads, but not so much when dealing with tender products like challah or brioche.

To shape the dough into a tight ball, use the palm of your hand to fold one end of the dough over the middle. Rotate the dough ever so slightly counterclockwise, then fold again. Repeat several times until you have a rounded dough with a top that has several seams. Flip the dough upside down so the seam is now touching the work surface and use your hand to lightly rotate in a circular motion. This motion creates some friction with the work surface, sealing those seams. This works the same for larger doughs like boules or smaller pieces of dough.

If the recipe calls for rolling the dough, like for Sourdough Pizza Margherita (page 294) or any of the breads made with enriched doughs like brioche or Danish, you will notice that the outer edges of the dough tend to crack and split while rolling. Again, this happens because gluten-free doughs don't have much stretch. This is normal. I try to correct it by lightly patting the palms of my hands against those cracks, even if it doesn't eliminate it fully.

A note about bench flour. Bench flour is the flour that is sprinkled on a work surface to prevent the dough from sticking during kneading or shaping. For crusty breads where I want more texture, I use whatever whole-grain flour is already in the recipe. For tender breads, I like to use tapioca starch because it doesn't add much weight or texture to the surface of the dough.

PROOFING

Gluten-free doughs are much more finicky and delicate than gluten-containing doughs because of their lack of elasticity. Proper proofing is also not always apparent to the eye, especially with sourdough breads, so it requires a bit of practice to find the proper balance of time and temperature. Overproofing causes the dough to expand aggressively and then collapse because of lack of structure. In crusty doughs this will result in a big air pocket below the crust and a dense and gummy crumb. If your enriched dough has a compressed bottom, that is also likely caused by overproofing. On the contrary, if your dough is underproofed, you will not have enough aeration in the crumb.

Breads made with baker's yeast proof faster than those made with sourdough starter. The proofing times listed in the recipes are for environments that hover around 68°F (20°C). If your kitchen is warmer or you decide to proof in the oven at a higher temperature, know that your dough will proof more quickly. Breads made with baker's yeast rise in volume significantly. The dough is ready when it has nearly doubled and feels marshmallow-like to the touch, light and airy without being completely expanded and ready to collapse.

My oven has a proofing setting, which I set at 75°F (24°C). Just that bit of difference compared to my kitchen air temperature makes an impact, as starters, sponges, and doughs proof faster this way. If your oven doesn't have a proofing setting, you can easily re-create it. Place a small pot of boiling-hot water in the oven, then place your dough next to it. This creates a moist and warm environment for the dough to rise. As mentioned earlier, sourdough doughs don't always appear to have significantly increased in volume while proofing, yet they really expand in the oven while baking. They should feel slightly lighter to the touch even if not puffed up.

You can also slow down fermentation by proofing doughs in the fridge, also known as retarding fermentation. This can be done in the bulk fermentation step (for example, with enriched doughs like brioche or Danish), but also once the dough has been shaped (for example, proofing the shaped sourdough boules in their baskets in the fridge for up to 12 hours or more). Colder fermentation develops the yeast flavor in recipes using baker's yeast, and in sourdough breads, it promotes a more acidic profile. Cold fermentation also improves dough hydration, making it slightly more elastic, and also helps retain the shape of the dough while baking. In my experience, sourdough breads that have been fermented in the refrigerator rise upward rather than sideways, whereas doughs that are baked right after proofing tend to expand outward. I also find that crumb structure is better after cold fermentation.

Gluten-free breads tend to expand sideways more than upward and that is why the vessel we proof them in makes an impact on the shape of the final bread. Read about the proofing baskets I like to use on page 17. Or how to create a parchment paper "mold" for challah to proof and keep its shape better (see Note, page 339). This is also why proofing and baking gluten-free breads in loaf pans and molds results in taller products, because the vessels provide a wall structure upon which the dough can rise.

Finally, a note about how to cover your dough while it proofs. Throughout the book I mention to cover the doughs with linen kitchen towels or plastic wrap or by wrapping a whole sheet pan in a large bag. When proofing doughs made with baker's yeast, which will be proofed relatively quickly, I cover the pan or dough with a light linen towel. It's quick enough that the surface of the dough will not dry. On the other hand, if I need to proof a dough for longer, and especially if it goes in the refrigerator, I cover the pan or the dough with plastic wrap or a large plastic bag so the surface of the dough doesn't dry out. If the surface of your dough is very dry when it goes in the oven, your bread can crack while baking (this is especially true for enriched doughs). I might get some pushback on this, but my preferred large plastic bags that wrap entire sheet pans are thin, transparent garbage bags (make sure they are not treated with odor-killing chemicals). They seal the moisture really well and allow for some airflow. And of course, I reuse my plastic bags over and over.

SCORING

High heat expands existing air bubbles in the dough and causes even more bubbles to be produced. This is called *oven spring.* The force of this expansion often breaks open the crust as it is baking. This is the reason why we score: to facilitate the expansion of the dough without the surface cracking in multiple places at once. Gluten-free crusty doughs will not expand as spectacularly as gluten-containing ones because there simply isn't that kind of elasticity, but your dough can still crack if not scored properly, and that crack, if it's really aggressive, could potentially cause your crumb to collapse onto itself.

A lame (see page 16) will be your go-to tool for scoring. It produces thin, deep, and sharp cuts. In a pinch, you can use a very

sharp knife with a thin blade, but a lame will be one of the most used tools in your bread-baking kit.

For crusty boules, I like to use a simple round lame holder (see Resources, page 390). If you are fairly new to scoring, flip your dough out of the proofing basket onto a piece of parchment. This will give you time for scoring, especially if you are doing intricate slashes, and the ability to move the dough around. If you prefer fully brown color all over the crust, leave the dough as is (lightly brush off any flour residue from the proofing basket). However, if you want to create intricate scoring details and need some contrast (a top that is light with darker brown tones that show through scoring), lightly dust the surface of the dough with white rice flour (darker flours will turn even darker while baking) and then proceed to score. The easiest way to score the dough is to first trace lines with string, which helps mark evenly spaced sections, then cut over the marked lines with your lame. The cuts should be about ½ inch (1.3 cm) deep, although smaller slashes can be somewhat shallower. A large cut off-center of a loaf is often at a 45-degree angle to the dough's surface; this expands that area of the loaf and can sometimes create an "ear." For a grid pattern on top of your dough, a square of slashes, or small cuts, hold your lame at a 90-degree angle and cut straight into the dough.

For baguettes, I like to use a long-handled lame holder (see Resources, page 390) where the razor itself is placed in the holder with a slight rounded angle. This helps lift up the dough when scoring, creating small ears in the baguette. Hold your lame in your hand and turn your wrist to a 45-degree angle. Score the dough at an angle, making 5 nearly vertical ¼-inch-deep (6 mm) slashes on the top of the baguette. The slashes should overlap about a third of the way. The biggest mistakes with scoring baguettes are to not overlap the slashes and to cut slashes that are more crosswise than lengthwise.

BAKING

Crusty breads require intense and moist heat to help with oven spring and crust caramelization. Always preheat your oven beyond the ding you hear or the green light you see indicating it has reached your desired temperature. You need the walls and metal elements inside the oven to heat thoroughly. Let your oven heat at least 15 minutes beyond when it says it's ready. Go to Equipment and Baking Tools (page 17) to read more about my oven. In general, I prefer electric ovens for bread baking. One of the most common troubleshooting questions I receive has to do with gas ovens that don't heat evenly and crusts not caramelizing deeply. Get an internal oven thermometer to make sure your oven is calibrated and let it get hot, hot, hot. I also keep a square pizza stone at the bottom of the oven for extra heat retention and because I like to bake directly on a pizza stone when making flatbreads like the Turmeric and Cumin Sourdough Lavash (page 278), Sourdough Pizza Margherita (page 294), or Pillowy Pita (page 272).

Unless the recipe states otherwise, I keep my oven rack in the lower third of the oven. This gives space for Dutch ovens and for good airflow.

CREATING STEAM

Steam is an important component in creating bread that has a desirable, flaky, and caramelized crust. Steam is particularly vital during the initial oven spring so that the surface of the bread remains moist and expands easily. Many of the breads in this book are baked in a cast-iron Dutch oven with ice cubes next to the bread so the heat and the trapped moisture create mini steam-chambers for the dough. But what about recipes like baguettes, which are too large to fit into a standard Dutch oven, or what if you simply don't have a Dutch oven? Preheat your oven to the desired temperature and set a cast-iron skillet on the rack below. Continue heating the oven for at least 15 minutes after it says it has reached temperature. It is important that the walls of the oven, not just the air within it, are really hot so you can create steam. Load your bread into the oven and place a handful of ice cubes in the skillet below. For baguettes, where steam is applied several times, add a handful of ice cubes every time the recipe calls for steam to be injected. You can also cover your bread with a large upside-down metal bowl, which will act as a lid and trap the steam. Close the oven door immediately.

COOLING

It is imperative you let your bread cool before cutting into it, especially for the high-hydration doughs, such as Rosemary Focaccia (page 266), Sourdough Ciabatta Rolls (page 93), Seeded Whole-Grain Teff Sourdough Boule (page 61), and Butter-Toasted Oat and Poppy Seed Loaf (page 71). The crumb on these breads needs time to set. The moisture evaporates as the bread cools, softening the crust slightly and setting the crumb into place. If you try to cut the bread and apply pressure before the crumb has dried out, your crumb will collapse and become gummy. For enriched doughs, the cooling times are not as long (although it's still recommended to wait a few minutes before cutting). The crumb in enriched doughs is softer while the dough is slightly warm. For best results, follow the cooling times indicated in the recipes.

STORING AND REFRESHING BREAD

I store most breads (especially crusty ones) in a brown paper bag at room temperature. I have tried linen bread bags as well as waxed linen wraps, but brown paper bags seem to work best. Sometimes I don't even cover the bread and simply leave it, cut-side down, on a cutting board on my kitchen counter. Freezing extra loaves or leftover bread is also another way to store it for a later time. Wrap the bread tightly in a plastic bag to eliminate any contact with air and then place it inside a freezer bag. Make sure that your bread is completely cool before you freeze it, because any warmth trapped in plastic wrap will end up as condensation and later turn to ice in the freezer. Thaw out frozen loaves at room temperature overnight and follow the steps below to refresh them.

To refresh crusty bread, run the entire loaf under cold water for 10 seconds and then bake it at 350°F (180°C) for 10 to 15 minutes. You will end up with a crispy crust and moist crumb once again. This can be done to loaves that have been frozen and thawed as well as those that have been sitting on your counter for a couple of days. If you have a few slices of stale bread on your counter, the quickest way to reheat and refresh it is to spray the slices with a little bit of water and toast them on a hot cast-iron pan. You will have a moist crumb with a thin layer of toasted surface that is delicious.

To refresh enriched doughs, such as croissants or brioche, place them on a sheet pan, spray them with water, and bake until tender and moist, 8 to 10 minutes. You can also reheat enriched doughs in the microwave by wrapping them in a wet paper towel and heating for 30 seconds to 1 minute, depending on the size of the bread.

BROWN RICE - TEFF
BUCKWHEAT
CHESTNUT

Sourdough Starters

Millet

Teff

Oat Flour

Flaxseed Meal

Xanthan Gum

Brown Rice Flour

Psyllium Powder

There is something very magical about a sourdough starter. It is the process of cultivating wild yeast and bacteria when fermenting flour and water. These microorganisms, which live all around us—in flour, on fruit skins, on our hands—eat the carbohydrates and sugars that the flour and water provide and in turn release gases, which leaven bread. Every sourdough starter is unique because it is influenced by environmental factors, such as temperature, the flour you are using, the soil in which the flour was grown, your own hands and body, humidity in the air, and even the bowl you are using to mix it in. A gluten-free sourdough starter is no different than one containing gluten. They have different flavor profiles depending on the flour you use and their hydration ratio (a gluten starter rises more and retains the trapped gases for much longer), but the process of building them is the same.

A sourdough starter requires your attention and care, and you will develop a strong bond with it and a sixth sense for its well-being. I have tweaked my sourdough process over the many years I have been baking, and I am constantly learning and adapting. My oldest gluten-free starter is a brown rice starter that dates back to 2016 that I grew following Naomi Devlin's recipe in her book *River Cottage Gluten Free*. I have reduced its hydration ratio since then (it is now 119%), and I have introduced some teff flour to give it an earthier and more sour flavor. My original mother starter is still called Amatxu, which means "mommy" in Basque. I have not named any of my other starters, but they have all been carefully labeled because there have been so many of them. The sourdough bread recipes in this book use either the Whole-Grain Brown Rice–Teff Sourdough Starter (page 48) or the Grain-Free Buckwheat-Chestnut Sourdough Starter (page 50). You can use your own gluten-free sourdough starter even if it is made with different flours, but make sure that it has the same hydration ratio as called for in the recipe or you will have to adjust the amount of water in the recipe to reflect that difference.

Your sourdough starter is a colony of microorganisms, but the two most important microbes are yeast and lactic acid bacteria. Both of these live symbiotically in your starter, working together to make it uninhabitable for any other harmful microbes.

WILD YEAST

Yeasts are single-celled fungi that represent about 1 percent of the entire fungus world. There are thousands of yeast species, but *Saccharomyces cerevisiae* are the ones used in bread baking and beer production. Yeast is primarily responsible for leavening bread. During the fermentation process, yeast microbes eat the simple carbohydrates in the flour and produce carbon dioxide and ethanol. These gas bubbles get trapped in the dough, which results in bread expanding.

LACTIC ACID BACTERIA

Sourdough starters contain lactic acid bacteria, which are responsible for the gut-health benefits of sourdough as they digest the simple carbohydrates in flour, turning your dough into prebiotic heaven—easier digestion and, therefore, less inflammation.
Lactic acid bacteria are also responsible for the distinct flavor profile of your sourdough starter. There are two categories of lactic acid bacteria: homofermentative and heterofermentative. Homofermentative lactic acid bacteria produce only lactic acid, which develops milky and mild notes. They prefer temperatures in the range of 86° to 95°F (30° to 35°C), though they grow at lower temperatures as well. Heterofermentative lactic acid bacteria, on the other hand, produce both lactic and acetic acid, yielding sour and tangy flavor profiles due to the acetic acid. These bacteria thrive at temperatures between 59° and 72°F (15° and 22°C) but can grow over a much wider range as well. When I research how lactic acid bacteria affect the flavor of bread, I find the literature overwhelming and sometimes even contradicting. In my experience, higher-hydration starters that are kept in the fridge in between feedings and cold-fermented doughs produce tangy and sour flavors. On the contrary, lower-hydration starters that are fermented at warm temperatures (such as a sweet stiff sponge) yield milder and milkier flavor notes. This is clearly a simplified categorization, as other factors like the type of flour you are using also have an impact.

WHAT GLUTEN-FREE FLOUR TO USE FOR YOUR STARTER

You can create a gluten-free sourdough starter with basically any gluten-free flour. Different flours will provide different flavors, and the colony of yeast and bacteria they support will be different. I have grown many different starters with single flours and flour combinations mainly to test how they behave and taste, but in all truth, I am only able to keep two or three going at one time because of the maintenance they require. You can currently find in my refrigerator the Whole-Grain Brown Rice–Teff Sourdough Starter (page 48), the Grain-Free Buckwheat-Chestnut Sourdough Starter (page 50), my 2016 brown rice sourdough starter, an oat starter that was converted from my old brown rice starter but that I will likely stop maintaining soon, and a 100 percent teff starter I am playing around with. The main starter I use now is the brown rice and teff starter. It is the most active and has a slightly more sour flavor than my original brown rice flour starter.

HYDRATION RATIO

You have probably heard the term *hydration ratio* many times when it comes to sourdough starters. It refers to the ratio of water to flour in your starter. If you have equal amounts of flour and water, your hydration ratio, expressed as a percentage, is 100%. Simply divide the amount of water (in grams) in the starter by the amount of flour (in grams) and you will know what your hydration ratio is. For example, the brown rice and teff starter uses 95 grams of water and 80 grams of flour (95/80 = 1.1875, therefore 118.75%, or to round up, 119% hydration). Gluten-free flours vary in their water-absorption capacity and that is why you will find different ratios.

GLUTEN-FREE SOURDOUGH STARTERS

Here are some sourdough starters I have tested to give you some ideas to help create your own:

Gluten-Free Sourdough Starter	Flour	Water	Hydration Ratio	Fermentation Speed*
BROWN RICE–TEFF	70 grams brown rice flour + 10 grams teff flour	95 grams filtered water	119%	Quick
BUCKWHEAT-CHESTNUT	35 grams light buckwheat flour + 35 grams chestnut flour	70 grams filtered water	100%	Fairly slow
SORGHUM	70 grams sorghum flour	80 grams filtered water	114%	Fairly quick
BUCKWHEAT	70 grams light buckwheat flour	70 grams filtered water	100%	Slow
OAT	70 grams oat flour	60 grams filtered water	86%	Quick

**Fermentation speed will depend on many different factors, mainly how mature your starter is and the temperature and moisture in your environment. This speed rating is based simply on observing my different starters and how they compare to one another. For example, after I feed my mature brown rice–teff starter, it takes 6 to 8 hours to double in the jar, whereas the buckwheat-chestnut starter can take 10 to 12 hours.*

GROWING THE SOURDOUGH STARTER

Growing your sourdough starter is not difficult. You can follow this process for any single flour or flour combinations you like. Some will ferment faster and produce more air bubbles and others will take longer. For example, brown rice flour–based starters grow really well with airy gas bubbles. In contrast, starters grown exclusively with buckwheat flour tend to be the slowest and might appear to produce fewer gas bubbles, although this doesn't mean they are not as productive.

You can create a starter in a glass mason jar, but I like to begin in a bowl and transfer to a jar at the very end, when the starter is established. I like to run a spatula through my starter as it ferments, and having it in a bowl allows me to see the mousse-like texture I am looking for.

Find a warm spot in your home where the temperature is consistent. Anywhere between 70° and 85°F (21° and 29°C) is ideal, but I have grown starters in my kitchen when it has been 65°F (18°C)—it just takes longer. A bread proofer, a heating pad, or nearby a warm space will work well.

Finally, write down feeding times in a notebook, because after a couple of days, you may lose track of which feeding you just did. The process (see Whole-Grain Brown Rice–Teff Sourdough Starter, page 48) dictates feedings every 12 hours for 5 days (10 feedings total). Don't get discouraged if your starter doesn't feel established after 5 days. It might take longer depending on your environment and the flour you are using. Continue feeding and discarding until your starter has a mousse-like consistency. Collect your discard in a mason jar and keep it in the refrigerator. This first discard will not be active enough to leaven recipes like Sourdough Crumpets Two Ways (page 131), but you can definitely use it in recipes like Sourdough Chocolate-Miso Cookies (page 115) or Fresh Sourdough Egg Pasta (page 139).

A NOTE ABOUT WATER

Since you are trying to cultivate yeast and bacteria in your starter, you should really pay attention to the chlorine level in your tap water. Having elevated chlorine levels could hinder bacteria and yeast growth and even kill it. I have a filter in my kitchen tap and that is the water I always use. If you don't have a filter for your tap water, leave a large pitcher of straight-from-the-tap water on your kitchen counter overnight; chlorine dissipates from the water as it sits. In the recipes that use sourdough, I list the water as "filtered water." I don't do this for the ones involving baker's yeast, because commercially grown yeast is very robust and can withstand some chlorine.

STORING THE STARTER

If you are going to be making bread every day, you can keep your starter at room temperature and feed it every 12 hours so it stays active and healthy, but for those of you who make bread every other day or even once a week, it's best to store your starter in the refrigerator. Catch your starter at its peak of fermentation and transfer it to the refrigerator then. The starter will slow down and become dormant once chilled.

HOW TO USE THE SOURDOUGH STARTER

After you build your starter after 10 feedings or so, it should be ready. I encourage you to make bread right away so you keep taking and feeding the mother starter; the more you use your starter, the healthier it will be. I store mine in the refrigerator when I am not using it, but since I make bread every 2 days or so, the starter is still bubbly in the fridge. If you don't make bread often and keep your starter in the fridge for days at a time, it will likely not be active enough, so refresh it the day before making your bread (see Feeding the Starter, below). If you are using room-temperature starter, you will likely need a shorter fermentation time.

My sourdough bread recipes begin with creating a sponge, which means you will be taking some starter out of your fridge and feeding it flour and water to activate it (each recipe will tell you how much flour and water to feed it). Give your starter a good stir before taking some out to make bread. The bottom of the starter tends to become wetter and the top drier as it sits. Once you have taken what you need to make your sponge, you will feed your remaining mother starter to multiply it so you have enough starter the next time you need to bake bread. You will have two starters on your counter at once—the starter that you are feeding to turn into dough and the mother starter that you are feeding for next time. Any time you take some starter away, you should feed it some to keep it going.

FEEDING THE STARTER

Your refrigerated mother starter will have to be fed at least once a week to keep it healthy; ideally, use it every 2 days.

The feeding ratio is simple:

1 part starter + 1 part flour + x (hydration ratio) parts water (1:1:x)

For example, the Whole-Grain Brown Rice–Teff Sourdough Starter (page 48) has a hydration ratio of 119%, so the x value in the equation above will be 1.19 (see chart, page 47). If you are using a starter that is 100% hydration, such as the Grain-Free Buckwheat-

Chestnut Sourdough Starter (page 50), then you will have equal parts starter, flour, and water. And so on. It's that simple.

For the recipes in this book, I like to keep a base of 150 grams of mother starter. That means that for the brown rice–teff starter, I will collect 150 grams of mother starter and feed it 130 grams of superfine brown flour plus 20 grams of teff flour and 178.5 grams of water (it's okay to round the water to 180 grams). And for the buckwheat-chestnut starter, 150 grams of starter, 75 grams of buckwheat flour plus 75 grams of chestnut flour, and 150 grams of water.

For this feeding process, I use a ceramic bowl with a spout. (The spout helps direct the starter into the mason jar without spillage.) Whisk the starter, flour, and water vigorously, making sure you incorporate a bit of air. Rinse your mason jar with water to remove any dried pieces of starter. Pour the starter back into the mason jar. Place a rubber band around the jar to mark where the starter is so you know how much it's growing and let it ferment at room temperature until it's grown in size. You will watch the starter grow and at some point notice that it is slightly deflating. It's at that point, or a bit sooner, that you want to return it to the fridge. While it's in the fridge, the starter slows down and goes dormant until you feed it again.

CONVERTING STARTERS

One of the most frequent questions I receive from bread bakers is whether they can convert an existing gluten-containing starter into a gluten-free one. The answer is yes, and it's quite simple. Treat the gluten starter as you would a gluten-free one and start feeding it gluten-free flour and water. How long it will take for the starter to be 100 percent free of gluten particles is difficult to say. I would do

How to Handle Your Starter When You're Traveling

I have left my starter in the refrigerator unfed for up to 3 weeks and it has been absolutely fine. In fact, a healthy sourdough starter can live in the refrigerator for months and you will likely be able to revive it with one or two refreshing feedings. To refresh it, repeat the basic feeding step. In a bowl, whisk 150 grams of starter with 150 grams flour and 178.5 grams of water (or however much water you need to maintain your starter's hydration). Pour it back into the mason jar and let it ferment at room temperature. Discard the rest of the starter. If your starter has been unfed for a long time, you might need to repeat the process one more time. Simply watch how it grows and decide if it needs another refreshing feed.

multiple feedings (discarding in between just as you do in the recipe for Whole-Grain Brown Rice–Teff Sourdough Starter on page 48), and if you want to be completely sure it is gluten-free, test it with gluten-detecting test strips.

You can also take your established gluten-free starter and begin feeding it a different flour to create a completely new starter. I have done this multiple times. Watch how the starter behaves. If you are converting a brown rice flour starter into a buckwheat one, for example, the first feeding might be very active but consecutive ones not as much, and that is because buckwheat flour doesn't ferment as quickly or get as bubbly as brown rice flour. That is completely normal.

Above all, remember, always keep enough of your healthy mother starter to get going. Don't use up all of it on experiments and deplete your source. A healthy starter is gold!

CONVERTING RECIPES FROM BAKER'S YEAST TO SOURDOUGH STARTER

It is fairly simple to convert a recipe that uses baker's yeast to sourdough starter. It will definitely require one or two trial tests, but in general terms, 8 grams of active dry yeast is equivalent to 150 grams of Whole-Grain Brown Rice–Teff Sourdough Starter (page 48). Remember that your sourdough starter will also have lactic acid bacteria and other microbes in addition to yeast, so it will be more complex in flavor and will require longer fermentation times.

You will have to do some math to compensate for the flour and water that already exist in your sourdough starter and subtract that from the flour and water that are called for in the recipe. For example, if your recipe calls for 8 grams of yeast, replace it with 150 grams of sourdough starter. Then, calculate how much flour and water are in your starter. In the case of the brown rice and teff starter, which has a hydration ratio of 119%, we have 1 part brown rice and 1.19 parts water. In the equation below, x will be the amount of flour and $1.19x$ will be the amount of water. Below are the amounts of flour and water you will need to subtract from the recipe that uses baker's yeast.

$$150 \text{ grams (total starter)} = x \text{ (flour)} + 1.19x \text{ (water)}$$
$$150 \text{ grams} = 2.19x$$
$$x \text{ (flour)} = 150/2.19 = 68.49 \text{ grams (rounded up to 68.5 grams)}$$
$$1.19x \text{ (water)} = 1.19 \times 68.49 = 81.5 \text{ grams water}$$

To confirm your results:

68.5 grams of flour + 81.5 grams of water = 150 grams total starter

As an example, if your recipe calls for 8 grams of active dry yeast, 500 grams of flour, and 500 grams of water, your new recipe will look like this.

	Recipe using baker's yeast (in grams)	Recipe using sourdough starter (in grams)
Yeast / Sourdough Starter	8	150
Flour	500	500 – 68.5 = 431.5
Water	500	500 – 81.5 = 418.5

Once you have determined what your recipe looks like, you must change the process a bit because that sourdough starter will have to be activated before you make your dough. Take some of the flour and water in the original recipe, whisk it with starter, and let it ferment at room temperature until it is active, bubbly, and has a mousse-like texture. After that, make your dough with the remaining ingredients and proof again as you would in your original recipe.

As you see, it's a bit of math, but once you understand the concept and process, you can apply this to many recipes. You can also use these principles to convert recipes using sourdough starter to baker's yeast.

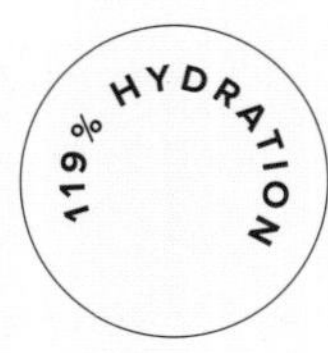

Whole-Grain Brown Rice–Teff Sourdough Starter

70 grams superfine brown rice flour

10 grams ivory teff flour

95 grams filtered water, at around 80°F (27°C)

This sourdough starter has become my go-to since I started developing gluten-free bread recipes. The teff adds a very nuanced earthiness that balances the sweetness of the brown rice. I use ivory teff, but you can use dark teff, which will result in a darker starter.

MAKES ENOUGH STARTER FOR 1 LOAF, PLUS MORE TO KEEP GOING

FEEDING 1 In a medium bowl, whisk together the brown rice flour, teff flour, and water until you have a paste that has the consistency of hummus. If your paste is thicker, add a very small amount of water and whisk. Make sure to incorporate air into it. Cover the bowl with a kitchen towel and let it ferment for about 12 hours or until the sponge has a mousse-like texture when you run a spoon through it. It might not be very bubbly after the first feeding.

FEEDING 2 Measure 75 grams of the starter into a medium bowl. Discard the rest. Whisk in the same amount of brown rice flour, teff flour, and water as in the first feeding. Cover the bowl with a kitchen towel and ferment for about 12 hours or until it has a mousse-like texture. Again, depending on your flour, you might not see many bubbles after this second feeding and that is okay. Continue with the remaining feedings.

FEEDINGS 3 THROUGH 10 Repeat the process as stated above every 12 hours for a total of 10 feedings (5 days). By day 3, you should see bubbles and aeration after 12 hours. Right after the tenth feeding, transfer the starter to a mason jar (anything from a 12-ounce/340 ml to a 1-quart/1 L jar will work well) and let it ferment there for up to 12 hours or until it is bubbly. The starter is ready to be used.

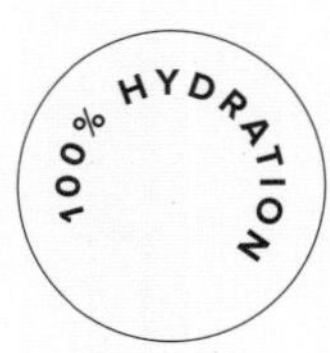

Grain-Free Buckwheat-Chestnut Sourdough Starter

35 grams light buckwheat flour

35 grams chestnut flour

70 grams filtered water, at around 80°F (27°C)

This grain-free sourdough starter follows the same steps as the Whole-Grain Brown Rice–Teff Sourdough Starter (page 48), but it uses buckwheat and chestnut flours instead, which are grain-free. This starter feels different than the one made with brown rice and teff; it is thicker and stretchier. I always use light buckwheat flour in my starters as I have found the darker varieties take longer to grow and are not as elastic. If you can't source chestnut flour, you can make a starter that is 100% buckwheat. In my experience, 100% buckwheat sourdough starters are a bit harder to establish.

MAKES ENOUGH STARTER FOR 1 BOULE, PLUS MORE TO KEEP GOING

FEEDING 1 In a medium bowl, whisk together the buckwheat flour, chestnut flour, and water until you have a thick paste that is a little gummy and stretchy. Make sure to incorporate air into it. Cover the bowl with a kitchen towel and let it ferment for about 12 hours or until it has a mousse-like texture when you run a spoon through it. It might not be very bubbly after the first feeding.

FEEDING 2 Measure 70 grams of the starter into a medium bowl. Discard the rest. Whisk in the same amount of buckwheat flour, chestnut flour, and water as in the first feeding. Cover the bowl with a kitchen towel and ferment for about 12 hours or until it has a mousse-like texture. Again, depending on your flour, you might not see many bubbles after this second feeding and that is okay. Continue with the remaining feedings.

FEEDINGS 3 THROUGH 10 Repeat the process as stated above every 12 hours for a total of 10 feedings (5 days). By day 3, you should see bubbles and aeration after 12 hours. Right after the tenth feeding, transfer the starter to a mason jar (anything from a 12-ounce/340 ml to a 1-quart/1 L jar will work well) and let it ferment there for up to 12 hours or until it is bubbly. The starter is ready to be used.

Sweet Stiff Sourdough Starter

A sweet stiff sourdough starter is a starter with a very low hydration ratio that also contains sugar. When I make it with brown rice flour, the hydration is about 64%, but when I use oat flour it's even lower at 56%. This creates a very milky starter with lots of lactic acid bacteria and yeast. It is used for enriched doughs, such as the Sourdough Brioche (page 198) or Oat and Honey Sourdough Hot Cross Buns (page 313). This is not a starter that I maintain, but one I build out of the Whole-Grain Brown Rice–Teff Sourdough Starter (page 48) just when I am going to make a recipe that calls for it. (Think of it as a sponge.) As always, make sure your starter is active before making the sweet stiff starter sponge. You can use starter that is refrigerated, but it needs to have bubbles when you run a spoon through it, ideally having been fed 1 day before. If your starter is not bubbly in the fridge or has hooch (see page 52) sitting on top, then make sure to feed it the day before starting the process. I use a 12-ounce (340 ml) wide-mouth mason jar or plastic container where the sweet stiff starter can rise. The sides help give it structure and you can see better how it's fermenting versus doing it in a bowl and waiting for bubbles. Make sure it has enough space on the top for air.

Troubleshooting Your Sourdough Starter

Here are some tips to help you troubleshoot the most common issues with starters.

Starter doesn't bubble. Temperature is very important, especially in the very beginning or when trying to revive your starter. Make sure to keep the starter in a warm environment (ideally, between 75° and 85°F/24° and 29°C). If your oven has a proofing setting, consider yourself lucky. Otherwise, place your starter in the oven with a pot of boiling-hot water next to it. If it's warm in your environment and the starter doesn't bubble, it could be that your flour is not fermenting well for various reasons. Try switching your flour brand. I have seen this happen with bakers who use bulk-bin flours (not to say all bulk-bin flours will do this). If you are trying to revive a mature starter that seems to be struggling, increase the feeding to a higher ratio. For the brown rice–teff starter, for instance, instead of the 1:1:1.19 ratio, you can do 1:2:2.38.

Is this smell okay? A healthy starter will smell like a mixture of yogurt and wine. But sometimes, when you use earthier flours like teff and buckwheat, the smell could be more pungent and you might be wondering if you are doing something wrong. Don't panic. It's very hard to kill a starter, and unless it smells like rotten food or has mold on it, it should be okay.

Mold. If you see pink or green spots or any fuzzy things growing on your starter, throw it away. That is mold. I have seen this happen when there is soap residue in the bowl or mason jar, which kills healthy microbes and allows mold to take over. Rinse your jar only with water in between feedings to avoid any soap residue.

Starter seems very liquid. It's okay if your starter becomes liquid. As the starter hydrates and ferments, it tends to loosen up. It also can become more or less liquid as seasons change and temperature changes. You could add a bit less water if you find your starter is too liquid, but it's not imperative.

Liquid collects on top of my starter. There are two reasons why liquid collects on top of your starter. The more common one is that it's a liquid called hooch, the mixture of water, acids, and ethanol that wild yeast produces during fermentation. This is completely normal and it indicates that your starter is hungry. If you have kept your starter in the refrigerator for a while without feeding, an accumulation of hooch is a good indicator that you need to refresh it. Another reason for liquid collecting on top of your starter is that water is not getting absorbed. This usually happens when your flour is overhydrated or too coarse and not hydrating well. In this case, you can reduce the amount of water you are feeding your starter by 10% and see if it keeps happening.

Starter is not very sour. When you begin making sourdough bread you might have a specific taste in mind that you are looking for. Remember that gluten-free flours have different flavor profiles than wheat flour, which will impact the flavor of your bread. Adding a little bit of teff and buckwheat will add a slightly more sour flavor to your starter, but it's not the only thing that will impact it (colder temperatures result in slightly more sour starters). Embrace the flavor of gluten-free flours and don't try to mimic wheat. Also, the hooch that collects on top of your starter can add sourness, so don't throw it away. Stir it back in.

Starter rises and falls. It is normal for your starter to rise and fall. Remember that there is no gluten in your starter, therefore no elastic strands to trap the gases formed during fermentation. Bubbles form, but they fall quickly due to lack of elasticity. Always watch your starter and see when it has reached peak fermentation. Peak fermentation will happen right before you see the starter deflate. The top will dome and crack, then begin to slowly deflate. With time, you will develop an intuition or sense for when that moment is by watching how the starter rises. This is when you want to either use it (if you are dealing with the sponge to make bread) or refrigerate it.

No big bubbles. How big the bubbles in your starter are is not necessarily a good indicator of whether it's healthy. Different flours have different elasticity and some of them will be able to trap gases a little bit better. For example, an oat flour starter will have much larger bubbles than a buckwheat one.

The float test doesn't work for gluten-free starter. Can you do the float test that is done for gluten starters to determine if your gluten-free starter is at its peak? The float test only works if your starter has specific density, but remember that your gluten-free starter doesn't trap gases the same as a gluten one, so that test is not an accurate tool in this case. Your gluten-free starter is denser than the gluten one. Also, there is no "glue" holding the starter together, so it will dissolve in water.

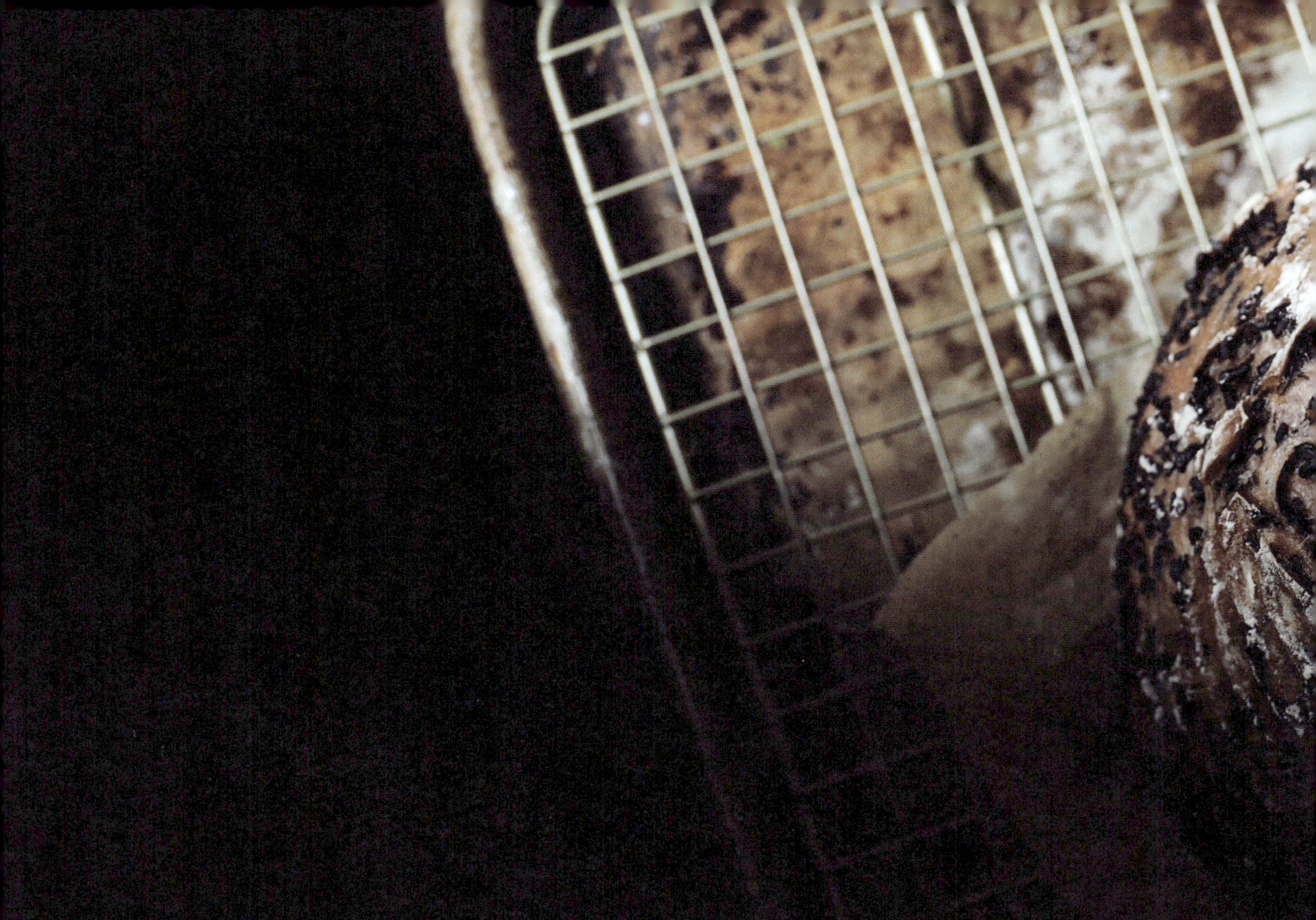

No. 2

Sourdough Breads

Grain-Free Buckwheat Chestnut Baguettes

Once you have established an active sourdough starter and understand how it lives and breeds, baking sourdough bread is really simple. My sourdough bread recipes begin by creating a sponge (traditionally also known as levain or pre-ferment) where the sourdough starter is mixed with flour and water to activate it to make that particular recipe. You will notice that even if a recipe calls for the same starter, I feed it different flours depending on the recipe. For example, the Seeded Whole-Grain Teff Sourdough Boule (page 61) begins with a sponge made with Whole-Grain Brown Rice–Teff Sourdough Starter (page 48) fed with teff, but the Sourdough Salted Miso Baguettes (page 81), which use the same starter, are fed sorghum flour. That is because I am looking for a different flavor profile in each recipe; the starter will eat whichever flour you feed it. Make sure your starter is active before you begin making the recipe. If your starter has been in the refrigerator for a few days and doesn't seem active (no bubbles when you stir it), feed it the day before you are going to make bread.

The chapter begins with the recipes with a higher percentage of whole-grain flours (for example, Grain-Free Buckwheat-Chestnut Batard on page 63) and then moves on to lighter ones with higher starch content (for example, Sourdough Ciabatta Rolls on page 93).

Seeded Whole-Grain Teff Sourdough Boule

FOR THE SPONGE

150 grams filtered water, at around 75° to 80°F (24° to 29°C)

125 grams Whole-Grain Brown Rice–Teff Sourdough Starter (page 48)

125 grams ivory teff flour

FOR THE DOUGH

90 grams oat flour, plus more for dusting

90 grams sorghum flour

60 grams tapioca starch

8 grams kosher salt

20 grams flaxseed meal

20 grams psyllium husk powder

325 grams filtered water, at around 75° to 80°F (24° to 29°C)

20 grams maple syrup

35 grams sunflower seeds, plus more for coating

35 grams pumpkin seeds, plus more for coating

35 grams white sesame seeds, plus more for coating

15 grams black sesame seeds

This long-fermentation sourdough boule is nutritious and full of nutty flavor. It contains about 86% whole-grain flours and only 14% starch, so don't expect a crumb with large pockets of air. This is bread in the tradition of dense and flavorful rye loaves. The seeds on the crust add texture and crunch. You can use a combination of different seeds if you have some to use up in your pantry.

MAKES 1 BOULE

Make the sponge. In a medium bowl, whisk together the water, starter, and teff flour until smooth. Cover with a kitchen towel and proof at around 75° to 80°F (24° to 29°C) for 3 to 6 hours, until it has a mousse-like texture when you run a spoon through it.

Make the dough. In a stand mixer, stir together the oat flour, sorghum flour, tapioca starch, and salt. Add the active sponge to this bowl. In the same bowl you used to make the sponge, combine the flaxseed and psyllium. Pour in the water while you simultaneously whisk until smooth. Let it gel for 5 minutes. Add this gel to the bowl with the flour. Add the maple syrup. Snap the dough hook onto the mixer and mix the dough on medium speed until it is smooth, 2 to 3 minutes. The dough should feel moist and bouncy and hold its shape. Add the sunflower, pumpkin, and white and black sesame seeds. Continue mixing on medium speed until the seeds are well distributed through the dough, about 1 minute. Transfer the dough to your work surface and knead it a couple of times. Shape it into a tight ball.

Cover the dough with seeds. Place a handful of mixed sunflower, pumpkin, and white sesame seeds on a plate and dip the top of the dough to coat. The surface of your dough should be fairly moist so the seeds will stick to it, but if that is not the case, spray the dough with a little bit of water before dipping it into the seeds.

Proof the dough. Lightly dust a proofing basket with some oat flour and place the dough in it upside down so the seed-coated surface is on the bottom and the seam of the dough is on the top. Cover the proofing basket with a kitchen towel. At this point, you can proof your dough at room temperature for 1½ to 2½ hours or do a cold fermentation in the refrigerator anywhere from 10 to 20 hours. If you decide to proof the dough in the refrigerator, it is best to cover the basket with plastic wrap tightly secured with a rubber band so the surface of the dough doesn't dry out.

Preheat the oven. About 45 minutes before your dough is ready, position a rack in the bottom third of the oven and place a 5.5-quart (5.2 L) cast-iron Dutch oven on the rack. Preheat the oven to 500°F (260°C). Once the oven has reached temperature, let the Dutch oven continue heating for 15 minutes.

Score the dough. When the dough is ready, lay out a piece of parchment on your work surface and carefully invert the dough onto the parchment. Score your dough (either one large score in the middle or a grid pattern on top).

Bake the bread. Carefully lift the dough along with the parchment paper and place both in the preheated Dutch oven. Add 2 or 3 ice cubes next to it. Cover with the lid and bake for 45 minutes. Remove the lid, reduce the oven temperature to 425°F (220°C), and bake for 10 minutes, or until the bread is dark golden brown.

Cool the bread. Transfer the bread to a wire rack and let it cool for at least 30 minutes before cutting into it. Be patient, it pays off. Store the bread at room temperature wrapped in a paper bag for up to 2 days.

Grain-Free Buckwheat-Chestnut Batard

Buckwheat and chestnut together create a nutty, naturally sweet, and intensely flavorful bread. The crust in this loaf is dark, with a dense and moist crumb that has a slightly purple tone to it. The sponge in this recipe takes a bit of time to ferment, so start the process the night before. In the morning, make the dough, proof, and bake. You can shape it into a batard or a boule. See How to Make Chestnut Flour at Home (page 20) for making your own.

MAKES 1 BATARD

FOR THE SPONGE

170 grams filtered water, at around 75° to 80°F (24° to 29°C)

150 grams Grain-Free Buckwheat-Chestnut Sourdough Starter (page 50)

75 grams light buckwheat flour

75 grams chestnut flour

FOR THE DOUGH

20 grams psyllium husk powder

15 grams flaxseed meal

340 grams filtered water, at around 75° to 80°F (24° to 29°C)

150 grams chestnut flour

90 grams light buckwheat flour

90 grams tapioca starch

10 grams kosher salt

20 grams maple syrup

White rice flour, for dusting

Make the sponge. In a medium bowl, whisk together the water, starter, buckwheat flour, and chestnut flour until smooth, creating a stretchy paste. Cover the bowl with a kitchen towel or plate and let it ferment for 8 to 10 hours at room temperature. The sponge will puff up slightly and will have a mousse-like texture.

Make the dough. In a medium bowl, combine the psyllium and flaxseed. Add the water while whisking vigorously until smooth. Let it gel for 5 minutes. In a stand mixer, stir together the chestnut flour, buckwheat flour, tapioca starch, and salt. Add the psyllium-flaxseed gel along with the sponge and maple syrup. Snap on the dough hook and mix on medium speed until the dough comes together, 2 to 3 minutes. The dough will be sticky and moist but should hold together nicely.

Shape and proof the dough. Transfer the dough to a work surface and knead a few times. Shape into a tight ball and then into an oval. Lightly dust an oval banneton with some white rice flour and place the dough in it seam-side up. Cover with a kitchen towel or plastic wrap and proof for 3 to 4 hours. The dough will not rise significantly. It will feel slightly soft to the touch but not as noticeably as other doughs. Don't worry, this is normal.

Preheat the oven. Position a rack in the bottom third of the oven and place a cast-iron Dutch oven on the rack. Preheat the oven to 450°F (230°C). Once the oven has reached temperature, let the Dutch oven continue heating for 15 minutes.

(Recipe continues)

Score the dough. Place a piece of parchment paper on your work surface and invert the dough onto it. Dust a little more white rice flour on top of the dough. Score the top of the bread.

Bake the bread. Lift the parchment paper with the dough and place both in the preheated Dutch oven. Add 2 or 3 ice cubes next to the dough and cover the Dutch oven. Bake for 45 minutes. Remove the lid, reduce the oven temperature to 400°F (200°C), and bake for an additional 15 minutes, or until the crust is a deep brown color but not burned.

Cool the bread. Transfer the bread to a wire rack and let it cool completely, at least 30 minutes. Store the bread at room temperature wrapped in a paper bag for up to 2 days.

VARIATIONS

Chocolate-Walnut Chestnut Batard

90 grams chocolate (70% cacao), cut into ¼-inch (6 mm) squares

60 grams coarsely chopped walnuts

7 grams cacao powder

Once the dough is mixed, fold in the chocolate, walnuts, and cacao powder. Then proceed with the recipe as directed.

Apple-Raisin-Rosemary Chestnut Batard

90 grams red apple (leave skin on), cut into ½-inch (1.3 cm) cubes

60 grams plump raisins

2 teaspoons (1 g) finely chopped fresh rosemary leaves

Once the dough is mixed, fold in the apple, raisins, and rosemary. Then proceed with the recipe as directed.

Nordic-Style Seed Bread

FOR THE SPONGE

170 grams filtered water, at around 75° to 80°F (24° to 29°C)

150 grams Whole-Grain Brown Rice–Teff Sourdough Starter (page 48)

70 grams superfine brown rice flour

70 grams ivory or brown teff flour

FOR THE DOUGH

Olive oil, for greasing

20 grams psyllium husk powder

450 grams filtered water, at around 75° to 80°F (24° to 29°C)

140 grams ivory or brown teff flour

120 grams oat flour

35 grams sesame seeds

35 grams flaxseeds

35 grams chia seeds

35 grams pumpkin seeds

35 grams sunflower seeds

10 grams kosher salt

40 grams blackstrap molasses

If you enjoy rugbrød or the Nordic-style rye loaves, you will love this recipe made with whole-grain flours, lots of seeds, and no starches. Slice it thinly, toast it, and serve it as a base for an open-faced sandwich. It's a very flavorful and textural little bread.

MAKES 1 LOAF

Make the sponge. In a medium bowl, whisk together the water, starter, brown rice flour, and teff flour until you have a smooth paste. Cover the bowl with a kitchen towel or plate and proof for 3 to 5 hours, until the top is domed and the inside has a mousse-like texture when you run a spoon through it.

Prepare the pan. Grease the bottom and sides of a 9-by-4-inch (23 by 10 cm) Pullman loaf pan with some olive oil.

Make the dough. In a medium bowl, vigorously whisk together the psyllium and water until smooth. Let it gel for 5 minutes. In a large bowl, stir together the teff flour, oat flour, sesame seeds, flaxseeds, chia seeds, pumpkin seeds, sunflower seeds, and salt. Add the molasses, the psyllium gel, and the sponge. Stir everything together with a wooden spoon. Continue mixing with your hand until you have a very sticky and loose dough. Scoop the dough into the prepared pan.

Proof the dough. Cover the pan with a kitchen towel and proof for 3 to 5 hours until the dough has risen nearly to the top of the pan. (Alternatively, proof at room temperature for 2 hours and then 8 to 12 hours in the refrigerator.)

Bake the bread. Preheat the oven to 450°F (230°C). Bake the bread for 45 minutes. Carefully remove the bread from the pan, return it to the oven, and place directly on the oven rack. Reduce the oven temperature to 400°F (200°C) and bake for 20 minutes, or until the bread is golden brown and sounds hollow when tapped on the bottom.

Cool the bread. Transfer to a wire rack and cool completely before cutting. Store the bread at room temperature wrapped in a paper bag for up to 3 days.

Sourdough Teff-Oat Seeded Rolls

These hearty and crunchy rolls remind me of Germany and all the bakeries I visited there many moons ago. A spread of butter and a thin slice of cheese on the seeded rolls that lined the bakery windows sustained me as I hopped from city to city on a summer holiday. You can use whatever seeds and grains you have on hand—they will make a crunchy and flavorful crust for the rolls.

MAKES 8 ROLLS

FOR THE SPONGE

150 grams Whole-Grain Brown Rice–Teff Sourdough Starter (page 48)

85 grams filtered water, at around 75° to 80°F (24° to 29°C)

70 grams ivory or brown teff flour

FOR THE DOUGH

20 grams psyllium husk powder

7 grams flaxseed meal

325 grams filtered water, at around 75° to 80°F (24° to 29°C)

12 grams extra-virgin olive oil

160 grams tapioca starch

120 grams oat flour

35 grams sorghum flour

12 grams granulated sugar

8 grams kosher salt

FOR THE TOPPING

100 grams rolled oats, millet grain, flaxseeds, sesame seeds, poppy seeds, or sunflower seeds

Make the sponge. In a medium bowl, whisk together the starter, water, and teff flour until smooth. Cover with a kitchen towel and proof for 3 to 4 hours, until it has puffed up and has a mousse-like texture.

Make the dough. In a medium bowl, whisk together the psyllium and flaxseed. Add the water and olive oil and whisk until smooth and thick. Let it gel for 5 minutes. In a stand mixer, stir together the tapioca starch, oat flour, sorghum flour, sugar, and salt. Add the sponge and psyllium-flaxseed gel. Snap on the dough hook and mix on medium speed until you have a smooth and bouncy dough, 3 to 4 minutes.

Shape the dough. Transfer the dough to your work surface. Knead it a few times to bring it together. Cut the dough into 8 equal pieces (about 125 g each). Knead each piece of dough and shape into a tight ball. The dough pieces should hold together but feel slightly moist.

Cover the rolls in seeds. Combine the grains and seeds on a large plate. If you used flour to roll your dough pieces and they don't feel moist to the touch, spray them with a little bit of water. Roll the dough in the seed and grain mixture, making sure it is sticking to the surface well. Place the dough pieces on a sheet pan.

Proof the rolls. Cover the pan with a large kitchen towel or wrap it in a thin plastic bag. Proof for 2 to 3 hours, until the dough feels slightly lighter. Because they are whole-grain rolls, the dough won't expand much or feel marshmallow-like, but don't worry, they will expand in the oven.

(Recipe continues)

Preheat the oven. Position a rack in the bottom third of the oven and preheat the oven to 500°F (260°C). Let the oven continue heating for at least 15 minutes after it has reached temperature.

Score the rolls. Cut a slash ¼ inch (6 mm) deep on the center of each roll.

Bake the rolls. Place the pan in the oven and reduce the oven temperature to 450°F (230°C). Bake for 25 to 30 minutes, until the rolls are crispy and dark brown but not burned, injecting steam three times in 5-minute intervals (at 1 minute, 6 minutes, and 11 minutes). If you don't have steam in your oven, see Creating Steam (page 32).

Cool the rolls. Transfer the rolls to a wire rack and let cool for at least 30 minutes before cutting into them. Store them tightly wrapped in a paper bag for up to 2 days.

Butter-Toasted Oat and Poppy Seed Loaf

FOR THE SWEET STIFF SPONGE

75 grams Whole-Grain Brown Rice–Teff Sourdough Starter (page 48)

45 grams filtered water, at around 75° to 80°F (24° to 29°C)

20 grams maple syrup

70 grams superfine brown rice flour

FOR THE BUTTER-TOASTED OATS

55 grams unsalted butter or vegan butter

90 grams rolled oats, plus more for topping

12 grams poppy seeds

40 grams maple syrup

FOR THE DOUGH

30 grams psyllium husk powder

450 grams filtered water, at around 75° to 80°F (24° to 29°C)

150 grams tapioca starch

125 grams oat flour

45 grams sorghum flour

10 grams kosher salt

Olive oil, for greasing

FOR THE TOPPING

25 grams rolled oats

This loaf is one of my favorites. It's light and airy, yet chewy and textural from the oats and poppy seeds. It uses a sweet stiff sponge, which will create a starter that is milky and buttery. The bread is a little sweet, but not so much that you cannot use it for a savory sandwich, and it's delicious toasted and spread with butter. The dough is a little bit delicate and can easily overproof because of its high water content. You will know it was overproofed if there is compression on the bottom and a pocket of air on the top. If this happens, you can reduce the water amount by 10% and proof for a slightly shorter time.

Note that this bread will require a bit of time. I like to start the sweet stiff sponge in the morning of the day before I am going to bake the bread. Let the sweet stiff starter proof during the day, make and proof the dough in the evening, refrigerate overnight, and bake the following morning.

MAKES 1 LOAF

Make the sweet stiff sponge. In a medium bowl, whisk together the starter, water, and maple syrup until smooth. Add the brown rice flour and mix with a spatula until you have a very thick paste. Knead it a few times. Place the sponge in a wide-mouth 12-ounce (340 ml) mason jar or plastic container, gently pressing it down into the bottom. Place a rubber band around the jar right where the top of the sponge sits so you will be able to see how much it has grown. Loosely cover the jar with a small kitchen towel or the lid without sealing.

Ferment the sponge. Let the sponge sit until it has risen by about 50 percent and the top feels very springy and soft to the touch, 8 to 10 hours. This stiff sponge does best around 75° to 80°F (24° to 29°C), so in the wintertime I like to keep it in the oven with the light on and a small pot with boiling-hot water that I reheat every 30 to 45 minutes to keep at a constant temperature.

Make the butter-toasted oats. Heat a medium sauté pan over medium heat. Add the butter and swirl it around until it melts completely and begins to lightly bubble. Add the oats and poppy seeds and stir to coat in the butter. Keep cooking and stirring until the oats are lightly toasted and smell slightly nutty, 3 to 4 minutes. Be careful not to burn them. Add the maple syrup and stir to coat the oats. Cook for a minute until the oats are completely coated in the maple syrup. Transfer to a plate and let cool completely. When cool, break up any large clusters with your fingers. Set aside.

Make the dough. In a medium bowl, whisk together the psyllium and water vigorously. Let it gel for 5 minutes. In a stand mixer, stir together the tapioca starch, oat flour, sorghum flour, and salt. Add the sponge, psyllium gel, and butter-toasted oats. Snap on the dough hook and mix on medium speed until you have a soft and smooth dough, 3 to 4 minutes.

Shape the dough. Transfer the dough to a work surface and knead it a few times. Dust the work surface with tapioca starch if needed. Shape the dough into a tight ball, then roll slightly until you have a loaf that is about 8 inches (20 cm) long.

Cover the dough in rolled oats. Place the untoasted rolled oats on a large plate and roll the dough on them so they stick to all sides.

Proof the dough. Grease an 8 ½-by-4½-inch (22 by 11 cm) loaf pan with olive oil. Place the dough in it. Cover with a kitchen towel and proof at room temperature for 30 minutes to 1 hour, then transfer to the refrigerator for 8 hours. The dough will not puff up significantly or feel much lighter to the touch, but it will rise in the oven.

Preheat the oven. Position a rack in the bottom third of the oven and preheat the oven to 450°F (230°C).

Bake the bread. Transfer the pan to the oven and bake for 45 minutes. Reduce the oven temperature to 400°F (200°C) and bake for 30 minutes, or until golden brown.

Cool the bread. Let the bread cool in the pan for 15 minutes, then invert onto a wire rack to cool completely before cutting into it. It is normal if the sides cave in slightly. Store the bread at room temperature wrapped in a paper bag for up to 2 days.

Black Rice and Sesame Mochi Bread

PICTURED ON PAGES 76–77

FOR THE STIFF SPONGE

115 grams filtered water, at around 75° to 80°F (24° to 29°C)

75 grams Whole-Grain Brown Rice–Teff Sourdough Starter (page 48)

140 grams superfine brown rice flour

FOR THE BLACK RICE

1,000 grams water

65 grams uncooked black rice

6 grams kosher salt

FOR THE DOUGH

20 grams psyllium husk powder

395 grams cooking water from the black rice

140 grams superfine white rice flour, plus more for dusting

80 grams tapioca starch

70 grams sorghum flour

10 grams kosher salt

125 grams cooked black rice

35 grams toasted black sesame seeds

You might consider this boule a bit unusual because of its color and slightly gummy yet crunchy texture, but it's delicious. A little on the dense side, this is not a loaf with an open crumb, but it is very moist. The cooked rice provides chewiness, a nice bite, and nuttiness. You can of course use this bread to make sandwiches, but I like to eat it by itself or as a side with a salad.

MAKES 1 LOAF

Make the stiff sponge. In a medium bowl, whisk together the water and starter. Add the brown rice flour and stir together until you have a shaggy dough. Knead the dough until smooth. Place the stiff sponge in a wide-mouth 12-ounce (340 ml) mason jar or plastic container, gently pressing it down into the bottom. Place a rubber band around the jar right at the top of where the sponge sits so you can see how much it has grown. Cover with a kitchen towel or a lid and proof at room temperature for 8 to 10 hours, until it rises about 50 percent. This stiff sponge does best around 75° to 80°F (24° to 29°C), so in the winter, I like to keep it in the oven with the light on and a small pot with boiling-hot water that I reheat every 30 to 45 minutes to keep at a constant temperature.

Cook the black rice. In a pot, combine the water, black rice, and salt and bring to a high simmer over high heat. Turn the heat down to medium-low, cover, and cook until the rice is tender, about 30 minutes. Set a sieve over a large bowl and drain the black rice. Reserve both the cooking water and the cooked black rice. Measure 395 grams cooking liquid. If you are short, simply add a touch of water until you have the right amount of liquid. Measure 125 grams of cooked black rice. You might have a bit extra. (You can cook the black rice a day in advance and keep both the liquid and rice refrigerated until ready to use. Make sure they are cooled to room temperature before using in the dough.)

Make the dough. Place the psyllium in a medium bowl. Add the rice cooking water and vigorously whisk until smooth. Let it gel for 5 minutes. In a stand mixer, stir together the white rice flour, tapioca starch, sorghum flour, and salt. Add the stiff sponge and psyllium gel. Snap on the dough hook and mix on medium speed until the dough comes together, 2 to 3 minutes. The dough will be smooth and moist.

Shape the dough. Lightly dust a work surface with some white rice flour. Transfer the dough to the work surface and knead a few times. Pat it down and roll it into a roughly 11-inch (28 cm) square that is ½ inch (1.3 cm) thick. It's okay if it's not the exact size. Top the dough with the cooked black rice and sesame seeds. Fold one-third of the dough over the middle and then the other third over it, creating a letter fold. Pat the dough down to a 1-inch (2.5 cm) thickness. Rotate 90 degrees and give it another letter fold. Roll the dough into a log and then shape into ball. If the dough cracks in some spots revealing the rice, it's okay. Knead a couple of times to shape it into a ball. This will create a swirl pattern inside the bread and some of the rice will be exposed on the surface while baking, which gives a nice texture.

Proof the dough. Dust the inside of a proofing basket with some white rice flour and place the dough in it seam-side up. Cover with a kitchen towel. Proof the dough at room temperature for 2 to 3 hours. (Alternatively, proof for 1 hour at room temperature and then 8 to 12 hours in the refrigerator.)

Preheat the oven. Position a rack in the bottom third of the oven and place a cast-iron Dutch oven on the rack. Preheat the oven to 500°F (260°C). Continue heating for at least 15 minutes after the oven has come to temperature.

Score the bread. Place an 8-inch (20 cm) square piece of parchment on your work surface. Gently invert the dough onto it. Dust the top of the dough with white rice flour. Score the dough using a lame.

Bake the bread. Lift the parchment paper with the dough on it and place it in the Dutch oven. Add 2 or 3 ice cubes next to the dough, cover with the lid, and bake for 50 minutes. Remove the lid, reduce the oven temperature to 425°F (220°C), and bake for 15 minutes, or until the bread is deeply caramelized and crusty.

Cool the bread. Transfer the bread to a wire rack and let it cool completely. The crust will soften considerably as it cools. Store the bread at room temperature wrapped in a paper bag for up to 2 days.

Flourless Fermented Buckwheat and Red Lentil Bread

350 grams buckwheat groats (not toasted), rinsed

165 grams red lentils, rinsed

230 grams filtered water, at around 75° to 80°F (24° to 29°C)

65 grams unsweetened applesauce

25 grams sesame seeds

12 grams extra-virgin olive oil

8 grams kosher salt

This is a high-fiber and high-protein bread loaf that is grain-free, starch-free, and easy to digest. The bread is sour, earthy, and a little funky, too, making it great for veggie sandwiches—think the kind you'd get in the 1970s at a vegetarian cafe. It is inspired by a flatbread I've been making for years where buckwheat groats and red lentils are blended into a batter and fermented for up to 2 days, so it doesn't require an established sourdough starter. The batter can also be made into flatbread by thinning it out with a little bit of water and cooking it on a cast-iron pan like a crêpe.

MAKES 1 LOAF

Soak the buckwheat and lentils. In a large bowl, combine the buckwheat and lentils. Cover them with an abundance of cold water and soak for 4 hours. Drain the buckwheat and lentils.

Make the batter. In a high-powered blender or food processor, combine half of the buckwheat and lentils with 115 grams water and puree until you have a smooth batter. Start blending on low and increase the speed slowly. Stop the blender if needed, scrape the sides, and blend again until you have a smooth batter. It's okay if it's a little gritty. Pour the batter into a large bowl. Blend the remaining buckwheat and lentils with 115 grams water to a smooth batter and add it to the bowl. Stir in the applesauce.

Ferment the batter. Cover the bowl with a kitchen towel or a plate and let it ferment anywhere from 12 to 36 hours. The warmer the environment, the faster it will ferment. I like to put the batter in the oven with a pot of boiling-hot water next to it, especially in the very beginning to get it going. The batter is ready when it has a mousse-like texture.

Preheat the oven. When the batter is ready, position a rack in the bottom third of the oven and preheat the oven to 400°F (200°C). Line a 9-by-4-inch (23 by 10 cm) Pullman loaf pan with a strip of parchment paper, letting some hang over the sides.

(Recipe continues)

Bake the bread. Stir 15 grams of the sesame seeds, the olive oil, and the salt into the batter and pour into the prepared loaf pan. Sprinkle the top with the remaining 10 grams sesame seeds. Bake the bread for 45 to 50 minutes, until it has risen, the top has cracked, and an instant-read thermometer inserted in the center reads 200° to 210°F (93° to 99°C).

Cool the bread. Let the bread cool in the pan for 10 minutes, then lift it out onto a wire rack to cool for 30 minutes before slicing. Store the bread at room temperature tightly wrapped for up to 3 days. This loaf is best served toasted.

Sourdough Salted Miso Baguettes

FOR THE SPONGE

150 grams Whole-Grain Brown Rice–Teff Sourdough Starter (page 48)

85 grams filtered water, at around 75° to 80°F (24° to 29°C)

70 grams sorghum flour, plus more for dusting

FOR THE DOUGH

20 grams psyllium husk powder

7 grams flaxseed meal

300 grams filtered water, at around 75° to 80°F (24° to 29°C)

200 grams potato starch

120 grams tapioca starch, plus more for dusting

20 grams white (shiro) miso

10 grams granulated sugar

8 grams kosher salt

FOR THE TOPPING

140 grams sesame seeds, preferably unhulled

10 grams coarse sea salt flakes

8 grams nori sheets (optional)

70 grams hemp seeds (optional)

In the film *Pig*, Nicolas Cage stars as a retired chef out for vengeance, looking for the people who kidnapped his truffle-sniffing pig, and he dreams about the salted baguette served at a fictional bakery in Portland, Oregon. I was intrigued. "Are salted baguettes a thing? Do they use seawater? But wouldn't that hinder fermentation?" I had so many questions. After doing some research, I discovered that salted baguettes aren't really a thing, but the idea had already triggered my curiosity and so I decided to experiment. By adding miso to my trusty baguette recipe and topping it with a mixture of nori and sesame seeds to give it a deeper flavor, I got a salty baguette! Everyone who tries it cannot believe it is gluten-free.

MAKES 2 BAGUETTES

Make the sponge. In a medium bowl, whisk together the starter, water, and sorghum flour until you have a smooth paste. Cover the bowl with a towel or a plate and proof at room temperature for 3 to 4 hours, until the starter is bubbly and has a mousse-like texture.

Make the dough. In a medium bowl, combine the psyllium and flaxseed. Add the water and immediately whisk together vigorously until smooth. Let it gel for 5 minutes. In a stand mixer, combine the potato starch, tapioca starch, miso, sugar, and salt. Add the sponge and psyllium-flaxseed gel. Snap on the dough hook and mix on medium speed until all the flours are well hydrated and the dough comes together smoothly, 2 to 3 minutes.

Make the topping. In a food processor, combine the sesame seeds, coarse salt, and nori (if using) and pulse 3 to 4 times. Add the hemp seeds (if using) and pulse once to combine. If you don't have a food processor, use a mortar and pestle. This will make more than you need for these baguettes. Keep the unused mixture in an airtight jar for another time.

Shape the dough. Transfer the dough to a work surface and cut into 2 equal pieces. Shape each piece of dough into a tight ball and then roll it into a log that is about 15 inches (38 cm) long with tapered ends. You can dust the work surface with a bit of tapioca starch as you roll, but do not add too much, as you need a bit of friction to be able to roll it. Spray or brush the top of the dough with a small amount of water (only enough so the topping sticks). Place the topping mixture on a sheet pan and dip the moist side of the dough in it. Transfer both baguettes to another sheet pan seed-side up.

Proof the baguettes. Cover the pan with a kitchen towel or wrap it in a thin plastic bag. Proof for 2 to 3 hours, until the dough feels soft and marshmallow-like. You can do this in the oven with a pot of boiling-hot water next to it.

Preheat the oven. About 30 minutes before the dough is done proofing, position a rack in the bottom third of the oven and preheat the oven to 500°F (260°C).

Score the baguettes. Hold your lame in your hand and turn your hand to a 45-degree angle. You want an angled cut so the dough can expand and create nice ears at each slash. Score the dough, making five ¼-inch-deep (6 mm) slashes lengthwise on the top of the baguette. The slashes should overlap about a third of the way.

Bake the baguettes. Place the pan in the oven and reduce the oven temperature to 450°F (230°C). Bake the baguettes for 35 minutes, or until deep golden brown and crusty, injecting steam three times in 5-minute intervals (at 1 minute, 6 minutes, and 11 minutes). If you don't have steam in your oven, see Creating Steam (page 32).

Cool the baguettes. Transfer the baguettes to a wire rack to cool for at least 30 minutes. It's important to let the internal steam release so the crumb can set and the crust can soften slightly. The bread will keep well at room temperature wrapped in parchment paper for 2 days, but it's best eaten the same day.

Note: If you want to make demi baguettes, which are perfect for sandwiches, cut the dough into 5 equal pieces (195 g each). Shape each piece into a mini baguette with a thick center and tapered ends. Proof, score, and bake with steam at 450°F (230°C) for 30 minutes.

Grain-Free Buckwheat-Chestnut Baguettes

PICTURED ON PAGE 57

FOR THE SPONGE

125 grams Grain-Free Buckwheat-Chestnut Sourdough Starter (page 50)

125 grams filtered water, at around 75° to 80°F (24° to 29°C)

70 grams light buckwheat flour

55 grams chestnut flour

FOR THE DOUGH

20 grams psyllium husk powder

7 grams flaxseed meal

280 grams filtered water, at around 75° to 80°F (24° to 29°C)

150 grams tapioca starch

70 grams light buckwheat flour

50 grams chestnut flour

8 grams kosher salt

White rice flour, for dusting (optional)

The Sourdough Salted Miso Baguettes (page 81) are airy, light, elastic, and mineral-y. These baguettes, on the other hand, are nutty, naturally sweet, and dense due to the higher amount of whole grain. Because the buckwheat-chestnut starter takes longer to ferment, make the sponge in the evening so it can ferment overnight, then make the dough, proof, and bake in the morning.

MAKES 2 BAGUETTES

Make the sponge. In a medium bowl, whisk together the starter, water, buckwheat flour, and chestnut flour until smooth. It will have the consistency of yogurt. Cover the bowl with a kitchen towel or plate and proof overnight, for 8 to 10 hours, until the sponge has a slight dome on the top and has a mousse-like texture when you run a spoon through it. If your room temperature is below 70°F (21°C), proof the starter in the oven with a small pot of boiling-hot water next to it.

Make the dough. The next morning, when the sponge is puffed up, in a medium bowl, whisk together the psyllium and flaxseed. Add the water and whisk vigorously. Let it gel for 5 minutes. In a stand mixer, stir together the tapioca starch, buckwheat flour, chestnut flour, and salt. Add the sponge and the psyllium-flaxseed gel. Snap on the dough hook and mix on medium speed until a moist, bouncy dough forms that holds together nicely, 3 to 4 minutes. You might have to scrape down the sides of the bowl halfway through.

Shape the dough. Transfer the dough to a work surface. Knead a few times and cut it in half. Knead each piece of dough a few times and shape into a tight ball. Begin rolling one piece of dough into a log that is roughly 15 inches (38 cm) long. If your dough is too wet, you can dust the work surface with a little white rice flour, but try not to use too much, as you need a bit of friction to roll the dough. Taper the ends of the log, giving it a baguette shape. Transfer the dough to a sheet pan. Repeat with the second piece of dough and place on the pan.

Proof the baguettes. Cover the pan with a kitchen towel or wrap it in a plastic bag. Proof at room temperature for 2 to 4 hours, ideally around 75° to 80°F (24° to 29°C). If your kitchen is cold, proof in your oven with a pot of boiling-hot water next to it. The dough will not puff up very much, but it will feel slightly lighter to the touch. Don't worry if it appears the same size as when you shaped it. It will expand while baking.

Preheat the oven. About 30 minutes before the dough is done proofing, position a rack in the bottom third of the oven and preheat the oven to 450°F (230°C).

Score the baguettes. When the dough has proofed, dust the tops with some white rice flour, if desired. (This will give you a nice contrast of color, but it's not necessary.) Hold your lame in your hand at a 45-degree angle. You want an angled cut so the dough can expand and create nice ears at each slash. Score the dough, making five ¼-inch-deep (6 mm) slashes lengthwise on the top of the baguette. The slashes should overlap about a third of the way.

Bake the baguettes. Bake the baguettes for 35 minutes, until deep golden brown and crusty, injecting steam three times in 5-minute intervals (at 1 minute, 6 minutes, and 11 minutes). If you don't have steam in your oven, see Creating Steam (page 32).

Cool the baguettes. Transfer the baguettes to a wire rack to cool for at least 30 minutes. It's important to let the internal steam release so the crumb can set and the crust can soften slightly. The bread will keep well at room temperature wrapped in parchment paper for 2 days, but it's best eaten the same day.

Country White Sourdough Bread

FOR THE SPONGE

170 grams filtered water, at around 75° to 80°F (24° to 29°C)

150 grams Whole-Grain Brown Rice–Teff Sourdough Starter (page 48)

70 grams sorghum flour

70 grams superfine brown rice flour

FOR THE DOUGH

25 grams psyllium husk powder

370 grams filtered water, at around 75° to 80°F (24° to 29°C)

20 grams maple syrup

12 grams extra-virgin olive oil

105 grams sorghum flour

90 grams millet flour

90 grams tapioca starch

10 grams kosher salt

White rice flour, for dusting

When I think of a basic white, tender, and soft sourdough bread, this is it. The crumb is moist and has small air pockets, and the crust is soft and golden. It is perfect for all kinds of sandwiches and even French toast. I've provided some suggestions for variations on the following pages, but you can add any other ingredients you like to create your own versions of this recipe. I like to proof the dough in an oval banneton (proofing basket) to create a batard shape, but of course a round boule will work as well.

MAKES 1 BATARD

Make the sponge. In a medium bowl, whisk together the water, starter, sorghum flour, and brown rice flour until smooth. Cover with a kitchen towel or plate and proof for 3 to 4 hours, until it has a mousse-like texture when you run a spoon through it.

Make the dough. In a medium bowl, whisk together the psyllium, water, maple syrup, and olive oil until smooth. Let it gel for 5 minutes. In a stand mixer, stir together the sorghum flour, millet flour, tapioca starch, and salt. Add the sponge and psyllium gel. Snap on the dough hook and mix on medium speed until the dough comes together, 3 to 4 minutes. The dough should be moist and hold together nicely.

Shape the dough. Transfer the dough to a work surface and knead a few times. Shape into a tight ball and then into an oval. Lightly dust an oval banneton with some white rice flour and place the dough in it seam-side up.

Proof the dough. Cover the banneton with a kitchen towel and proof until it feels slightly light to the touch, 2 to 4 hours. (Alternatively, proof for 1 hour at room temperature and then 10 to 12 hours in the refrigerator.) The dough will only rise about 25 percent, and don't worry if it doesn't seem that much lighter. It will rise in the oven.

Preheat the oven. Position a rack in the bottom third of the oven and place a cast-iron Dutch oven on the rack. Preheat the oven to 500°F (260°C). Once the oven has reached temperature, let the Dutch oven continue heating for 15 minutes.

(Recipe continues)

Country White Sourdough Bread (top) with Beet Swirl Variation (bottom)

Bake the bread. Cut an 8-inch (20 cm) square of parchment paper and place it on a work surface. Invert the dough onto the parchment. Dust the top with a bit of white rice flour and score the top of the dough. Lift the dough with the parchment into the Dutch oven. Add 2 or 3 ice cubes next to the dough, cover with the lid, and bake for 45 minutes. Remove the lid, reduce the oven temperature to 450°F (230°C), and bake for 15 minutes, or until golden brown.

Cool the bread. Place the bread on a wire rack to cool for at least 1 hour before cutting into it. Store the bread at room temperature wrapped in a paper bag for up to 2 days.

VARIATIONS

Country White Sandwich Bread

Make the dough as directed. Shape the dough into an oval and place it in a greased 8½-by-4½-inch (22 by 11 cm) loaf pan. Cover with a kitchen towel. Proof the dough until it feels light to the touch, 2 to 4 hours. Place a cast-iron pan in the bottom of the oven and preheat to 500°F (260°C). Score the top of the dough. Place the loaf pan in the oven and add 3 ice cubes to the hot cast-iron pan. Bake for 30 minutes, adding 3 more ice cubes to the cast-iron pan at the 6-minute mark, then reduce the heat to 450°F (230°C) and bake for 15 minutes more, until the top of the bread is deep golden brown. Let cool in the pan for 10 minutes, then transfer to a cooling rack and cool completely before slicing.

Country White Beet Swirl Bread

Cook the beets. In a small saucepan, cover 2 medium beets with water. Bring to a boil over high heat. Reduce the heat to medium-low and cook the beets until fork-tender, about 45 minutes. Drain the beets and when cool enough to handle, peel and chop them. Process in a food processor or blender to form a chunky paste.

Make the dough as directed. After the dough is mixed, add 120 grams of the beet puree and mix only until the beets are evenly distributed. If you mix longer, the entire dough will be pink; I prefer to leave a bit of a swirl effect in the crumb. Proceed with shaping, proofing, and baking as directed.

Country White Bread with Turmeric Leeks, Garlic, and Toasted Sesame Seeds

30 grams sesame seeds

25 grams extra-virgin olive oil

1 large leek, white and light-green parts only, washed and thinly sliced (about 90 g)

1 garlic clove, thinly sliced

¼ teaspoon (1 g) kosher salt

½ teaspoon (1 g) ground turmeric

Toast the sesame seeds. Heat a small sauté pan over medium heat. Add the sesame seeds and toast them until they begin to turn a golden color and smell nutty, about 2 minutes. Transfer them to a bowl and let them cool completely.

Cook the leek mixture. In the same sauté pan, combine the olive oil, leeks, garlic, and salt. Stir and cook over medium-low heat until the leeks and garlic begin to lightly caramelize, 5 to 6 minutes. Do not let them burn. Stir in the turmeric and transfer to a bowl to cool.

Make the dough as directed. When the dough has come together, add the leek mixture and sesame seeds and mix for a few seconds until they are distributed. I like to leave a swirl effect; if you mix for too long, the entire dough will turn yellow. Proceed with shaping, proofing, and baking as directed.

Country White Bread with Raspberry and Chocolate

Make the dough as directed. When the dough has come together, add 90 grams coarsely chopped chocolate (70% cacao) and 20 grams freeze-dried raspberries and mix for a few seconds until they are distributed. I like to leave a swirl effect; if you mix for too long, the entire dough will turn red. Proceed with shaping, proofing, and baking as directed.

Corn Milk Sourdough Bread

FOR THE SWEET STIFF SPONGE

75 grams Whole-Grain Brown Rice–Teff Sourdough Starter (page 48)

45 grams whole milk or oat milk, at around 75° to 80°F (24° to 29°C)

70 grams superfine brown rice flour

20 grams granulated sugar

FOR THE DOUGH

345 grams sweet corn kernels, fresh or thawed frozen

20 grams psyllium husk powder

280 grams filtered water, at around 75° to 80°F (24° to 29°C)

105 grams sorghum flour

80 grams tapioca starch

80 grams finely milled corn flour

40 grams medium-grind cornmeal

24 grams granulated sugar

10 grams kosher salt

15 grams unsalted butter or vegan butter, melted

You should make this bread when fresh corn is at its peak in summer. It's equally sweet and savory with a lot of texture that comes from the fresh corn and the coarse cornmeal. Use it for sandwiches, but also alongside grilled vegetables and meats and abundant salads.

MAKES 1 BOULE

Make the sweet stiff sponge. In a medium bowl, whisk together the starter and milk until smooth. Add the brown rice flour and sugar and mix with a spatula until you have a thick paste. Knead it a few times. Place the sponge in a wide-mouth 12-ounce (340 ml) mason jar or plastic container, gently pressing it down into the bottom. Place a rubber band around the jar right where the top of the sponge sits so you will be able to see how much it has grown. Loosely cover the jar with a small kitchen towel or the lid without sealing.

Ferment the sponge. Let the sponge sit until it has risen about 50 percent and the top feels very springy and soft to the touch, 8 to 10 hours. The sponge won't have large air pockets but should feel light when you touch the top. This stiff sponge does best at 75° to 80°F (24° to 29°C), so in the winter, I like to keep it in the oven with the light on and a small pot with boiling-hot water that I reheat every 30 to 45 minutes to keep at a constant temperature.

Make the corn milk. In a food processor or blender, process the corn kernels until pureed but slightly chunky. Transfer the corn puree to a nut milk bag or inside a thin kitchen towel and squeeze over a bowl to catch the juices. This will be your corn "milk" and you should have 100 grams. If you don't have enough, top it off with some water. Measure 100 grams of the leftover pulp (save the rest for another use). Set aside.

Make the dough. In a medium bowl, vigorously whisk together the psyllium, water, and corn "milk." Let it gel for 5 minutes. In a stand mixer, stir together the sorghum flour, tapioca starch, corn flour, cornmeal, sugar, and salt. Add the reserved corn pulp, sweet stiff sponge, psyllium gel, and melted butter. Snap on the dough hook

and mix on medium speed until the dough comes together, 3 to 4 minutes. The dough will be slightly soft and moist but should hold together. Knead a few times and place in a proofing basket seam-side up.

Proof the dough. Cover the proofing basket with a kitchen towel and proof the dough for 2 to 4 hours at room temperature. (Alternatively, proof for 1 hour at room temperature and then 8 to 12 hours in the refrigerator.)

Preheat the oven. Position a rack in the bottom third of the oven and place a cast-iron Dutch oven on the rack. Preheat the oven to 450°F (230°C). Once the oven has reached temperature, let the Dutch oven continue heating for 15 minutes.

Bake the bread. Place an 8-inch (20 cm) square piece of parchment paper on a work surface. Invert the dough onto it and score the top using a lame. Lift the parchment and transfer the dough to the Dutch oven. Add 2 or 3 ice cubes next to the dough, cover with the lid, and bake for 45 minutes. Remove the lid, reduce the oven temperature to 425°F (220°C), and bake for 10 minutes, or until golden brown.

Cool the bread. Transfer the bread to a wire rack to cool completely before cutting. Store the bread at room temperature wrapped in a paper bag for up to 2 days.

Sourdough Ciabatta Rolls

FOR THE SPONGE

150 grams Whole-Grain Brown Rice–Teff Sourdough Starter (page 48)

80 grams filtered water, at around 75° to 80°F (24° to 29°C)

70 grams superfine brown rice flour, plus more for dusting

FOR THE DOUGH

20 grams psyllium husk powder

325 grams filtered water, at around 75° to 80°F (24° to 29°C)

25 grams extra-virgin olive oil, plus more for greasing

12 grams apple cider vinegar

120 grams tapioca starch

120 grams potato starch

90 grams sorghum flour

8 grams kosher salt

Ciabatta, which in Italian means "slipper," is a high-hydration bread with a very airy and moist crumb and a thin and crispy crust. It stays moist for a couple of days and is the perfect roll for sandwiches, especially Charred Broccolini and Marinated Artichokes with Romesco on Ciabatta (page 385).

MAKES 6 CIABATTA ROLLS

Make the sponge. In a medium bowl, whisk together the starter, water, and brown rice flour until smooth. Cover with a kitchen towel and let it ferment at around 75° to 80°F (24° to 29°C) until it is airy and mousse-like. It might be anywhere from 3 hours to 6 hours depending on your starter and your environment.

Make the dough. In a medium bowl, whisk together the psyllium, water, olive oil, and vinegar. Let it gel for 5 minutes. In a stand mixer, stir together the tapioca starch, potato starch, sorghum flour, and salt. Add the sponge and psyllium gel. Snap on the dough hook and mix on medium speed until you have a smooth, bouncy, and moist dough, 3 to 4 minutes.

Proof the dough. Grease a medium bowl with some olive oil. Add the dough to the bowl and roll it around to coat the entire surface with olive oil. Cover tightly with plastic wrap and refrigerate for 12 to 15 hours. The dough will not appear to have grown significantly after this time, which is okay.

Cut the dough. Lightly dust a work surface with brown rice flour. Gently roll the dough (or pat down) into a rectangle that is roughly 6 by 9 inches (15 by 23 cm). It's okay if the edges are not sharp and your rectangle is not perfect. Cut the dough in half lengthwise, then cut each piece into thirds. You will have 6 pieces of dough that are roughly 3 inches (7.5 cm) square.

Proof the rolls. Line a sheet pan with parchment paper and place the pieces of dough on it. Cover with a kitchen towel or plastic wrap or place the pan inside a large plastic bag and ferment at room temperature until the dough feels lighter and slightly marshmallow-like to the touch, 1½ to 2½ hours (depending on your room temperature).

(Recipe continues)

Preheat the oven. About 30 minutes before the rolls are done proofing, position a rack in the bottom third of the oven and preheat the oven to 500°F (260°C). Let the oven continue heating for at least 15 minutes after it has reached temperature.

Bake the rolls. Dust the tops of the rolls with a light sprinkle of brown rice flour. Place the pan in the oven and reduce the oven temperature to 450°F (230°C). Bake the ciabatta rolls until golden brown, 25 to 30 minutes, injecting steam three times in 5-minute intervals (at 1 minute, 6 minutes, and 11 minutes). If you don't have steam in your oven, see Creating Steam (page 32).

Cool the rolls. Let the rolls cool for 30 minutes before cutting into them. They are best eaten within 2 days. Store them in a brown paper bag at room temperature.

Whole-Grain Sourdough Cinnamon-Raisin Loaf

FOR THE SPONGE

150 grams Whole-Grain Brown Rice–Teff Sourdough Starter (page 48)

125 grams filtered water, at around 75° to 80°F (24° to 29°C)

105 grams ivory or brown teff flour

FOR THE AUTOLYZE

140 grams ivory or brown teff flour, plus more for dusting

120 grams oat flour

120 grams tapioca starch

280 grams filtered water, at around 75° to 80°F (24° to 29°C)

FOR THE DOUGH

115 grams filtered water, at around 75° to 80°F (24° to 29°C)

20 grams psyllium husk powder

40 grams maple syrup

12 grams extra-virgin olive oil, plus more for greasing

10 grams kosher salt

7 grams flaxseed meal

110 grams raisins

This is a dark and earthy cinnamon-raisin loaf made with teff and oat. If you prefer a lighter and softer bread, try the Cinnamon-Raisin Pain de Mie (page 160). This recipe includes an autolyze, which is a process of mixing part of the flour and water in the recipe and letting it rest before adding the rest of ingredients. Including this step can help improve the elasticity and texture of the bread, especially in a recipe, like this one, that uses whole-grain flours such as teff and oat. It is not something that I often do and I haven't seen a tremendous difference when I have introduced an autolyze to my process, but wanted to highlight it so you can try it, too. You can read more about autolyze on page 27.

MAKES 1 LOAF

Make the sponge. In a medium bowl, whisk together the starter, water, and teff flour until smooth. Cover with a kitchen towel and proof at room temperature until it has a mousse-like texture, 3 to 4 hours.

Autolyze. At the same time you make the sponge, in the bowl of a stand mixer, stir together the teff flour, oat flour, and tapioca starch. Add the water and mix with a spatula until you have a thick paste. Let the flour and water hydrate while the sponge is proofing.

Make the dough. To the stand mixer bowl with the autolyze add the water, psyllium, maple syrup, olive oil, salt, flaxseed, and sponge. Snap on the dough hook and beat on medium speed for 2 to 3 minutes. The dough will appear very wet and more like batter than dough. Don't fret. This is normal and it happens because the psyllium needs time to absorb all the water. Turn off the mixer and let the dough rest for 10 minutes. Start the mixer again and add the raisins. Mix until thoroughly combined. The dough will be moist and sticky but should hold together.

Make the cinnamon-sugar swirl. In a small bowl, stir together the sugar and cinnamon.

(Recipe continues)

FOR THE CINNAMON-SUGAR SWIRL

50 grams granulated sugar

15 grams ground cinnamon

Prep the pan. Grease an 8 ½-by-4½-inch (22 by 11 cm) loaf pan with some olive oil and line with a strip of parchment paper that hangs over the sides.

Shape the dough. Lightly dust a work surface with some teff flour. Scrape the dough onto it and dust the top with a bit more teff flour. The dough will be sticky, so you can be generous with the flour. Pat down the dough to a rectangle that is roughly 7 by 12 inches (18 by 30 cm). Sprinkle half of the cinnamon sugar on top and lightly press down with your hand so it sticks to the dough. Starting on a short side, fold one-third of the dough over the center and then the other end over it, creating a letter fold. Rotate the dough 90 degrees and pat it down again to a rectangle that is roughly 7 by 12 inches (18 by 30 cm). Sprinkle the remaining cinnamon sugar on top. Starting from a short side, roll the dough into a log.

Proof the dough. Place the dough in the loaf pan, pat it down so it fits the pan, cover with a towel, and proof for 3 to 4 hours. (Alternatively, proof for 1 to 2 hours at room temperature and then 8 to 12 hours in the refrigerator.) The dough won't puff up as much as other doughs and it won't rise much, but you should see an increase in volume of about 50 percent.

Preheat the oven. About 30 minutes before the dough is done proofing, position a rack in the bottom third of the oven and preheat the oven to 425°F (220°C).

Bake the bread. Transfer the loaf pan to the oven. Bake for 45 minutes, then invert the bread out of the pan, place it directly on the oven rack, and bake for 15 minutes, or until deep golden brown.

Cool the bread. Transfer the bread to a wire rack to cool completely. The bread will last 2 days in a paper bag and after that is best toasted.

Chewy Sourdough Bagels

A freshly baked bagel is one of life's greatest pleasures. They don't really even need to be toasted, although I have to admit, I prefer a toasted bagel even when freshly made. You can make these all in one day, but if you are like me and you like to wake up your household with the smell of bagels in the oven, I recommend you start the sponge the afternoon before, make the dough in the evening, and proof the bagels in the refrigerator overnight. The cold ferment helps harden the bagels, too, which makes it easier to handle them when boiling.

MAKES 8 BAGELS

FOR THE SPONGE

170 grams filtered water, at around 75° to 80°F (24° to 29°C)

150 grams Whole-Grain Brown Rice–Teff Sourdough Starter (page 48)

70 grams superfine brown rice flour

70 grams sorghum flour

FOR THE DOUGH

20 grams psyllium husk powder

7 grams flaxseed meal

270 grams filtered water, at around 75° to 80°F (24° to 29°C)

150 grams oat flour

90 grams tapioca starch

40 grams potato starch

8 grams kosher salt

20 grams maple syrup

12 grams extra-virgin olive oil

FOR THE WATER BATH

1,350 grams water

20 grams blackstrap molasses

25 grams baking soda

4 grams kosher salt

Make the sponge. In a medium bowl, whisk together the water, starter, brown rice flour, and sorghum flour until you have a smooth paste. Cover the bowl with a kitchen towel or plate and proof until the top is domed and the sponge has a mousse-like texture, 3 to 4 hours.

Make the dough. In a medium bowl, whisk together the psyllium and flaxseed. Add the water and whisk vigorously until smooth. Let it gel for 5 minutes. In a stand mixer, stir together the oat flour, tapioca starch, potato starch, and salt. Add the sponge, psyllium-flaxseed gel, maple syrup, and olive oil. Snap on the dough hook and mix on medium speed until you have a smooth and moist dough, 2 to 3 minutes.

Shape the dough. Line a sheet pan with parchment paper. Turn the dough out onto a work surface. Cut the dough into 8 equal pieces (about 135 g each). Shape each piece into a ball, then use the end of a wooden spoon or your thumb (lightly floured to avoid sticking) to press a hole through the center of the dough, gently expanding it to 1½ inches (4 cm) in diameter. Repeat with all the dough pieces. Place the bagels on the lined pan.

Proof the dough. Wrap the pan in a large plastic bag or kitchen towel and proof at room temperature until the dough feels light, 2 to 3 hours. (Alternatively, proof for 1 hour at room temperature and then 8 to 12 hours in the refrigerator. If proofing in the fridge, cover the pan with a plastic bag or wrap with plastic wrap.)

(Recipe continues)

FOR THE TOPPING

135 grams seeds and spices (sesame seeds, pumpkin seeds, poppy seeds, dried onion, dried garlic, fennel seeds, black pepper, flaky sea salt, etc.)

Preheat the oven. Position one rack in the bottom third of the oven and another at the lowest position in the oven. Place a cast-iron pan or tray on the bottom rack. Preheat the oven to 500°F (260°C). Let the oven heat for at least 15 minutes after it comes to temperature.

Prepare the water bath. In a large deep pot, bring the water to a boil over high heat, then reduce the heat to maintain a simmer. When you are ready to boil the bagels, add the molasses, baking soda, and salt to the water. The water will bubble up, so be careful.

Boil the bagels. If you have proofed your bagels at room temperature, chill them in the freezer for 5 minutes so they are easier to handle when boiling. If you have proofed them in the refrigerator, they should feel sturdy and solid enough to handle. Working in two batches, gently lower 4 bagels into the simmering water and cook for 20 seconds on each side. Boil no more than 4 bagels at a time. Remove them with a slotted spoon and return them to the sheet pan. Sprinkle the seeds and spices on top.

Bake the bagels. Place the sheet pan in the oven, reduce the oven temperature to 450°F (230°C), and toss 4 or 5 ice cubes in the cast-iron pan at the bottom of the oven. Close the door and bake for 20 to 22 minutes, until the bagels are deep golden brown.

Cool the bagels. Transfer them to a wire rack to cool for at least 30 minutes before serving. The bagels are best eaten the same day, but they can be frozen, tightly wrapped, for up to 3 months.

VARIATION

Blueberry Sourdough Bagels

Add 50 grams freeze-dried blueberries after mixing the dough. Mix again until the dough is smooth and takes on a purple color. Shape, proof, and cook the bagels as directed. Omit the topping.

No. 3

Ways to Use Sourdough Discard

Sourdough discard is a portion of the sourdough starter that is removed before feeding it in order to manage the starter's growth and refresh the acidity levels. The discard is not active enough to leaven bread, but you can use it in other recipes—from pancakes to cookies—as it's nothing more than flour, water, and beneficial microbes.

I like to store my sourdough discard in a glass jar in the refrigerator (make sure you label it as discard), and every time I refresh my starter and have any left, I add it to the discard jar. You can keep your discard in the refrigerator for as long as it doesn't spoil. It will start to develop hooch after a while, which will contribute a lot of tangy flavor to whatever recipe you use it in. Simply stir the hooch back in every time you add more discard to your jar. You will know your discard has gone bad if the hooch on top turns dark or if you see any pink or gray spots (mold), or if it smells like rotten food.

If your discard is fresh, you could even create a new starter with it; see Converting Starters (page 45).

The recipes in this chapter can be made with discard that is active (meaning discard that came from starter that was recently fed) or inactive (discard that has sat in the fridge for a while). Some are as simple as whisking in your discard and baking, like the Lacy Sourdough Crêpes (page 122) or Sourdough Chocolate-Miso Cookies (page 115), while others require activating the starter, as in Sourdough Crumpets Two Ways (page 131).

Lemon–Poppy Seed Sourdough Pound Cake

Classic lemon–poppy seed cake becomes extra tangy and flavorful with the addition of sourdough discard.

MAKES 1 POUND CAKE

FOR THE CAKE BATTER

110 grams extra-virgin olive oil, plus more for greasing

25 grams poppy seeds

140 grams superfine brown rice flour

100 grams almond flour

30 grams tapioca starch

1 teaspoon (4 g) kosher salt

½ teaspoon (2 g) baking soda

½ teaspoon (2 g) xanthan gum (optional)

150 grams granulated sugar

10 grams finely grated lemon zest (from 2 to 3 lemons)

40 grams honey or maple syrup

3 large eggs, at room temperature

200 grams discard from Whole-Grain Brown Rice–Teff Sourdough Starter (page 48)

55 grams fresh lemon juice

FOR THE CLEAR GLAZE

50 grams granulated sugar

55 grams fresh lemon juice

FOR THE POWDERED SUGAR GLAZE (OPTIONAL)

240 grams powdered sugar

25 to 35 grams fresh lemon juice

Preheat the oven. Position a rack in the center of the oven and preheat the oven to 350°F (180°C). Grease a loaf pan with olive oil and line with a strip of parchment paper, leaving some overhang.

Grind the poppy seeds. In a coffee grinder or blender, grind the poppy seeds to a fine powder. Set aside.

Mix the batter. In a large bowl, stir together the brown rice flour, almond flour, tapioca starch, salt, baking soda, and xanthan gum (if using). In a medium bowl, rub the sugar and lemon zest together until the sugar feels sandy. Whisk in the honey, eggs, sourdough discard, olive oil, and lemon juice until smooth. Add the wet ingredients to the dry ingredients and whisk until you have a smooth and pourable batter.

Swirl the batter. Pour half of the batter into a separate bowl and stir in the ground poppy seeds. Alternate adding spoonfuls of the two different batters into the prepared pan. Run the tip of a knife through the batter to create swirls.

Bake the cake. Bake for 45 to 50 minutes, until a toothpick inserted in the middle comes out clean.

Make the clear glaze. In a small saucepan, heat the sugar and lemon juice until the sugar is dissolved. When the cake comes out of the oven, use a toothpick to puncture some holes in it. Brush the cake with the glaze.

Cool the cake. Let the cake cool in the pan for 10 minutes. Use the parchment to transfer the cake to a wire rack to cool completely.

Make the powdered sugar glaze. In a medium bowl, whisk together the powdered sugar and lemon juice until smooth. Make sure to wait until the cake is completely cooled to glaze it. Pour the glaze over the top of the cake, letting it drip over the sides. Slice the cake and serve. Store the cake tightly wrapped in the fridge for up to 3 days.

Banana Sourdough Bread

115 grams extra-virgin olive oil, plus more for greasing

350 grams mashed banana (from 3 very ripe bananas)

200 grams light brown sugar

3 large eggs, at room temperature

100 grams discard from Whole-Grain Brown Rice–Teff Sourdough Starter (page 48)

2 teaspoons (8 g) vanilla extract

105 grams superfine brown rice flour

100 grams almond flour

60 grams tapioca starch

1 teaspoon (4 g) baking soda

½ teaspoon (2 g) kosher salt

1 firm-ripe banana (optional), halved lengthwise

2 tablespoons (20 g) finely chopped walnuts (optional)

I have made a variety of banana bread recipes throughout my years as a baker and cookbook author. Here is a new recipe adapted to include sourdough discard. The cake is equally moist and has a slight tang that is delicious. The recipe is intentionally simple, but you could add walnuts, chopped chocolate, and even a crumble on top; see the Variation. If you are avoiding starch, omit the tapioca and use an additional 75 grams almond flour.

MAKES 1 LOAF

Preheat the oven. Position a rack in the center of the oven and preheat the oven to 350°F (180°C). Grease a 9-by-4-inch (23 by 10 cm) loaf pan with olive oil and line with a strip of parchment paper, leaving some overhang.

Make the batter. In a large bowl, whisk together the mashed banana, brown sugar, eggs, olive oil, sourdough discard, and vanilla until smooth. In a medium bowl, stir together the brown rice flour, almond flour, tapioca starch, baking soda, and salt. Add the dry ingredients to the wet and whisk until you have a smooth batter. Pour the batter into the prepared pan. If desired, place the banana halves and sprinkle the walnuts (if using) on top of the batter.

Bake the bread. Bake for 60 to 65 minutes, until a toothpick inserted in the center comes out clean. Check the banana bread at around 45 minutes and if it seems to be getting too dark, tent the top with aluminum foil.

Cool the bread. Let the banana bread cool in the pan for 10 minutes, then lift out onto a wire rack to cool completely. Store the banana bread tightly wrapped in the refrigerator for up to 3 days.

VARIATION

Banana and Chocolate Sourdough Bread

Add 15 grams cacao powder to the dry ingredients and fold 90 grams chopped chocolate (70% cacao) into the batter. Bake as directed.

Fudgy Sourdough Brownies

3 large eggs, at room temperature

200 grams granulated sugar

2 teaspoons (8 g) vanilla extract

180 grams chocolate (70% cacao), coarsely chopped

110 grams unsalted butter or vegan butter or extra-virgin olive oil

50 grams unsweetened cocoa powder

150 grams discard from Whole-Grain Brown Rice–Teff Sourdough Starter (page 48)

1 teaspoon (4 g) kosher salt

Flaky sea salt (optional), for sprinkling

This is a gooey and fudgy brownie with a thin crust. Not all sugars are equal when it comes to how shiny the brownie's crust is. If you like a shiny, thin crust, use superfine sugar rather than plain old granulated. If you are not worried about shine and you prefer to focus on flavor, you could use half granulated sugar and half dark brown sugar or even coconut sugar.

SERVES 8

Preheat the oven. Position a rack in the center of the oven and preheat the oven to 350°F (180°C). Line a 9-inch (23 cm) square cake pan with parchment paper.

Whip the eggs. In a stand mixer fitted with the whisk, beat the eggs, sugar, and vanilla on medium-high speed for 10 minutes until the mixture is thick and pale in color.

Melt the chocolate. Meanwhile, place the chopped chocolate and butter in a heatproof bowl and melt over a pan with simmering water. Remove the bowl from the heat and whisk in the cocoa powder until smooth.

Make the batter. Add the chocolate mixture, sourdough discard, and salt to the egg mixture and whip on high speed until you have a smooth batter, about 30 seconds.

Bake the brownies. Pour the batter into the prepared pan. Sprinkle with the sea salt, if using. Bake for 20 to 25 minutes, until the top cracks.

Cool the brownies. Let cool in the pan for 15 minutes, then lift out of the pan and cut into squares. If you want them especially fudgy, refrigerate them overnight and serve the next day. The brownies will keep for 5 days tightly wrapped into the refrigerator.

Sourdough Chocolate-Miso Cookies

110 grams unsalted butter or vegan butter, at room temperature

120 grams dark brown sugar

100 grams granulated sugar

20 grams white (shiro) miso

2 teaspoons (8 g) vanilla extract

120 grams discard from Whole-Grain Brown Rice–Teff Sourdough Starter (page 48)

105 grams superfine brown rice flour

50 grams almond flour

30 grams tapioca starch

½ teaspoon (2 g) baking soda

¼ teaspoon (1 g) baking powder

170 grams chocolate (70% cacao), coarsely chopped

Flaky sea salt (optional), for sprinkling

The combination of sourdough discard and miso adds another layer of umami to these cookies, which balances their sweetness. These are classic cookies with a crispy edge and soft center, and I promise you that you will not be able to stop eating them. You can replace the almond flour with unsweetened finely shredded coconut for a slightly chewier texture.

MAKES 16 COOKIES

Preheat the oven. Position two racks in the center and lower third of the oven and preheat the oven to 350°F (180°C). Line two sheet pans with parchment paper.

Make the dough. In a stand mixer fitted with the paddle, cream the butter, brown sugar, granulated sugar, miso, and vanilla on medium speed until smooth, about 1 minute. Scrape the paddle and sides of the bowl. Add the sourdough discard and continue mixing until creamy. In a medium bowl, stir together the brown rice flour, almond flour, tapioca starch, baking soda, and baking powder. Add to the mixer bowl and mix on medium speed until combined. Add the chocolate chunks and mix until they are evenly distributed.

Shape the cookies. Using a 3-tablespoon ice cream scoop, drop 8 balls of the dough onto each sheet pan leaving 2 inches (5 cm) between the cookies. If desired, sprinkle a little flaky sea salt on top.

Bake the cookies. Bake for 13 to 15 minutes, until the edges of the cookies are golden brown and the center feels a little underbaked, rotating the pans front to back and switching racks halfway through. The cookies will be slightly puffed in the center but they will deflate and crack as they sit.

Cool the cookies. Let the cookies cool on the pan for 5 minutes, otherwise they will fall apart, then transfer them to a wire rack. The cookies will keep in an airtight container at room temperature for up to 3 days.

Ginger Molasses Sourdough Cookies with Chocolate Chunks

FOR THE COOKIE DOUGH

110 grams unsalted butter or 85 grams vegan butter, melted

75 grams light brown sugar

75 grams granulated sugar

1 large egg yolk or 1½ tablespoons (20 g) unsweetened applesauce

1 tablespoon (6 g) finely grated fresh ginger

150 grams discard from Whole-Grain Brown Rice–Teff Sourdough Starter (page 48)

80 grams blackstrap molasses

105 grams superfine brown rice flour

90 grams light buckwheat flour

1 teaspoon (4 g) baking soda

1 teaspoon (4 g) kosher salt

½ teaspoon (2 g) ground cinnamon

½ teaspoon (2 g) ground ginger

¼ teaspoon (1 g) ground cloves

90 grams chocolate (70% cacao), coarsely chopped

During the winter months, I make these cookies at least once a week. My family prefers them to any other cookie. They are crunchy on the exterior and spongy on the interior. Personally, I like them better when they cool and the chocolate pieces are hard rather than gooey, but I might be the outlier on this. Note that I list two different amounts for butter whether you are using unsalted butter or vegan butter. That is because the unsalted butter can be browned and, in the process, you lose some of it. If you are using vegan butter instead, simply melt it; do not try to brown it. For a vegan version, replace the egg yolk with applesauce.

MAKES 15 COOKIES

Make the brown butter (only if using unsalted butter). In a small saucepan, cook the unsalted butter over medium-high heat. Stir it occasionally as it melts and sizzles, and then more frequently as the bubbles get smaller and the sizzle peters out. The milk solids will caramelize and release a nutty aroma. Remove the pan from the heat and pour the brown butter into a small bowl. Set aside and allow to cool for 10 minutes.

Make the cookie dough. In a medium bowl, whisk together the brown butter (or melted vegan butter), brown sugar, granulated sugar, egg yolk (or applesauce), and fresh ginger. Mix in the sourdough discard, and molasses. In a small bowl, stir together the brown rice flour, buckwheat flour, baking soda, salt, cinnamon, ground ginger, and cloves. Add the dry ingredients to the wet and stir together until you have a smooth dough. Mix in the chopped chocolate until thoroughly distributed. Cover the bowl with plastic wrap and refrigerate the dough for at least 2 hours to chill.

Make the sugar coating. In a small bowl, stir together the granulated sugar, cinnamon, and ground ginger. Set aside.

FOR THE SUGAR COATING

½ cup (100 g) granulated sugar

1 teaspoon (3 g) ground cinnamon

1 teaspoon (3 g) ground ginger

Preheat the oven. Position racks in the center and lower third of the oven and preheat the oven to 350°F (180°C). Line two sheet pans with parchment paper.

Shape the cookies. Using a 3-tablespoon ice cream scoop, form the dough into balls. Roll them in the sugar coating mixture and place them on the lined sheet pans leaving 3 inches (7.5 cm) between the cookies.

Bake the cookies. Bake for 12 to 15 minutes, until the exterior feels set, but they are still soft in the center. Rotate the pans front to back and switch racks halfway through to ensure they bake evenly.

Cool the cookies. Let the cookies cool on the pans for 10 minutes before lifting them or they can crumble. Store them in an airtight container for up to 5 days.

Fruit and Nut Sourdough Crackers

Olive oil, for greasing

180 grams oat flour

140 grams raisins or coarsely chopped apricots

75 grams pumpkin seeds (or any coarsely chopped nuts)

50 grams light brown sugar

30 grams flaxseed meal

2 teaspoons (8 g) baking soda

1 teaspoon (4 g) psyllium husk powder

1 teaspoon (4 g) kosher salt

1 to 2 teaspoons (1 to 2 g) fresh rosemary leaves (optional), finely chopped

375 grams whole milk or oat milk

150 grams discard from Whole-Grain Brown Rice–Teff Sourdough Starter (page 48)

80 grams maple syrup or honey

If you are anything like me, you probably could live on cheese and crackers. Not just any crackers, but those incredibly thin, store-bought fruit- and nut-filled crackers. They are irresistible alongside a salty cheese. Now you can make them at home. They are really easy to pull together and they last a long time if you keep them in an airtight container. The process is similar to making biscotti where you bake a loaf, slice it, and bake it again until the crackers are dry. I bake it in a traditional 8½-by-4½-inch (22 by 11 cm) loaf pan, but you can bake it in two smaller loaf pans.

MAKES ABOUT 40 CRACKERS

Preheat the oven. Position a rack in the center of the oven and preheat the oven to 350°F (180°C). Grease an 8½-by-4½-inch (22 by 11 cm) loaf pan with olive oil and line with a strip of parchment, letting some hang over the edges.

Make the batter. In a large bowl, stir together the oat flour, raisins, pumpkin seeds, brown sugar, flaxseed, baking soda, psyllium, salt, and rosemary (if using). Add the milk, starter, and maple syrup. Stir everything to combine. You will have a very liquid batter. Let it sit for 5 minutes so the mixture thickens and resembles cake batter. Pour into the prepared pan. Smooth out the top.

Bake the loaf. Place the loaf pan in the oven and bake for 1 hour to 1 hour 10 minutes, until a toothpick inserted in the center comes out clean. If the top becomes too dark toward the end, tent it with a piece of aluminum foil.

Cool the bread. Let the bread cool in the pan for 10 minutes, then lift it up holding the parchment and transfer to a wire rack to cool completely. After the bread has cooled, freeze it for 30 to 40 minutes. (Alternatively, wrap the bread in plastic and store at room temperature for a day. The cooler the bread, the easier it is to slice.)

Preheat the oven. Position a rack in the center of the oven and preheat the oven to 275°F (140°C).

Slice the loaf. Using a very sharp knife, cut the bread into very thin slices (about ⅛ inch/3mm thick) and place them on a single layer on two sheet pans (you might even need a third). It's important they be as thin as possible so they dry properly and become crispy. Some of the slices might crack around the edges while cutting or some of the raisins might pop off, which is normal.

Bake the crackers. Transfer the pans to the oven and bake for 15 minutes. Flip the crackers over and bake for 15 to 20 minutes more, until they are dry and golden brown throughout. The crackers will shrink and warp slightly as they dry. They might not appear completely crispy after the baking time, but they will continue to dry as they cool, so take that into account if you feel they need a few more minutes of baking time. Store them in an airtight container, at room temperature, for up to 2 weeks.

Grain-Free Sourdough Seeded Crackers

- 125 grams discard from Grain-Free Buckwheat-Chestnut Sourdough Starter (page 50); see Note
- 280 grams water
- 120 grams light buckwheat flour
- 55 grams extra-virgin olive oil
- 50 grams almond flour
- 1 teaspoon (4 g) kosher salt
- 70 grams assorted seeds (sesame, pumpkin, flax, sunflower, cumin, coriander, nigella)
- 2 teaspoons (6 g) sumac (optional), for sprinkling
- Flaky sea salt, for sprinkling
- Freshly ground black pepper, for sprinkling

I make these crackers whenever we host friends and family. It is probably one of my most popular recipes in the mezze and appetizer arena. They are impossibly thin, crispy, and very nutty and complement recipes like Muhammara (page 365) or Roasted Cauliflower Hummus with Fried Chickpeas (page 367). There is no rolling involved with these crackers; simply whisk all ingredients together into a thin batter, pour onto a sheet pan, and bake.

MAKES 2 LARGE SHEETS

Make the batter. In a medium bowl, whisk together the starter, water, buckwheat flour, olive oil, almond flour, and salt until smooth. The batter will be runny, like a very thin pancake batter or heavy cream. Cover the bowl and let the batter rest for 20 minutes. (The batter keeps in the fridge for 24 hours, so you could make it ahead of time. Note that if you chill the batter, it will take a few minutes longer to bake.)

Preheat the oven. Position racks in the middle and lower third of the oven and preheat the oven to 300°F (150°C). Line two 13-by-18-inch (33 by 46 cm) sheet pans with parchment paper.

Pour the batter. After 20 minutes, the batter will have thickened slightly, but will remain pourable and thin. Pour half of the batter onto one of the sheet pans. Using an offset spatula, evenly spread the batter to reach the edges of the pan. You want the batter paper-thin so it gets crispy when it bakes. Make sure it is as even as possible. Sprinkle half of the seeds all over the top of the batter and gently press them down. Sprinkle a little bit of sumac (if using), flaky salt, and pepper over the top. Repeat with remaining batter on the second prepared sheet pan.

Bake the crackers. Place the pans in the oven and bake for 20 minutes. Switch racks and bake for 15 to 20 minutes, until the crackers are golden brown and dry. Be careful when you open the oven door because a lot of steam will come out. If they are still pale, add 5 to 10 more minutes of baking time. Gently remove the crackers, while still on the parchment paper, from the pan and place them directly on the oven racks. Bake for 5 to 10 minutes, until completely dry on the bottom.

Cool the crackers. Transfer to a wire rack to cool completely. Break the crackers into large shards. Store them in an airtight container for up to 7 days.

Note: If the only discard you have available is from Whole-Grain Brown Rice–Teff Sourdough Starter (page 48), you can use it, but reduce the amount of water in this recipe to 250 grams. On the contrary, if you don't have any sourdough starter at all, omit it and use 185 grams light buckwheat flour and 345 grams water.

Lacy Sourdough Crêpes with Banana and Miso Caramel

PICTURED ON PAGE 124

FOR THE CRÊPE BATTER

150 grams discard from Whole-Grain Brown Rice–Teff Sourdough Starter (page 48) or Grain-Free Buckwheat-Chestnut Sourdough Starter (page 50)

1 large egg or 1 flax egg (see page 26)

15 grams unsalted butter, vegan butter, or coconut oil, melted and cooled, plus more for greasing

10 grams granulated sugar

⅛ teaspoon (0.5 g) kosher salt

FOR THE MISO CARAMEL

150 grams granulated sugar

55 grams water

115 grams heavy cream or canned full-fat coconut milk, lightly warmed

40 grams white (shiro) miso

TO SERVE

2 bananas, thinly sliced

35 grams salted roasted peanuts, coarsely chopped

This recipe should be called *lazy* lacy crêpes. Traditional crêpes require that the batter rest overnight so the flour can hydrate properly. In this case, since the sourdough discard is well hydrated, once you whisk all the ingredients together, your batter is ready to go. Of all the recipes that use discard, these are the easiest things to make. The discard adds a distinct milky sour note that is delicious. As is the case with most crêpes, the first, and even second, crêpe doesn't turn out. Don't be discouraged; throw it out and start again. You will have to adjust your heat a bit until you get the perfect pan temperature. You want the pan to be hot enough that the batter sizzles but not so hot that the crêpes burn.

You don't necessarily need a special crêpe pan for this—a regular nonstick should work. Also, if you have enough starter, you can double the recipe and freeze the crêpes for a later time. If you don't want to make the miso caramel, serve the crêpes simply with the sliced bananas and toasted peanuts or even your favorite jam. See the Variation (opposite) to turn them into chocolate crêpes.

MAKES 5 OR 6 CRÊPES

Make the crêpe batter. In a medium bowl, whisk together the discard, egg (or flax egg), melted butter, sugar, and salt until smooth. The batter will be very thin, similar to the consistency of heavy cream. If using the buckwheat-chestnut starter discard, you will need to add 25 grams of water, since it has a lower hydration ratio.

Cook the crêpes. Heat a 7- to 8-inch (18 to 20 cm) nonstick pan over medium heat. To see if the pan is hot enough, sprinkle a few droplets of water on it and if they sizzle right away, it's ready. Take a small dab of butter and coat the bottom of the pan (I sometimes take the entire stick and just rub it all over the pan). Hold the pan with one hand and with the other, pour a bit less than ¼ cup (35 g) of batter into it. As you are adding the batter, swirl the pan so it spreads evenly all over the bottom into a thin layer. Cook until golden brown, about

1 minute. Then, using your fingers or the tip of a spatula, gently lift the crêpe and flip it over. Cook for another minute, then transfer to a plate. Remember that your first crêpe will be a test. If the batter seems thick and it's not spreading easily in the pan, add a bit more water. Cook the remaining batter. Store the crêpes in the refrigerator tightly wrapped for up to 2 days. You can also freeze them tightly wrapped for up to 1 month.

Make the miso caramel. In a medium saucepan, stir together the sugar and water. Bring to a boil over medium-high heat without stirring. Use a wet pastry brush to wash down any sugar crystals that form on the sides of the pan. Cook until the sugar turns a deep golden brown. Remove the pan from the heat and carefully pour in the warm cream. If the cream is cold, the caramel can harden. Return the pan to low heat and stir until it's liquid again. Whisk in the miso. Pour the caramel into a glass mason jar. It will harden as it cools. Melt it by placing the glass jar in some hot water or in the microwave, heating in 20-second intervals. Store in the refrigerator for up to 1 week.

Serve the crêpes. Place the crêpes on a platter and top with sliced bananas, a generous drizzle of caramel, and chopped peanuts. Serve immediately.

Note: If you want to make these crêpes but don't have sourdough starter, replace the starter with 70 grams brown rice flour and 80 grams water. Whisk all the ingredients together and refrigerate the batter overnight.

VARIATION

Chocolate Sourdough Crêpes

Whisk 7 grams unsweetened cacao powder and 15 grams water into the batter. Whisk until smooth. Cook as directed.

Sourdough Waffles or Pancakes

PICTURED ON PAGE 125

FOR THE SPONGE

225 grams discard (must still be bubbly) from Whole-Grain Brown Rice–Teff Sourdough Starter (page 48)

170 grams whole milk or oat milk

140 grams superfine brown rice flour

55 grams fresh lemon juice

30 grams tapioca starch

20 grams maple syrup

FOR THE BATTER

1 large egg, lightly beaten, or 1 flax egg (see page 26)

25 grams unsalted butter or vegan butter, melted, plus more for greasing

1 teaspoon (4 g) vanilla extract

1 teaspoon (4 g) baking soda

¾ teaspoon (3 g) kosher salt

FOR SERVING

Maple syrup

In this recipe, the sourdough discard is activated to get a bubblier and more sour pancake or waffle by letting the sponge ferment overnight. But if you are rushed for time, simply mix all the ingredients for the sponge and the batter together in a large bowl and skip the overnight fermentation. This version will be a little less bubbly and less sour but delicious, too. You can also try a grain-free version (see Variation) using discard from the Grain-Free Buckwheat-Chestnut Sourdough Starter.

MAKES 10 PANCAKES OR 8 WAFFLES

Make the sponge. The night before you are going to cook the waffles or pancakes, in a large bowl, whisk together the discard, milk, brown rice flour, lemon juice, tapioca starch, and maple syrup. Cover the bowl with a kitchen towel and ferment at room temperature overnight (8 to 10 hours). In the morning, the sponge should be puffed up and bubbly.

Make the batter. Whisk the egg (or flax egg), melted butter, vanilla, baking soda, and salt into the sponge right before you are going to cook it.

To make pancakes: Heat a nonstick or a well-seasoned cast-iron pan over medium-high heat. Add a dab of butter and pour in about ⅓ cup (65 g) of batter for each pancake. Cook until you see bubbles form on the surface and the bottom looks golden brown, about 2 minutes. Flip and finish cooking for another minute. Repeat with the remaining batter. Serve warm with maple syrup or any other toppings you prefer.

To make waffles: Heat a waffle iron over medium-high heat. When the waffle iron is ready, grease with some butter or pan spray and pour enough batter to fill the waffle iron (the amount will depend on the size). Cook until golden brown, 2 to 3 minutes. Repeat with the remaining batter. Serve warm with maple syrup or any other toppings you prefer.

VARIATION

Grain-Free Waffle and Pancake Batter

FOR THE GRAIN-FREE SPONGE

200 grams discard from Grain-Free Buckwheat-Chestnut Sourdough Starter (page 50)

100 grams almond flour or chestnut flour

90 grams light buckwheat flour

200 grams whole milk or oat milk

55 grams fresh lemon juice

20 grams maple syrup

FOR THE BATTER

1 large egg, lightly beaten, or 1 flax egg (see page 26)

25 grams unsalted butter or vegan butter, melted

1 teaspoon (4 g) vanilla extract

1 teaspoon (4 g) baking soda

¾ teaspoon (3 g) kosher salt

Follow the same steps as in the basic recipe.

Skillet Sourdough Mochi Corn Bread with Honey-Butter Glaze

210 grams superfine sweet white rice flour

150 grams medium-grind stone-ground cornmeal

100 grams light brown sugar

1½ teaspoons (6 g) baking powder

1 teaspoon (4 g) kosher salt

¼ teaspoon (1 g) baking soda

225 grams whole milk, oat milk, or canned full-fat coconut milk

150 grams discard from Whole-Grain Brown Rice–Teff Sourdough Starter (page 48)

55 grams unsalted butter, vegan butter, or coconut oil, melted

2 large eggs or 2 flax eggs (see page 26)

15 grams unsalted butter or vegan butter, at room temperature

FOR THE HONEY-BUTTER GLAZE

40 grams unsalted butter or vegan butter

40 grams honey

Mochi is a Japanese sticky cake made from sweet white rice flour. The combination of corn bread and mochi might seem unusual, but they are actually perfect partners—sticky and a little gummy from the sweet white rice flour in contrast to the crunchy and textural cornmeal.

MAKES ONE 10-INCH (25 CM) ROUND CORN BREAD

Preheat the oven. Position a rack in the center of the oven and preheat the oven to 425°F (220°C) with a 10-inch (25 cm) cast-iron skillet inside.

Make the batter. In a large bowl, stir together the sweet white rice flour, cornmeal, brown sugar, baking powder, salt, and baking soda. Whisk in the milk, sourdough discard, melted butter, and eggs until you have a thick smooth batter.

Bake the corn bread. Remove the heated skillet from the oven and add the room-temperature butter while swirling it around until it melts completely. It will sizzle and foam up slightly. Pour in the batter and smooth out the top with a spatula. Return the skillet to the oven and bake for 20 to 25 minutes, until the corn bread is puffed up and golden brown all over.

Make the honey-butter glaze. In a small saucepan, melt the butter and honey together over medium heat. When the corn bread comes out of the oven, glaze the top with the honey butter. Let the corn bread cool for 10 minutes, then slice and serve while warm. It is best eaten the same day.

Note: If you prefer a not-so-sweet corn bread, cut the amount of brown sugar in half. If you don't have sourdough discard, increase the sweet white rice flour to 280 grams and the milk to 340 grams, and add 4 grams apple cider vinegar.

Sourdough Crumpets Two Ways

Crumpets are the original English muffins, which evolved to be a bit more doughy and slightly chewier. They are extremely easy to make. You will need at least one English muffin ring that is about 4 inches (10 cm) wide and 1 inch (2.5 cm) deep. You could cook one at a time or as many as you can fit on your griddle. You can order the rings online, or in a pinch use a cookie cutter. Temperature is really important when cooking crumpets. You want to keep an even low heat so the crumpets cook on the inside without burning the outside; keep an eye on the heat and adjust accordingly.

Here are two ways to make crumpets. One batter requires overnight proofing and the other can be cooked right away. They are both delicious.

Overnight Sourdough Crumpets

MAKES 6 TO 8 CRUMPETS

150 grams whole milk or oat milk

150 grams discard (must still be bubbly) from Whole-Grain Brown Rice–Teff Sourdough Starter (page 48)

35 grams superfine brown rice flour

35 grams ivory teff flour

30 grams tapioca starch

10 grams granulated sugar

1 teaspoon (4 g) kosher salt

Olive oil, for greasing

½ teaspoon (2 g) baking soda

Cornmeal (optional)

Mix the batter. In a medium bowl, whisk together the milk, discard, brown rice flour, teff flour, tapioca starch, sugar, and salt in a medium bowl until you have a batter the consistency of heavy cream.

Proof the batter. Cover the bowl with a kitchen towel and ferment until bubbly and the batter has a mousse-like texture, about 8 hours or overnight.

Preheat the griddle. When your batter has fermented, grease the insides of 6 rings 4 inches (10 cm) in diameter and 1 inch (2.5 cm) deep with olive oil. Preheat a large cast-iron griddle or pan over medium-low heat. It's important to build heat slowly, otherwise the muffins will burn on the bottom and will not cook in the center. The pan is ready when a drop of water sizzles on the surface. Place the rings on the pan.

Cook the crumpets. When your griddle is ready, whisk the baking soda into the batter. If using the cornmeal, sprinkle a dusting on the pan where the ring is sitting. Pour ¼ to ⅓ cup (50 to 65 g) of batter into each ring mold (it should fill only half the ring). The batter will begin to bubble immediately. Cook over medium-low heat until you see bubbles appear on the top surface, 6 to 8 minutes. The edges of the top should appear matte and fairly dry when it's ready to flip over. Carefully lift off the rings and flip the crumpets. Continue cooking until the bottoms are golden brown and the centers are set, 4 to 5 minutes.

Cool the crumpets. Remove the crumpets from the pan and cool on a rack for 5 minutes. Serve them warm or at room temperature.

10-Minute Sourdough Crumpets

MAKES 6 CRUMPETS

Cooking spray or olive oil, for greasing

300 grams discard (must still be bubbly) from Whole-Grain Brown Rice–Teff Sourdough Starter (page 48)

1 teaspoon (4 g) granulated sugar

1 teaspoon (4 g) baking powder

½ teaspoon (2 g) kosher salt

Preheat the griddle. Preheat a large cast-iron griddle or pan over medium-low heat. It's important to build heat slowly, otherwise the muffins will burn on the bottom and will not cook in the center. Grease the insides of 6 rings 4 inches (10 cm) in diameter and 1 inch (2.5 cm) deep with cooking spray or olive oil. The pan is ready when a drop of water sizzles on the surface. Place the rings on the pan.

Mix the batter. In a medium bowl, whisk together the discard, sugar, baking powder, and salt until smooth. The batter should have the consistency of pancake batter or heavy cream; if it seems stiff, add a tablespoon of water at a time until you reach the desired consistency.

Cook the crumpets. Pour ¼ to ⅓ cup (50 to 65 g) of batter into each ring mold (it should fill only half the ring). The batter will begin to bubble immediately. Cook over medium-low heat until you see bubbles appear on the top surface, 6 to 8 minutes. The edges of the top should appear matte and fairly dry when it's ready to flip over. Carefully lift off the rings and flip the crumpets. Continue cooking until the bottoms are golden brown and the centers are set, 4 to 5 minutes.

Cool the crumpets. Remove the crumpets from the pan and cool on a rack for 5 minutes. Serve them warm or at room temperature.

Sourdough Biscuits

110 grams unsalted butter or vegan butter

60 grams tapioca starch, plus more for dusting

60 grams potato starch

50 grams sorghum flour

15 grams granulated sugar

2¼ teaspoons (9 g) baking powder

½ teaspoon (2 g) kosher salt

¼ teaspoon (1 g) baking soda

¼ teaspoon (1 g) xanthan gum (optional)

150 grams discard from Whole-Grain Brown Rice–Teff Sourdough Starter (page 48)

80 grams whole milk or oat milk

This is probably my children's favorite recipe and one they now make for their friends. The biscuits are savory and flaky and the addition of sourdough discard adds a distinct sour, almost yogurt-like flavor. The xanthan gum is optional, but it does help create a flakier biscuit with more distinct layers. The trick with biscuits is to not mix the butter into the flour too much and to keep the dough as cold as possible, hence the freezing and grating of the butter. But do not be afraid to mix it enough so the dough holds its shape. Do not leave it as a shaggy mass. Knead and press the dough together until you have a solid block that doesn't fall apart.

MAKES 6 BISCUITS

Place the butter in the freezer for at least 30 minutes. Line a sheet pan with parchment paper.

Make the dough. In a large bowl, whisk together the tapioca starch, potato starch, sorghum flour, sugar, baking powder, salt, baking soda, and xanthan gum (if using). Take the butter out of the freezer and grate it on the large holes of a box grater into the flour mixture. Toss the flour mixture and butter together. In a large bowl, stir together the discard and milk and pour into the flour-butter mixture. Using a fork, toss everything together until you have a shaggy dough.

Fold and cut the biscuits. Lightly dust a work surface with tapioca starch. Transfer the dough to the work surface and knead it a couple of times until it sticks together nicely. You should be able to see pieces of butter throughout the dough. Shape into a rectangle that is three times longer than it is wide (the exact size doesn't matter) and about 1 inch (2.5 cm) thick. With a long side facing you, fold one-third of the dough over the center third, then fold the other third over it, creating a letter fold. Rotate the dough 90 degrees, pat it down to 1 inch (2.5 cm) thick, and repeat the process one more time. The folding doesn't have to be precise. Pat down the dough until you have a square that is 1 inch (2.5 cm) thick. Cut the dough into 6 squares. (Alternatively, you can use a round cutter to cut out biscuits, then reroll any scraps and cut again.) Place the biscuits on the prepared sheet pan and refrigerate for 30 minutes to chill.

(Recipe continues)

Preheat the oven. Position a rack in the center of the oven and preheat the oven to 500°F (260°C).

Bake the biscuits. Place the pan in the oven and reduce the oven temperature to 450°F (230°C). Bake for 15 to 18 minutes, until the biscuits are golden brown. Serve while warm.

VARIATIONS

Sourdough Biscuits with Currants

Add 65 grams dried currants to the dry ingredients and proceed as directed.

Sourdough Buckwheat Scones with Caramelized Pear and Sesame Seeds

2 teaspoons (10 g) unsalted butter or vegan butter

1 tablespoon (12 g) granulated sugar

1 medium pear, peeled, cored, and cut into ⅛-inch (3 mm) slices

50 grams light buckwheat flour

1 tablespoon toasted sesame seeds

In a small sauté pan, melt the butter over medium heat. Add the sugar and stir until the sugar melts. Add the pear slices to the pan and try to keep them in a single layer. Cook until softened and very lightly caramelized, about 5 minutes, turning them over halfway through. Add a tablespoon of water if the slices are on the dry side and the pan seems not to have any moisture. Transfer the caramelized pear slices to a plate to cool completely.

Make the dough as directed, but replace the sorghum flour with the buckwheat flour. After kneading the dough and when it's patted down into the first rectangle, lay the cooled pear slices on top. Sprinkle with the toasted sesame seeds. Fold, cut, chill, and bake the dough as directed.

Fresh Sourdough Egg Pasta

140 grams superfine brown rice flour, plus more for dusting

90 grams potato starch

2½ teaspoons (10 g) xanthan gum

1½ teaspoons (6 g) kosher salt

150 grams discard from Whole-Grain Brown Rice–Teff Sourdough Starter (page 48)

4 large egg yolks

2 large eggs

20 grams extra-virgin olive oil

One of the biggest pleasures in my career as a gluten-free recipe developer has been to teach people how to make gluten-free sourdough pasta. I have taught hundreds of people how to make a food they thought they would never be able to enjoy again, and to watch their faces as they roll and cut pasta gives me tremendous joy. You can cut this pasta into whatever shape you like or keep it as sheets to make lasagna or ravioli. The possibilities are endless.

A pasta roller and cutter are not mandatory, but I highly recommend it if you want really thin sheets of pasta and evenly cut spaghetti or fettuccine. You can roll the pasta by hand with a rolling pin, but it might be more difficult to get it as thin and even as you can using a pasta roller.

MAKES ABOUT 600 GRAMS (ABOUT 8 SERVINGS)

Mix the pasta dough. In a large bowl, stir together the brown rice flour, potato starch, xanthan gum, and salt. Make a well in the center of the flour mixture and pour in the discard, egg yolks, whole eggs, and olive oil. Using a fork, begin by whisking the wet ingredients in the center and slowly working your way outward, incorporating some of the flour into the egg mixture. Continue mixing until you have a shaggy dough, then switch to kneading the dough with your hands. The dough will feel moist and have a consistency similar to Play-Doh, but the surface will be a bit rough. If your dough feels too wet, add a tablespoon of brown rice flour; if it feels too dry, add a tablespoon of water.

Knead the dough. Transfer the dough to a work surface. If your hands are covered in dough, wash them (any rough wet dough on your hands will give the dough a rough texture). I like to use a smooth wood surface or marble counter for kneading as it helps create a smooth surface on the dough. Dust the surface with a bit of brown rice flour and knead the dough together until it is completely smooth, about 10 minutes (don't cut corners here; it really does take a full 10 minutes to get a very smooth dough). If your dough feels dry, wet your hands lightly and knead the dough incorporating more water until you have a pliable dough. On the contrary, if your dough feels wet, dust the work surface with brown rice flour while kneading until you have the right consistency. Use a bench knife to clear the surface of any dry pieces of dough while you are kneading. Once smooth, the dough is ready to be rolled.

Roll the dough. Cut the dough into 8 equal pieces. Take one of the pieces of dough and flatten it into a roughly 3-inch (7.5 cm) square. Keep the remaining pieces of dough covered with a kitchen towel so the surface doesn't dry out. Roll the dough through the thickest setting in your pasta roller (number 0 in my machine). I try to keep the edges of the dough as square as possible. Reduce the thickness of the roller to the next setting and roll the dough through it. I like to roll the dough to the number 5 or 6 setting. As the dough gets thinner, it becomes more delicate. I like to dust the surface of the dough with a tiny bit of brown rice flour in between rolling so it doesn't stick to the roller. Trim any cracked edges, because cracks can expand as you roll the dough. For the best results, roll the dough slowly so it doesn't get stuck and rip. If the dough does rip, knead it back together and roll again. Make room on your kitchen counter and lay out the sheets of dough.

Dry the pasta. Even though this is considered fresh pasta, I like to dry it for at least 30 minutes at room temperature. It won't be completely dry, but it will become slightly firmer and easier to handle when cooking. The surface should feel more leathery after drying. This is when I like to cut the pasta into shapes. My machine has a spaghetti and fettuccine cutter. Run the pasta sheets through the cutter. (You can also cut the pasta by hand with a sharp knife or pizza cutter.) Lightly dust the cut pasta with some brown rice flour and place on a sheet pan or large container.

To store the pasta: If you are not going to cook the pasta right away, you can store it tightly wrapped on a sheet pan in the refrigerator for up to 3 days or freeze it for up to 3 months.

To cook the pasta: Bring a large pot of water to a boil and season it with a generous amount of salt. Add the pasta to the boiling water and cook until it is soft but still has some bite, 1 to 2 minutes. Drain and serve with your preferred sauce.

VARIATION

Vegan Pasta

Omit the eggs and egg yolks. Increase the xanthan gum in the dough to 12 grams. Add 160 grams of water to the dough along with the sourdough discard and olive oil.

If your dough feels dry, add a tiny bit of extra water by wetting your hands and kneading the dough with them. On the contrary, if your dough feels wet, dust your work surface with brown rice flour while kneading. This will give you control over how much flour or water you are adding and let you observe how the dough is changing.

The dough without eggs is much more delicate, so don't roll it as thinly (I stop at the number 4 setting in my roller). If the edges of the pasta begin to tear as you roll, trim the edges. These light tears can become more pronounced as you roll the dough thinner, so keep the edges of your pasta sheets very sharp.

Sourdough Sweet Pastry Dough

140 grams superfine brown rice flour, plus more for dusting

120 grams tapioca starch, plus more for dusting

25 grams granulated sugar

1 teaspoon (4 g) xanthan gum (optional)

½ teaspoon (2 g) kosher salt

225 grams cold unsalted butter or vegan butter, cut into ½-inch (1.3 cm) pieces

150 grams discard from Whole-Grain Brown Rice–Teff Sourdough Starter (page 48), well chilled

This pastry dough has become my go-to for sweet and savory tarts, pies, quiches, and galettes. I enjoy the sour note that the sourdough discard adds, but mostly I love the elasticity that a well-hydrated discard adds to the dough. The xanthan gum is optional but provides a bit more stretch to the dough, especially if you are going to use it for any lattice work.

MAKES ENOUGH FOR TWO 9-INCH (23 CM) TARTS

Mix the dough. In a large bowl, stir together the brown rice flour, tapioca starch, sugar, xanthan gum (if using), and salt. Toss the diced butter in the flour mixture to coat it. Using your fingers, work the butter into the flour until you have shards of butter and flour that are evenly distributed. Some pieces will be larger than others. Make a well in the center and add the discard. Using a fork, mix the starter into the flour and butter mixture until you have a shaggy dough.

Knead the dough. Turn the dough out onto a work surface and knead it lightly a couple of times. If your dough feels wet, dust the top with a tablespoon or so of brown rice flour or tapioca starch and lightly knead it in. Conversely, if the dough feels dry, add a few drops of water while you knead it together. The dough should still feel relatively shaggy. Use your hands to press the dough together.

Chill the dough. Cut the dough in half and shape each piece into a disk that is about 1 inch (2.5 cm) thick. Wrap in plastic or parchment paper and refrigerate until firm, at least 2 hours. The dough can also be frozen for up to 1 month tightly wrapped. Thaw in refrigerator overnight.

Roll the dough. If your dough is very cold, let it come to room temperature for about 10 minutes. Roll out and bake the dough according to the recipe you are using.

VARIATION

Sourdough Savory Pastry Dough

Make the dough as directed, but reduce the sugar to 5 grams.

Plum Galette

FOR THE FILLING

455 grams (1 pound) ripe yet firm plums, sliced

25 grams granulated sugar

1 teaspoon (3 g) ground cinnamon

½ teaspoon (1 g) ground ginger

¼ teaspoon (1 g) kosher salt

50 grams almond flour

FOR THE DOUGH

½ recipe Sourdough Sweet Pastry Dough (page 143), well chilled

Tapioca starch, for dusting

FOR THE EGG WASH

1 large egg, lightly beaten, or 1 tablespoon (20 g) maple syrup

Raw sugar (optional), for sprinkling

A galette is a free-form, rustic tart where pastry is rolled out thinly and topped with a nice pile of sweetened fruit, then the pastry is folded over the fruit. Any fruit will work, although you might have to adjust the sugar amounts depending on the sweetness of the fruit. If you are using very juicy fruit, add a tablespoon of tapioca starch to the filling.

MAKES ONE 8-INCH (20 CM) GALETTE

Preheat the oven. Position a rack in the bottom third of the oven and preheat the oven to 425°F (220°C). Line a sheet pan with parchment paper.

Make the filling. In a medium bowl, toss together the plums, sugar, cinnamon, ginger, and salt and set aside for 20 minutes for the sugar to dissolve.

Roll the dough. If your dough is very cold, let it come to room temperature for about 10 minutes before rolling out. Dust a work surface and a rolling pin with tapioca starch. Place the dough on the surface and roll it into a rough round ⅛ inch (3 mm) thick. Make sure to move the dough around so it doesn't stick to the surface, and keep the rolling pin and surface dusted. Gently lift the dough and transfer it to the lined sheet pan.

Fill the galette. Spread the almond flour in the center of the dough, leaving a 3-inch (7.5 cm) border. Arrange the plums over the almond flour and pour any juices from the bowl on top. Fold the edges of the dough over the plums. Transfer the pan to the refrigerator to chill the galette for 20 minutes, or you can place it in the freezer for 5 minutes.

Egg wash the dough. Use a pastry brush to lightly brush the beaten egg (or maple syrup) on the exposed dough. Sprinkle with raw sugar, if desired.

Bake the galette. Transfer to the oven and bake for 15 minutes. Reduce the oven temperature to 375°F (190°C) and bake for 25 to 30 minutes more, until the crust is golden brown and the filling is bubbling.

Cool the galette. Let the galette cool on the pan for 15 minutes before slicing. Serve warm or at room temperature. Store in the refrigerator tightly wrapped for up to 2 days.

Cheesy Potato and Leek Slab Pie

FOR THE DOUGH

Sourdough Savory Pastry Dough (page 143)

Tapioca starch, for dusting

FOR THE FILLING

2 medium Yukon Gold potatoes (10 ounces/280 g total), peeled and sliced paper thin (preferably using a mandoline)

3 tablespoons (38 g) extra-virgin olive oil

3 medium leeks (15 ounces/425 g total), white and light-green parts only, halved lengthwise

2 tablespoons (30 g) water

1½ teaspoons (6 g) kosher salt

1 teaspoon (2 g) freshly ground black pepper

4 ounces (110 g) soft goat cheese or vegan soft spreadable cheese

A small handful fresh dill leaves

4 ounces (110 g) Gruyère cheese or vegan Gruyère-style cheese, coarsely grated

FOR THE EGG WASH

1 large egg, lightly beaten

Small pinch of kosher salt

Make this savory tart during the cold months. Serve a slice along with some hearty greens and you have a delicious meal for any time of the day.

SERVES 6 TO 8

Make the dough. Make the pastry dough as directed through the kneading step. Pat it into a rectangle that is roughly 10 by 8 inches (25 by 20 cm). Wrap the pastry in parchment paper or plastic wrap and refrigerate for 1 hour.

Soak the potatoes. Place the sliced potatoes in a large bowl and cover them with cold water. Soak for 30 minutes.

Cook the leeks. Heat a large sauté pan over medium heat. Add 2 tablespoons of the oil and the leeks cut-sides down. Cook until they begin to brown, about 5 minutes. Turn the leeks over. Add the water, ½ teaspoon of the salt, and ½ teaspoon of the pepper. Cover the pan and cook the leeks until tender, about 15 minutes. Set aside and let the leeks cool.

Preheat the oven. Position a rack in the lower third of the oven and preheat the oven to 425°F (220°C).

Season the potatoes. Drain the potatoes and dry them as much as possible between paper towels. Place in a bowl and toss with the remaining 1 tablespoon olive oil, 1 teaspoon salt, and ½ teaspoon pepper. Set aside.

Roll out the pastry. Lay a large sheet of parchment paper on a work surface. Dust the paper and a rolling pin with a generous dusting of tapioca starch. Place the dough on the parchment and roll it into a rectangle roughly 18 by 14 inches (46 by 36 cm) and ⅛ inch (3 mm) thick. Make sure to move your dough around so it doesn't stick to the paper, and keep the rolling pin and surface dusted. Gently lift the paper with the dough and transfer it to a 13-by-9-inch (33 by 23 cm) sheet pan. The pastry edges will hang over the sides of the pan, but that is okay as we will fold these over the filling.

(Recipe continues)

Fill the tart. Spread the goat cheese over the pastry dough. Top with half of the dill. Scatter half of the Gruyère over the goat cheese. Arrange the seasoned potatoes and leeks on top and finish with the remaining Gruyère. Fold the edges of the pastry over the filling. If your pastry dough feels warm, put the pan in the refrigerator for 20 minutes or the freezer for 7 minutes.

Make the egg wash. Whisk the egg and salt together in a small bowl. Brush the top of the pastry with the egg wash.

Bake the pie. Bake the pie for 15 minutes. Reduce the oven temperature to 375°F (190°C) and bake for 25 to 30 minutes more, until the crust is golden brown.

Cool the pie. Let the pie cool for 10 minutes before cutting. Sprinkle the top with the remaining dill. Serve warm or at room temperature.

Sourdough Yorkshire Puddings or Popovers

60 grams potato starch

45 grams tapioca starch

1 teaspoon (4 g) kosher salt

¼ teaspoon (1 g) xanthan gum

240 grams whole milk or oat milk, at room temperature

75 grams discard from Whole-Grain Brown Rice–Teff Sourdough Starter (page 48)

4 large eggs, at room temperature

35 grams unsalted butter or vegan butter, melted, plus more for greasing

Yorkshire puddings or popovers are made by baking a crêpe-like batter of eggs, milk, and flour in a hot oven until you have these impossibly tall crispy shells with nearly hollow interiors. My first time trying a Yorkshire pudding was during a summer stay in London when I was twelve. It was served with gravy alongside a roast—I had never seen such a thing. Ever since, I associate them with drawn-out holiday meals or special occasions.

I use a 6-cavity nonstick popover pan that creates really big popovers. If you have a traditional cast-iron one, preheat it in your oven for 15 minutes before adding the batter. No need to preheat or grease nonstick pans. If you only have a standard muffin tin, see the Small Popovers variation on page 151.

It is crucial that the ingredients be at room temperature when you mix the batter. If your eggs are out of the refrigerator, place them (uncracked) in a bowl with warm water for 15 minutes. Make sure to warm up the milk to room temperature as well.

MAKES 6 LARGE POPOVERS

Preheat the oven. Position a rack in bottom third of the oven and preheat the oven to 450°F (230°C). Let the oven continue heating for at least 15 minutes after it has reached temperature. If using a cast-iron pan, preheat it in the oven for 15 minutes.

Make the batter. In a large bowl, stir together the potato starch, tapioca starch, salt, and xanthan gum. In a medium bowl, whisk together the milk, discard, eggs, and melted butter until smooth. Add the egg mixture to the dry ingredients and whisk to combine until very smooth and free of lumps. If you have lumps in your batter, strain it through a fine sieve and press down with a rubber spatula to get all the batter smooth. (Alternatively, mix the batter in a high-powered blender.) You can let the batter rest in the refrigerator overnight, but make sure you let it come back to room temperature before baking.

Bake the popovers. If using a cast-iron popover pan, grease 6 cups with butter. Pour the batter into the prepared pan, filling the cups

two-thirds of the way up. Transfer to the oven and bake for 20 minutes, or until the popovers are puffed up and begin to turn golden brown. Reduce the oven temperature to 350°F (180°C) and bake until golden brown and crispy, 15 to 20 minutes. The inside of the popover should be mainly hollow with a bit of eggy dough strands. The interior shouldn't be too wet, so make sure to give it time in the second half of baking. If you have never baked one, you may want to test to see if it's done by opening one after the 15 minutes to see how the interior feels. If it's too wet, add a few more minutes to let it dry out. Remove from the pan and serve immediately.

VARIATIONS

Small Popovers

You can make these in a standard muffin pan for 12 smaller popovers. Make the batter as directed and grease 12 cups of the muffin tin. Preheat the oven to 450°F (230°C). Bake for 15 minutes. Reduce the oven temperature to 350°F (180°C) and bake for 10 to 15 minutes, until golden and crispy.

Caramelized Apple Dutch Baby

- 25 grams unsalted butter or vegan butter
- 25 grams granulated sugar
- 1 apple, peeled and thinly sliced
- ½ teaspoon (2 g) ground cinnamon
- Powdered sugar, for dusting

Preheat the oven and make the batter as directed.

Cook the apples. In a 12-inch (30 cm) cast-iron skillet or 1.5-quart (1.4 L) cast-iron casserole, melt the butter over medium-high heat and swirl it around the pan. Add the sugar and stir until it begins to melt into the butter. Add the apples and cinnamon, stir, and cook until soft and caramelized, about 3 minutes.

Bake the Dutch baby. Pour the batter into the skillet and place in the preheated oven. Bake for 15 minutes. Reduce the oven temperature to 350°F (180°C) and bake for 10 to 15 minutes more, until golden and puffed up. Serve immediately with a generous dusting of powdered sugar.

No. 4

Breads Made with Baker's Yeast

(or Leavened with Baking Soda)

Sweet Potato and Millet Cross Bread with Cumin

Mini Whole-Grain Walnut Baguettes

I primarily bake breads using sourdough starter because the slower fermentation allows the breakdown of proteins and the bread is overall better for your health. I also greatly enjoy the smell of sourdough starter and the complex flavor it adds to bread. However, I *love* the smell of baker's yeast. I love its sweet yeasty aroma and umami flavor; there's just no other way to describe it. As a child, I would be sent to the bakery to buy our daily baguettes. I distinctly remember my nose barely reaching the height of the counter, where a block of fresh yeast sat wrapped in wax paper, and inhaling that aroma. I have not used fresh yeast in years now (it's very difficult to find in the US), but I can still distinguish clearly whether something baking in the oven is made with sourdough or commercial yeast.

Commercially grown baker's yeast is made from the species of yeast called *Saccharomyces cerevisiae*. Yeast is produced in a controlled environment to achieve the same consistent product every time. Baker's yeast ferments breads much faster, as fast as 30 minutes, providing commercial bakers predictability and better cost margins. Even though the popularity of sourdough bread baking has exploded among home bakers, there is still room for making bread using baker's yeast. Convenience is a major draw, but it can also make bread baking less intimidating for beginners.

The recipes in this chapter are all made with baker's yeast, except two that are leavened with baking soda (Leek and Cheddar Soda Bread, page 190, and Yeast-Free Sandwich Bread, page 188). I use active dry yeast in my recipes because for the longest time it was the most available kind on supermarket shelves. Instant yeast has become more popular in the US as of late, and you can use that as well. Read more about baker's yeast on pages 25 and 29.

Some of the recipes in this chapter are truly quick, such as the Leek and Cheddar Soda Bread, Caramelized Onion and Poppy Seed Bialys (page 184), or Pain de Mie (page 159). Others will take a bit longer to proof, such as the One-Bowl No-Knead Oat Chia Bread (page 165). If you want to make these recipes replacing the baker's yeast with sourdough starter, read Converting Recipes from Baker's Yeast to Sourdough Starter (page 46).

Cinnamon-Raisin Pain de Mie

Pain de Mie

- 2½ teaspoons (10 g) active dry yeast
- 300 grams water, heated to 105°F (41°C)
- 300 grams whole milk or oat milk, heated to 105°F (41°C)
- 40 grams honey or maple syrup
- 30 grams psyllium husk powder
- 280 grams sorghum flour
- 160 grams tapioca starch
- 100 grams potato starch
- 12 grams kosher salt
- 1 teaspoon (4 g) baking powder
- 55 grams unsalted butter or vegan butter, at room temperature, plus more for greasing

Pain de mie is the ultimate sandwich bread loaf. Baked in a 9-inch (23 cm) Pullman loaf pan with a lid, it has a perfectly rectangular shape with a thin crust and soft white crumb. It makes the best toast since there is quite a bit of butter in the dough.

This recipe doesn't require a bulk ferment step, meaning it is mixed, proofed in the pan, and baked, so you can make it fairly quickly. Note that it has quite a long baking time, so do account for that. Make sure to let the bread dry out in the oven as written in the recipe, otherwise the sides of the loaf tend to cave in. (It is not the end of the world if they do, but perfectly square slices are more aesthetically pleasing.) If you don't have a Pullman loaf, you can bake it in a standard loaf pan, but the crust might be a bit thicker as the lid protects the surface of the dough and creates a thinner crust.

MAKES 1 LOAF

Make the yeast-psyllium mixture. Sprinkle the yeast into a large bowl. Add the water, milk, and honey and whisk until dissolved. Let the mixture sit until frothy, about 10 minutes. Whisk in the psyllium. Let it gel for 5 minutes.

Make the dough. In a stand mixer, stir together the sorghum flour, tapioca starch, potato starch, salt, and baking powder. Add the yeast-psyllium mixture and butter to the dry ingredients. Snap on the dough hook and mix on medium-low speed until the dough comes together, 2 to 3 minutes. It will be moist but hold together nicely.

Shape and proof the dough. Transfer the dough to a work surface and knead a few times to shape into a tight ball. Roll this ball into an oval shape that is about 8 inches (20 cm) long. Grease the bottom and sides of a 9-inch (23 cm) Pullman loaf pan as well as the underside part of the lid with butter. Place the dough inside and cover the pan with a kitchen towel. Proof the dough until it almost reaches the top rim of the pan, about 30 minutes. Don't let it go past the top of the pan or it can overproof and collapse while baking.

Preheat the oven. Position a rack in the bottom third of the oven and preheat the oven to 425°F (220°C).

Bake the bread. Cover the Pullman pan with its lid. Bake for 30 minutes. Reduce the oven temperature to 375°F (190°C) and bake for 30 minutes. Turn the oven off, remove the lid, but leave the pan in the oven for 30 minutes.

Cool the bread. Invert the bread onto a wire rack and let it cool for at least 30 minutes before cutting. It is best eaten the same day, but it is also great toasted a couple of days after. Store at room temperature wrapped in a paper bag for up to 3 days.

VARIATIONS

Cinnamon-Raisin Pain de Mie

3½ teaspoons (10 g) ground cinnamon

80 grams plump raisins

50 grams granulated sugar

Make the dough. Make the pain de mie dough as directed, but add 1½ teaspoons (4 g) ground cinnamon along with the dry ingredients. Add the raisins at the end of the mixing time.

Shape the loaf. Dust a work surface with a bit of sorghum flour and knead a few times until you have a tight ball. Roll the dough into a rectangle that is roughly 12 by 10 inches (30 by 25 cm) and ½ inch (1.3 cm) thick. In a small bowl, mix together the sugar and remaining 2 teaspoons (6 g) ground cinnamon. Sprinkle the surface of the dough with about half of the cinnamon sugar. With a short side facing you, fold the top third onto the middle and the lower third up over it, creating a letter fold. Turn the dough 90 degrees. Roll the dough again into a rectangle that is roughly 13 by 8 inches (33 by 20 cm). Sprinkle the surface with the remaining cinnamon sugar and press lightly into the dough. Starting from a short side, roll the dough into a tight log, then roll the log on your surface to seal the seam. You should have a log that is about 9 inches (23 cm) long. Place the dough in the greased Pullman pan and proof and bake as directed.

Buttered Miso and Toasted Sesame Pain de Mie

35 grams unsalted butter or vegan butter, melted

40 grams white (shiro) miso

¼ teaspoon (1 g) toasted sesame oil

¼ teaspoon (1 g) freshly ground black pepper

35 grams toasted sesame seeds

Make the dough as directed up to the shaping step.

Shape and layer the dough. In a medium bowl, stir together the melted butter, miso, sesame oil, and black pepper. Dust a work surface with a bit of sorghum flour and knead the dough a few times until you have a tight ball. Roll the dough into a rectangle that is roughly 12 by 10 inches (30 by 25 cm) and ½ inch (1.3 cm) thick. Spread half of the butter mixture over the dough (it will be a thin layer) and sprinkle the top with half of the sesame seeds. With a short side facing you, fold the top third onto the middle and the lower third up over it, creating a letter fold. Turn the dough 90 degrees. Roll the dough again into a rectangle that is 13 by 8 inches (33 by 20 cm). Spread the remaining butter mixture over the dough and sprinkle with the remaining sesame seeds. Starting from a short side, roll the dough into a tight log, then roll the log on your surface to seal the seam. You should have a log that is about 9 inches (23 cm) long. Place the dough in the greased Pullman pan and proof and bake as directed.

Note: When you cut into the baked bread, you might notice that there is a slight separation between the layers of dough. This is normal. The butter prevents the dough layers from sticking to each other and they tend to separate while baking.

Marble Rye-Style Loaf

- 2 teaspoons (8 g) active dry yeast
- 280 grams water, heated to 105°F (41°C)
- 280 grams whole milk or oat milk, heated to 105°F (41°C)
- 25 grams granulated sugar
- 20 grams psyllium husk powder
- 12 grams apple cider vinegar
- 10 grams flaxseed meal
- 140 grams sorghum flour
- 140 grams superfine brown rice flour, plus more for dusting
- 120 grams potato starch
- 90 grams tapioca starch
- 15 grams caraway seeds
- 2 teaspoons (8 g) kosher salt
- 55 grams extra-virgin olive oil, plus more for greasing
- 20 grams blackstrap molasses
- 12 grams unsweetened cacao powder
- 12 grams ivory teff flour or light buckwheat flour
- Egg wash: 1 large egg, lightly beaten with 1 tablespoon (15 g) water (optional)

There is no Reuben sandwich without a beautifully swirled marble rye packed with caraway seeds. For this gluten-free version, I use a little bit of teff flour and apple cider vinegar in the dough. Don't be afraid of the cacao powder in the recipe; it will not sweeten the bread. It is there for color and also adds acidity. You might also notice that the molasses makes half of the dough a bit more elastic. Take note of this for your future bread experiments! Try the meatless Melty Beet and Sauerkraut Reuben (page 381); it's my favorite with a bowl of soup on a winter's day.

MAKES 1 LOAF

Make the yeast-psyllium mixture. Sprinkle the yeast into a medium bowl. Add the water, milk, and sugar and whisk until dissolved. Let the mixture sit until frothy, 5 to 10 minutes. Whisk in the psyllium, vinegar, and flaxseed until smooth. Let it gel for 5 minutes.

Make the dough. In a stand mixer, stir together the sorghum flour, brown rice flour, potato starch, tapioca starch, caraway seeds, and salt. Add the olive oil and yeast-psyllium mixture. Snap on the dough hook and mix on medium speed until you have a smooth dough, 2 to 3 minutes. It should be moist and bouncy. Leave the dough in the mixer bowl, cover with a kitchen towel, and ferment until doubled in size, about 1 hour. (Alternatively, ferment at room temperature for 30 minutes, then cover tightly with plastic wrap and refrigerate for 8 to 10 hours to develop flavor.)

Make the cacao dough. Return the bowl to the mixer and with the dough hook, beat it until the dough is smooth again, 30 seconds to 1 minute. Divide the dough in half. Place one of the halves on a floured piece of parchment and pat it down to a rectangle that is roughly 13 by 8 inches (33 by 20 cm). To the remaining dough in the bowl, add the molasses, cacao powder, and teff flour. Mix on medium speed for a minute until the dough is smooth and the cacao powder has been evenly incorporated. Place the dough on another floured piece of parchment paper and pat it down to a rectangle that is roughly 13 by 8 inches (33 by 20 cm). The dough can be slightly sticky, so make sure your hands are clean when handling it to prevent the dough sticking to them too much.

(Recipe continues)

Lightly grease an 8½-by-4½-inch (22 by 11 cm) loaf pan with olive oil.

Shape the dough. Place the cacao rectangle dough on top of the plain one, making sure the sides line up as much as possible. Pat down the doughs, applying a little pressure or roll a rolling pin over the doughs to make sure they stick to each other well. Starting with a short side, roll the dough into a log that is 8 inches (20 cm) long. Place the dough in the prepared pan.

Proof the dough. Cover the pan with a kitchen towel and ferment until nearly doubled, 30 to 45 minutes. (If you fermented the dough in the refrigerator overnight, it will be cold and will take a bit longer to ferment once rolled, about 1 hour.)

Preheat the oven. Position a rack in the bottom third of the oven and preheat the oven to 450°F (230°C).

Bake the bread. When the dough is ready, brush the top with the egg wash (or simply water if you are avoiding eggs). Bake for 15 minutes. Reduce the oven temperature to 400°F (200°C) and bake for 35 minutes. Gently slide the bread out of the pan and place directly on the oven rack. Bake for 10 minutes, or until golden brown.

Cool the bread. Transfer the bread to a wire rack and let it cool for at least 30 minutes. The crust will appear hard initially, but will soften as the bread cools. Store the bread at room temperature wrapped in a paper bag for up to 2 days.

One-Bowl No-Knead Oat Chia Bread

¾ teaspoon (3 g) active dry yeast

675 grams water, heated to 105°F (41°C)

1½ teaspoons (6 g) granulated sugar

195 grams oat flour, plus more for dusting

140 grams sorghum flour

120 grams potato starch

90 grams tapioca starch

80 grams rolled oats

70 grams chia seeds

12 grams kosher salt

1½ teaspoons (6 g) xanthan gum

This is one of the easiest breads you can make—no kneading, shaping, or scoring required. Toss all the ingredients together in a bowl, ferment, and bake. This bread has a thin and crunchy crust and a chewy and dense crumb with some nice texture from the oats and chia seeds. It is not a showstopper like other breads are, but it's really tasty! It uses a small amount of baker's yeast compared to other bread recipes and its long fermentation time results in a deep yeasty flavor. If you prefer not to use xanthan gum, you can replace it with 15 grams psyllium husk powder. The color and texture do change slightly, but it works well.

MAKES 1 LOAF

Activate the yeast. Sprinkle the yeast into a large bowl. Add the water and sugar and whisk to combine. Let the mixture sit until frothy, 5 to 10 minutes. It's a small amount of yeast, so you will only see a small pool of bubbles in the center.

Make the dough. Add the oat flour, sorghum flour, potato starch, tapioca starch, rolled oats, chia seeds, salt, and xanthan gum to the yeast mixture and quickly stir together with a spatula or wooden spoon until incorporated. The dough will feel very liquidy initially, then slightly more like cake batter. Using your spatula, fold the edges of the dough over the center top to create a round boule. The dough will have thickened by now.

Proof the dough. Cover the bowl with a kitchen towel and proof for 4 to 5 hours at room temperature, until doubled in size, or 12 hours in the refrigerator. The dough will smell yeasty and the surface will crack.

Shape the dough. Set a piece of parchment paper on your counter. Gently scrape the dough out of the bowl onto the parchment. The dough will be moist but should hold its shape nicely. Dust the top with a little bit of oat flour and shape it into a round boule without kneading. Cover the dough with a towel and let it proof for 30 to 45 minutes more, until your oven preheats.

(Recipe continues)

1896
LODGE

Preheat the oven. Position a rack in the bottom third of the oven and place a cast-iron Dutch oven on the rack. Preheat the oven to 450°F (230°C).

Bake the bread. Carefully lift the parchment with the dough on top and transfer to the preheated Dutch oven. Cover with the lid and bake for 40 minutes. Remove the lid and bake for 20 minutes more, or until the bread is golden brown. The crust might appear too hard but will soften as it cools.

Cool the bread. Place the bread on a wire rack to cool for at least 20 minutes before cutting into it. It's best eaten the same day.

Note: If you don't have a Dutch oven, you can bake this bread in a loaf pan. After mixing the dough, cover the bowl with a kitchen towel and proof for 4 to 5 hours. Preheat the oven to 450°F (230°C). Transfer the dough to a lightly greased loaf pan and let it proof for 30 to 45 minutes more. Bake for a full hour. The crust will be slightly thicker and won't have the same golden brown color.

Olive and Rosemary Fougasses

2 teaspoons (8 g) active dry yeast

475 grams water, heated to 105°F (41°C)

12 grams granulated sugar

20 grams psyllium husk powder

150 grams tapioca starch

150 grams potato starch

150 grams sorghum flour, plus more for dusting

Leaves from 2 rosemary sprigs, finely chopped

2 teaspoons (8 g) kosher salt

25 grams extra-virgin olive oil, plus more for brushing

70 grams pitted Kalamata or green olives, chopped

Flaky sea salt, for sprinkling

Freshly ground black pepper, for sprinkling

15 grams sesame seeds

Grabbing a loaf of olive fougasse—a crispy and chewy bread in the shape of a grain of wheat, originally from Provence—was always on the top of the to-do list anytime we traveled across the border to France when I was a kid. A loaf doesn't quite describe this bread; it's more like a light olive oil–tinged stalk. The best way to eat it is to break off pieces, finishing the whole thing while silently walking along cobblestone streets—this is how I remember it.

The bread has a crispy crust with a chewy bite and nice air pockets and is a close cousin to focaccia. The most important thing for achieving a crispy exterior is to preheat your oven for a good half hour or even longer. Give the oven a chance to get really hot by preheating it to 500°F (260°C), then lowering it to 450°F (230°C) when the bread goes in. You can even skip the sheet pan and bake the bread directly on a pizza stone.

MAKES 2 LARGE FOUGASSES

Make the yeast-psyllium mixture. Sprinkle the yeast into a medium bowl. Add the water and sugar and whisk until dissolved. Let the mixture sit until frothy, about 10 minutes. Whisk in the psyllium vigorously until smooth. Let it gel for 5 minutes.

Make the dough. In a stand mixer, stir together the tapioca starch, potato starch, sorghum flour, rosemary, salt, and yeast-psyllium mixture. Snap on the dough hook and begin mixing on medium speed. Add the olive oil and continue mixing until you have a smooth dough. It will look dry initially, but it should come together in 2 to 3 minutes. Add the olives and mix until they are thoroughly spread through the dough. The dough should feel moist and a little sticky but hold together nicely.

Proof the dough. Brush a large bowl with some olive oil and transfer the dough into it. Turn the dough around to coat in oil and shape into a ball. Cover the bowl and let it ferment until doubled in size, about 45 minutes.

Preheat the oven. Position a rack in the bottom third of the oven and preheat the oven to 500°F (260°C).

(Recipe continues)

Shape the fougasses. Lightly dust a work surface with some sorghum flour. Transfer the dough to the surface. Using your fingertips, press down on the dough to gently stretch it into a round that is ¼ to ½ inch (6 mm to 1.3 cm) thick. You can use a rolling pin if preferred, but be careful not to tear the dough. Using a bench knife or knife, vertically cut the dough in half. You should have two half-moons. Place one piece of dough on a sheet pan and the other on a second pan. Cut a center slash in the middle of each half-moon without cutting through the ends, then cut three slashes on each side. Gently pull apart the slashes so there is a nice opening in between. Again, be careful not to tear the dough. If you simply cut the slash but don't separate the dough enough, it will end up baking together and not give you a nice opening in the fougasse. The dough can easily tear because it doesn't have a lot of elasticity, so work gently.

Bake the fougasses. Loosely cover one pan with plastic wrap and refrigerate it while you bake the other. Brush the top of the fougasse with olive oil and sprinkle with flaky salt, black pepper, and half of the sesame seeds. Place the pan in the oven and reduce the oven temperature to 450°F (230°C). Bake for 25 to 30 minutes, until golden brown. Brush the second fougasse with olive oil, sprinkle with flaky salt, black pepper, and the remaining sesame seeds and bake for 25 to 30 minutes, until golden brown.

Cool the fougasses. Slide the fougasse loaves onto wire racks to cool for at least 30 minutes before cutting into them. They are best eaten the same day.

Mini Whole-Grain Walnut Baguettes

PICTURED ON PAGE 155

The Sourdough Salted Miso Baguettes (page 81) are my go-to baguettes, but this whole-grain baguette is a bit faster to throw together. Made with teff, oat, and sorghum flours, plus walnuts, the baguettes are dense, nutty, and very flavorful. I love them in the Mediterranean Artichoke and Spinach Omelet Sandwiches (page 378). You can, of course, make full-size baguettes: simply cut the dough into 2 pieces instead of 5 and bake them for 30 to 35 minutes.

MAKES 5 MINI BAGUETTES

FOR THE SPONGE

2 teaspoons (8 g) active dry yeast

225 grams water, heated to 105°F (41°C)

140 grams ivory or brown teff flour

FOR THE DOUGH

250 grams water, at room temperature

15 grams extra-virgin olive oil

12 grams apple cider vinegar

20 grams psyllium husk powder

7 grams flaxseed meal

120 grams oat flour

105 grams sorghum flour

90 grams tapioca starch

25 grams light brown sugar

2½ teaspoons (10 g) kosher salt

80 grams coarsely chopped walnuts

White rice flour (optional), for dusting

Make the sponge. Sprinkle the yeast into a medium bowl. Add the water and teff flour and whisk until smooth. Cover with a kitchen towel and proof until the sponge has puffed up significantly creating a dome and has a mousse-like texture, about 30 minutes.

Make the dough. Add the water, olive oil, and vinegar to the sponge and whisk to combine. Add the psyllium and flaxseed and vigorously whisk until dissolved. Let it gel for 5 minutes. In a stand mixer, stir together the oat flour, sorghum flour, tapioca starch, brown sugar, and salt. Add the yeast-gel mixture. Snap on the dough hook and mix on medium speed until it comes together into a smooth and moist dough, about 2 minutes. Add the walnuts and continue mixing until they are thoroughly incorporated.

Shape the baguettes. Cut the dough into 5 equal pieces (about 220 g each). Shape each piece of dough into a tight ball and then evenly roll into a log that is 8 inches (20 cm) long. Roll the ends of the log with the palms of your hands to taper them, creating the traditional baguette shape. Place them on a sheet pan, leaving 3 inches (7.5 cm) between the pieces. Cover with a kitchen towel and proof until the dough has increased about 50 percent and feels puffed up, 30 to 45 minutes.

Preheat the oven. Position a rack in the bottom third of the oven and preheat the oven to 450°F (230°C).

Score the baguettes. Dust the tops of the baguettes with a small amount of white rice flour, if desired. This will create a nice contrast on the surface after baking. Hold a lame between your fingers and turn your wrist about 45 degrees so that the blade is at an angle in relation to one of the baguettes. Score a lengthwise slash ¼ inch (6 mm) deep that runs nearly to the center of the baguette. Score another slash starting about 1 inch (2.5 cm) above the bottom of the previous slash so both slashes are overlapping. Repeat with the remaining baguettes.

Bake the baguettes. Place the pan in the oven and bake for about 25 minutes, or until the baguettes are deeply browned and crusty, injecting steam three times in 5-minute intervals (at 1 minute, 6 minutes, and 11 minutes). If you don't have steam in your oven, see Creating Steam (page 32).

Cool the baguettes. Transfer the baguettes to a wire rack to cool for at least 30 minutes. They are best eaten the same day. Store them in a brown paper bag at room temperature for up to 1 day.

Sweet Potato and Millet Cross Bread with Cumin

PICTURED ON PAGES 152–153

FOR THE ROASTED SWEET POTATO PUREE

1 medium sweet potato (12 ounces/340 g)

FOR THE SPONGE

1¼ teaspoons (5 g) active dry yeast

170 grams water, heated to 105°F (41°C)

175 grams millet flour, plus more for dusting

FOR THE DOUGH

160 grams potato starch

120 grams tapioca starch

75 grams millet grain

20 grams psyllium husk powder

7 grams flaxseed meal

2 teaspoons (8 g) kosher salt

1½ teaspoons (5 g) cumin seeds

170 grams water, at room temperature

12 grams extra-virgin olive oil

12 grams apple cider vinegar

This is one of those breads that is great to eat by itself or alongside a bowl of soup. The sweet potato adds natural sweetness and beautiful color, the millet gives it crunch, and the cumin lends a slight smokiness. You could make it with pumpkin puree, but you will likely have to reduce the water amount since pumpkin has more water than sweet potato. If you can't find millet grain, you can use quinoa.

MAKES 1 ROUND LOAF

Bake the sweet potato. Preheat the oven to 400°F (200°C). Place the sweet potato on a sheet pan and bake for 45 minutes to 1 hour, until cooked through. You should be able to slide the tip of a knife in without any resistance. Let the sweet potato cool completely. Peel and mash the flesh with a fork. Weigh out 225 grams of mashed sweet potato and set aside.

Make the sponge. Sprinkle the yeast into a medium bowl. Whisk in the water, then whisk in the millet flour until smooth. Cover with a kitchen towel and proof for about 30 minutes or until puffed up.

Make the dough. In a stand mixer, stir together the potato starch, tapioca starch, millet grain, psyllium, flaxseed, salt, and cumin. Add the sponge, the mashed sweet potato, the water, olive oil, and vinegar. Snap on the dough hook and mix on medium speed. Initially, the dough will look like a very runny batter, but it will set as the psyllium and flaxseed gel. Continue mixing for 2 to 3 minutes. Let the dough rest for 5 minutes. It will be moist but should hold together nicely. The moisture content of the sweet potato could vary and alter the moisture of the overall dough, so if the dough feels dry, add a touch more water, and if the dough feels wet, add a touch more millet flour.

Shape the dough. Dust a work surface with a little bit of millet flour. Shape the dough into a large ball sealing the seams tightly. Lightly dust a sheet pan with millet flour and place the dough on it. Using a sharp knife or bench knife, make a slash 2 inches (5 cm) deep down the center of the dough, then make another slash perpendicular to that to create a cross.

Proof the dough. Loosely cover the dough with plastic wrap, place in the refrigerator, and proof until the dough has nearly doubled and feels light and marshmallow-like to the touch, 2 to 4 hours.

Preheat the oven. Position a rack in the bottom third of the oven and preheat the oven to 500°F (260°C).

Bake the bread. Remove the plastic wrap and place the pan in the oven. Reduce the oven temperature to 450°F (230°C) and bake for 40 to 45 minutes, until golden brown, injecting steam three times in 5-minute intervals (at 1 minute, 6 minutes, and 11 minutes). If you don't have steam in your oven, see Creating Steam (page 32).

Cool the bread. Transfer the bread to a wire rack to cool completely before cutting into it. Store the bread at room temperature wrapped in a paper bag for up to 2 days.

Note: If you have trouble creating steam in your oven, you could easily bake this loaf in a Dutch oven. The Dutch oven will create a steam environment. Instead of proofing the shaped dough on a sheet pan, place it in a parchment paper–lined Dutch oven and follow the steps as directed. Bake it with the lid on for 30 minutes, then remove the lid and bake uncovered for 10 to 15 minutes.

Jerusalem Bagels

2 teaspoons (8 g) active dry yeast

280 grams water, heated to 105°F (41°C)

225 grams oat milk or whole milk, heated to 105°F (41°C)

40 grams honey

12 grams extra-virgin olive oil, plus more for brushing

20 grams psyllium husk powder

7 grams flaxseed meal

185 grams sorghum flour

140 grams superfine brown rice flour

120 grams tapioca starch

2 teaspoons (8 g) kosher salt

FOR THE SESAME TOPPING

150 grams sesame seeds

25 grams hot water

60 grams runny honey or pomegranate molasses

These bagels are soft and chewy. They are perfect for breakfast, or serve them with olive oil and za'atar or hummus for a snack.

MAKES 6 BAGELS

Make the yeast-psyllium mixture. Sprinkle the yeast into a medium bowl. Add the water, milk, honey, and olive oil and whisk until dissolved. Let the mixture sit until frothy, 5 to 10 minutes. Whisk in the psyllium and flaxseed. Let it gel for 5 minutes.

Make the dough. In a stand mixer, stir together the sorghum flour, brown rice flour, tapioca starch, and salt. Add the yeast-psyllium mixture. Snap on the dough hook and mix on medium speed until the dough comes together, 2 to 3 minutes. It should feel moist but not super sticky. Transfer the dough to a lightly oiled bowl, cover with a kitchen towel, and proof until doubled in volume, 45 minutes to 1 hour.

Preheat the oven. Position racks in the center and lower third of the oven and preheat the oven to 450°F (230°C). Line two sheet pans with parchment paper.

Prepare the sesame topping. Spread the sesame seeds on a large plate. In a small bowl, stir together the hot water and honey.

Shape the bagels. Transfer the dough to a work surface and knead it a few times to deflate it and bring back some smoothness. Cut the dough into 6 equal pieces and shape each piece into a tight ball. Roll each piece into a log about 18 inches (46 cm) long. If you find the dough is tearing easily, bring it together and knead a few more times. Take a log, flatten one end, place it on top of the opposite end, and pinch them together. Brush the top with the honey water and dip into the sesame seeds, covering the entire surface. Place the dough on one of the prepared sheet pans and proceed with the remaining logs.

Proof the bagels. Cover the pans with kitchen towels and proof for 20 to 25 minutes.

Bake the bagels. Place the pans in the oven and reduce the temperature to 425°F (220°C). Bake for 18 to 22 minutes, switching racks halfway, until the bagels are light golden brown. Brush the tops with olive oil.

Cool the bagels. Transfer the bagels to a wire rack and let cool for 15 minutes before serving. They are best eaten the same day.

Soft Pretzels

FOR THE SPONGE

1 teaspoon (4 g) active dry yeast

170 grams water, heated to 105°F (41°C)

70 grams superfine brown rice flour, plus more for dusting

70 grams sorghum flour

FOR THE DOUGH

15 grams psyllium husk powder

130 grams water, at room temperature

80 grams potato starch

60 grams tapioca starch

25 grams light brown sugar

1½ teaspoons (6 g) kosher salt

¾ teaspoon (3 g) xanthan gum

16 grams unsalted butter or vegan butter, melted, plus more for brushing

1 large egg white

FOR THE WATER BATH

2 quarts (1.8 L) water

80 grams baking soda

15 grams dark brown sugar

FOR THE TOPPING

Pretzel salt or assorted seeds, such as poppy, sesame, or pumpkin

This recipe produces pretzels that are soft and tender. The trick for that shiny and dark crust on pretzels is dipping them in a lye bath. If you are careful and up for the task, try it, as the lye gives the crust a glaze and adds a bit of chew to the pretzel. (You'll find some instructions on how to work with food-grade lye on page 181. The recipe includes a baking soda and brown sugar water bath, too.

MAKES 4 PRETZELS

Make the sponge. Sprinkle the yeast into a medium bowl. Add the water, brown rice flour, and sorghum flour and whisk until you have a smooth paste. Scrape the sides of the bowl and smooth out the top. Cover with a kitchen towel or plate and proof until the sponge puffs up and has a mousse-like texture, about 30 minutes.

Make the dough. Sprinkle the psyllium into a medium bowl. Whisk in the water. The mixture will gel right away, so work quickly. In a stand mixer, stir together the potato starch, tapioca starch, light brown sugar, salt, and xanthan gum. Add the sponge, psyllium gel, melted butter, and egg white to the dry ingredients. Snap on the dough hook and mix on medium speed until the dough comes together, 2 to 3 minutes. The dough will be soft and moist but hold together nicely.

Proof the dough. Cover the bowl with a kitchen towel and proof until the dough has nearly doubled in size, 30 to 45 minutes.

Prepare the water bath. About 5 minutes before the dough is done proofing, set a large pot with enough space for the water to bubble up on the stove. Add the water and bring it to a simmer over high heat. Wait to add the baking soda and brown sugar until you are ready to boil the pretzels. Reduce the heat if needed to keep it at a simmer.

Shape the pretzels. Lightly grease a sheet pan with pan spray or olive oil. Dust a work surface with brown rice flour. Scrape the dough from the bowl onto the work surface. Knead the dough a few times to deflate any air inside of it. Cut the dough into 4 equal pieces (about 165 g each). Knead each piece of dough a few times to deflate and shape into a tight ball. The dough is soft, so dust your surface with flour as needed. Roll the dough into a rope that is about 22 inches (56 cm) long, leaving the center part slightly thicker and tapering the ends off. Create a U shape with your dough. Lift both ends, twist

CHICAGO

them around each other once, then fold down, letting the ends rest over the thicker part of the dough at about 4 o'clock and 8 o'clock. Carefully transfer to the prepared sheet pan and gently spread out the "shoulders" of the pretzel. Repeat with the remaining dough.

Chill the pretzels. Transfer the sheet pan to the refrigerator for 30 minutes or freezer for 15 minutes.

Preheat the oven. Position a rack in the bottom third of the oven and preheat the oven to 450°F (230°C).

Boil the pretzels. Add the baking soda and dark brown sugar to the simmering water. Be careful because the baking soda will foam up. Gently lift a pretzel from the pan and lower it into the simmering water. Boil for 5 to 10 seconds and quickly lift it out of the water using a slotted silicone spatula or any flat slotted utensil. Return it to the pan. Repeat with the rest of the pretzels. Once they are all boiled, if your pretzels seem a bit misshapen, spread out the "shoulders" a bit before they go in the oven.

Note: For a vegan version, omit the egg white, increase the water in the dough to 150 grams, and increase the xanthan gum to 1 teaspoon (4 g).

Top and bake the pretzels. Sprinkle the tops with pretzel salt or seeds. For soft, light golden brown pretzels, bake for 20 minutes. For darker, crispier pretzels, bake for 25 minutes. If desired, brush the pretzels with melted butter as soon as they come out of the oven, which will soften them. Let the pretzels cool on the pan for 15 minutes before eating. They are best eaten while warm.

Using Food-Grade Lye for Pretzels

Food-grade lye (sodium hydroxide) is an alkaline compound used in food production. It must be properly handled as it can cause severe burns and damage upon contact with skin or eyes, but with proper handling, it creates delicious pretzels. You can get food-grade lye from specialty baking shops (see Resources, page 390). Use safety gear while handling lye (wear gloves and protect any exposed skin with clothing). Lye must be added to water and not the other way around. Use a solution of 8 cups (1.8 liters) of water and 2.5 ounces (75 g) of food-grade lye for this pretzel recipe. Fill a large stainless steel stockpot with water. Add the lye and bring it to a simmer over high heat. When the water is at a simmer, dip the chilled pretzels in the solution for 10 seconds (use a slotted spoon or spatula to help you submerge the pretzels in the solution). The lye bath will turn the dough yellow. Bake the pretzels as directed. You can store the lye water in the refrigerator for up to 3 days. You can safely dispose of it down your sink drain.

Rosemary Grissini

1 teaspoon (4 g) active dry yeast

280 grams water, heated to 105°F (41°C)

2 teaspoons (8 g) granulated sugar

25 grams extra-virgin olive oil, plus more for brushing

10 grams psyllium husk powder

140 grams sorghum flour

80 grams potato starch

60 grams tapioca starch, plus more for dusting

Leaves from 2 rosemary sprigs, finely chopped

1½ teaspoons (6 g) kosher salt

Poppy seeds, sesame seeds, and flaky sea salt, for topping (optional)

Grissini are crispy breadsticks with a pronounced olive oil flavor. These have a touch of rosemary, too, and sesame and poppy seeds as a topping. Serve them as part of a large appetizer spread with cheeses, charcuterie, pickled vegetables, and dips.

MAKES ABOUT 25 GRISSINI

Make the yeast-psyllium mixture. Sprinkle the yeast into a large bowl. Add the water and sugar and whisk until dissolved. Let the mixture sit until frothy, about 10 minutes. Whisk in the olive oil and psyllium until smooth. Let it gel for 5 minutes.

Make the dough. To the bowl with the yeast-psyllium mixture, add the sorghum flour, potato starch, tapioca starch, rosemary, and salt. Use a wooden spoon or spatula to stir everything together, then use your hands to knead the dough. It will appear slightly dry initially, but continue kneading for 3 to 5 minutes until smooth and moist. It will have the consistency of soft pasta dough. Add a touch of water if needed.

Proof the dough. Shape the dough into a tight ball and leave in the bowl. Cover the bowl with a kitchen towel and proof until doubled in size, about 1 hour.

Cut the dough. Dust a work surface with some tapioca starch. Place the dough on it and roll it into a rectangle roughly 10 by 11 inches (25 by 28 cm) and ¼ inch (6 mm) thick. It's okay if it is not exactly a rectangle. Brush the dough with a little bit of olive oil. Cut the dough into strips ¼ to ½ inch (6 mm to 1.3 cm) wide. Roll each strip of dough to round it and stretch it slightly. Transfer the grissini to a sheet pan, leaving about ½ inch (1.3 cm) between them. It's okay if your strips of dough are slightly longer than your sheet pan, just cut the ends off and reserve the scraps. Repeat with all the dough strips. Gather up all the scraps and reroll to make more grissini. You will have enough to fill two sheet pans. Cover the pans with kitchen towels or loosely cover with plastic wrap and proof for 45 minutes.

Preheat the oven. About 30 minutes before the dough is done proofing, position racks in the center and lower third of the oven and preheat the oven to 450°F (230°C).

Bake the grissini. Lightly brush the tops with more olive oil and sprinkle with any toppings (if using). Bake for 15 to 20 minutes, switching racks halfway through, until the grissini are dry and golden brown. They may curve a little toward the end of baking time. If you prefer that they remain straight, reduce the baking time by a couple of minutes.

Cool the grissini. Transfer the grissini to a wire rack to cool for at least 30 minutes. They will be crispy on the outside but slightly chewy on the inside. Store them in a paper bag or airtight container for up to 5 days.

Caramelized Onion and Poppy Seed Bialys

PICTURED ON PAGE 186

A bialy is a flat roll with an onion and poppy seed filling in the center; it's traditional in Ashkenazi Jewish cuisine. You can serve bialys for breakfast. The dough is similar to that of bagels, but unlike bagels, bialys are not boiled before baking.

MAKES 8 BIALYS

FOR THE DOUGH

2 teaspoons (8 g) active dry yeast

530 grams water, heated to 105°F (41°C)

1 teaspoon (4 g) granulated sugar

20 grams psyllium husk powder

12 grams apple cider vinegar

7 grams flaxseed meal

160 grams oat flour

160 grams millet flour

90 grams tapioca starch

90 grams potato starch

2½ teaspoons (10 g) kosher salt

Superfine brown rice flour, for dusting

FOR THE ONION–POPPY SEED FILLING

40 grams extra-virgin olive oil

½ medium yellow onion, diced

½ teaspoon (2 g) kosher salt

Small pinch of freshly ground black pepper

1½ teaspoons (4 g) poppy seeds

Sesame seeds, for sprinkling

Make the yeast-psyllium mixture. Sprinkle the yeast into a medium bowl. Add the water and sugar and whisk until dissolved. Let the mixture sit until frothy, about 10 minutes. Vigorously whisk in the psyllium, vinegar, and flaxseed until smooth. Let it gel for 5 minutes.

Make the dough. In a stand mixer, stir together the oat flour, millet flour, tapioca starch, potato starch, and salt. Add the yeast-psyllium mixture. Snap on the dough hook and mix over medium speed until the dough comes together, 2 to 3 minutes. The dough will feel moist and sticky but should hold together nicely.

Cut the dough. Cut the dough into 8 equal pieces (about 130 g each). Dust a work surface with some brown rice flour. Shape each piece of dough into a tight ball. Lightly dust a sheet pan with brown rice flour and place the dough pieces on it.

Proof the dough. Cover the sheet pan with a kitchen towel and proof at room temperature for 45 minutes to 1 hour. (Alternatively, cover the sheet pan with a large plastic bag or cover loosely with plastic wrap and refrigerate overnight for 8 to 12 hours.)

Make the onion-poppy seed topping. In a sauté pan, heat the olive oil over medium heat. Add the onion, salt, and pepper and cook until the onion begins to soften, 2 to 3 minutes. Do not brown the onions too much or they will burn in the oven. Remove the pan from the heat and mix in the poppy seeds. Let the filling cool before using.

Preheat the oven. Position a rack in the bottom third of the oven and place a cast-iron pan on the bottom of the oven. Preheat the oven to 500°F (260°C). Let the oven continue heating for 15 minutes after it has reached temperature.

Add the bialy filling. Dust your fingers with brown rice flour. Hold each piece of dough in your hands, pinching the center of the dough between your thumbs, creating disks that are about 5 inches (12 cm) across with a raised border and a crater in the center for the filling that is about 2½ inches (6 cm) wide. Place them on the sheet pan as you form them. Make sure the center cavity is deep and flat or it will puff up too much during baking, pushing the filling up and out. Add 1 teaspoon of the onion–poppy seed filling in the center of each bialy. Do not overfill. Sprinkle the tops with a pinch of sesame seeds.

Bake the bialys. Place the sheet pan in the oven and toss 5 or 6 ice cubes in the cast-iron pan. Bake for 22 to 25 minutes, until golden brown.

Cool the bialys. Transfer the bialys to a wire rack and let cool completely before cutting. Initially, the crust will seem very hard, but it will soften as the bialys cool. They are best eaten the same day.

Yeast-Free Sandwich Bread

PICTURED ON PAGE 187

- Olive oil, for greasing
- 210 grams superfine brown rice flour
- 140 grams sorghum flour
- 120 grams tapioca starch
- 12 grams baking powder
- 2 teaspoons (8 g) kosher salt
- ¾ teaspoon (3 g) baking soda
- 25 grams psyllium husk powder
- 10 grams flaxseed meal
- 620 grams water
- 20 grams maple syrup
- 15 grams apple cider vinegar

I get a lot of requests for yeast-free bread recipes. This is a loaf leavened with baking powder and baking soda. It doesn't have the yeasty flavor that I so love in bread, but it has great texture and comes together quickly. It's a basic recipe, but see the Variations that follow for some suggestions to dress it up.

MAKES 1 LOAF

Preheat the oven. Position a rack in the bottom third of the oven and preheat the oven to 450°F (230°C). Grease an 8 ½-by-4½-inch (22 by 11 cm) loaf pan with olive oil.

Make the dough. In a stand mixer, stir together the brown rice flour, sorghum flour, tapioca starch, baking powder, salt, and baking soda. In a medium bowl, combine the psyllium and flaxseed. Whisk in the water until smooth. Let it gel for 5 minutes. Pour the mixture into the dry ingredients along with the maple syrup and vinegar. If you're going to add in any additional ingredients, now is the time. Snap on the dough hook and mix on medium-high speed until the dough comes together and is smooth, 2 to 3 minutes. Transfer the dough to a work surface. Knead it a few times and shape it into an oval. Place it in the prepared pan.

Bake the bread. Bake until lightly golden brown, about 45 minutes.

Cool the bread. Let the bread cool in the pan for 5 minutes, then invert onto a wire rack to cool completely. Store the bread at room temperature wrapped in a paper bag for up to 3 days.

VARIATIONS

Seeded Sandwich Bread

Make the dough as directed, adding 85 grams assorted seeds (pumpkin, sunflower, sesame, chia, flax) when you mix the dough with the dough hook. Shape, bake, and cool as directed.

Green Olive and Rosemary Sandwich Bread

Make the dough as directed, adding 105 grams coarsely chopped pitted green olives (make sure you drain and pat dry them before adding into the dough) and coarsely chopped leaves from 2 sprigs of rosemary when you mix the dough with the dough hook. Shape, bake, and cool as directed.

Fig-Walnut Sandwich Bread

Make the dough as directed, adding 60 grams coarsely chopped walnuts and 60 grams coarsely chopped dried figs when you mix the dough with the dough hook. Shape, bake, and cool as directed.

Leek and Cheddar Soda Bread

This leek and Cheddar bread is like a giant scone, cheesy and buttery. There is no yeast in this bread, which instead relies on baking soda as a leavener. It comes together in no time, making it a perfect recipe when you want to have bread on the table quickly.

SERVES 6 TO 8

FOR THE LEEKS

1 tablespoon (15 g) extra-virgin olive oil

2 medium leeks (10 ounces/280 g total), white and light-green parts only, halved lengthwise and thinly sliced

½ teaspoon (2 g) kosher salt

FOR THE DOUGH

210 grams millet flour or sorghum flour, plus more for dusting

180 grams tapioca starch

110 grams oat flour

12 grams baking powder

10 grams psyllium husk powder

2 teaspoons (8 g) kosher salt

1 teaspoon (4 g) baking soda

1 teaspoon (2 g) dried oregano

180 grams English white Cheddar or vegan Cheddar-style cheese

110 grams very cold unsalted butter or vegan butter

280 grams cold water

15 grams whole milk or oat milk

Preheat the oven. Position a rack in the bottom third of the oven and preheat the oven to 425°F (220°C).

Cook the leeks. Heat a medium sauté pan over medium-high heat. Add the olive oil, leeks, and salt. Stir and cook until the leeks are softened and begin to caramelize, about 5 minutes. Don't let the leeks turn brown. Set aside and cool completely.

Make the dough. In a large bowl, stir together the millet flour, tapioca starch, oat flour, baking powder, psyllium, salt, baking soda, and oregano. Using a large grater, shred the Cheddar into the flour mixture. Toss the cheese into the flour as you go. Grate the cold butter into the flour and toss together to distribute it throughout. Add the cooked leeks and water. Toss everything together with a fork to distribute the moisture, then switch to your hands to knead the dough together.

Knead the dough. Transfer the dough to a work surface and knead until it all sticks together like a giant scone. Add water if the dough feels dry, but do it slowly while you knead. If the dough feels wet, add a dusting of millet or sorghum flour and knead it.

Shape the dough. Line a sheet pan with parchment paper. Transfer the dough onto it and shape into an 8-inch (20 cm) disk that is about 1½ inches (4 cm) high. Brush the top of the dough with the milk.

Score and bake the bread. Using a knife or bench knife, score a cross in the top of the dough ½ inch (1.3 cm) deep. Bake for 22 to 25 minutes, until golden brown.

Cool the bread. Let the bread cool on the pan for 15 minutes before slicing. It is best eaten while warm as it tends to dry out after a while.

No. 5

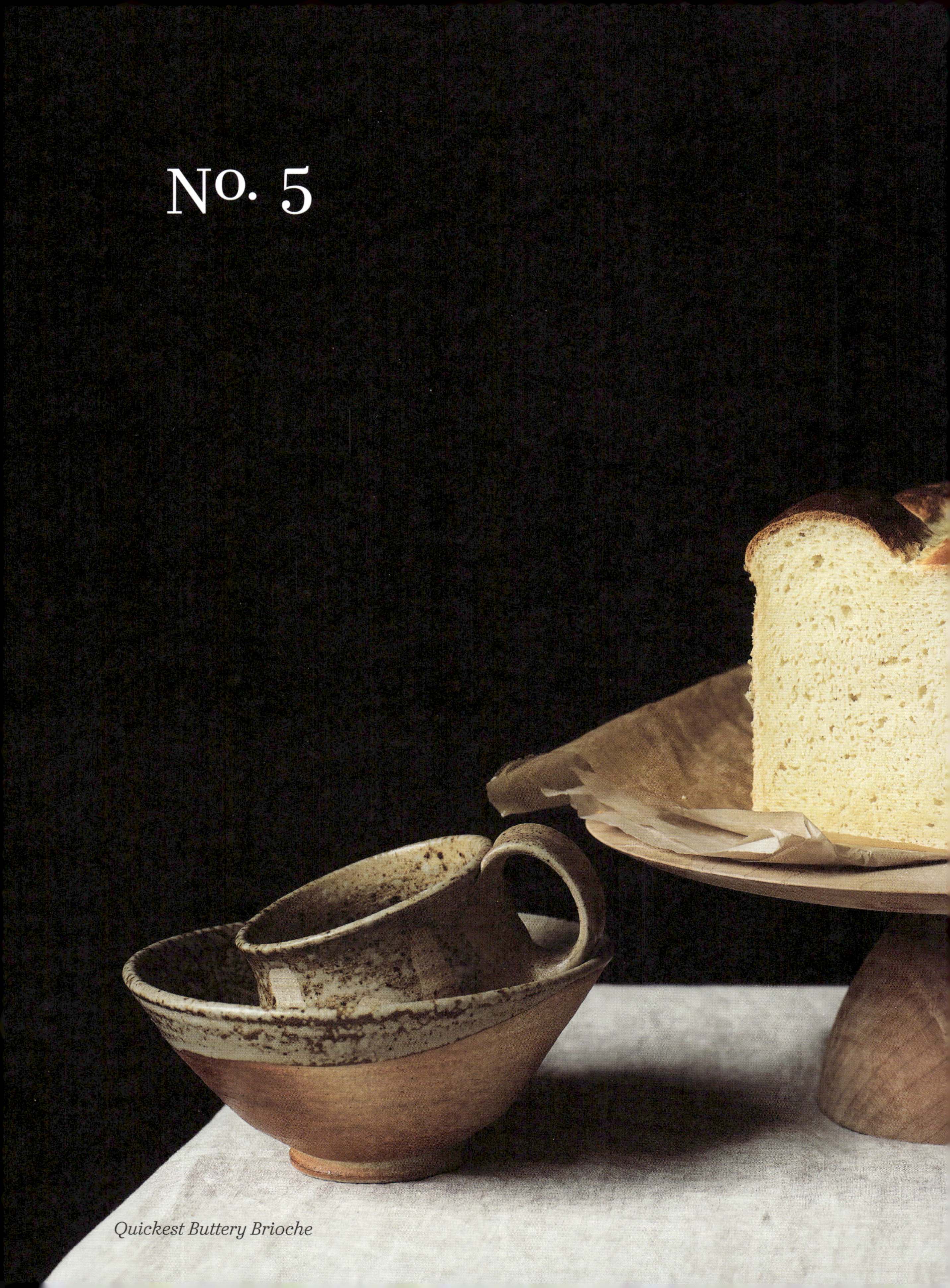

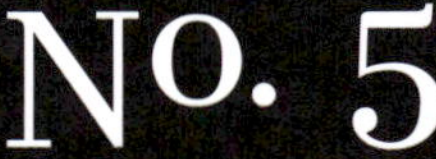

Quickest Buttery Brioche

Sweet and Savory Enriched Breads

My family's pastry shop in the Basque Country is known for its bollos de mantequilla: little buttery brioche buns sprinkled with a sugary topping and filled with the fluffiest buttercream. People line up every morning for these bollos, and children flock to the shop after school lets out to get them as an afternoon treat. I dunked one in warm milk for breakfast every day when I was a kid. My grandmother Miren was in charge of the bollo dough. I can still picture her clear as day, alone in the pastry kitchen at dusk with one dim overhead light above her. My grandmother whistled while she kneaded the buttery dough. If you have made brioche in a professional setting, you know it takes strength to knead and fold pounds of dough. That was my grandmother's job well into her sixties. The dough fermented overnight, and my grandfather and uncles came in at 4 a.m. to shape, proof, and bake.

The breads in this chapter are meant to be light and tender and that is why you will notice a higher percentage of starches in the flour mixture. If you alter the flour ratios and introduce more whole grains to the mix, you will end up with a completely different crust and crumb. Enriched breads rely on eggs and butter or oil for elasticity and richness and so it is trickier to make them vegan. For a Vegan Brioche recipe, turn to page 220; it can be used in place of the traditional version.

There are four basic dough recipes that are used throughout this chapter: Sourdough Brioche (page 198), Quickest Buttery Brioche (page 208), Danish Dough (page 222), and Soft and Fluffy Potato Rolls (page 244). But the brioche doughs are pretty much interchangeable. For example, if a recipe calls for dough from Quickest Buttery Brioche or Soft and Fluffy Potato Rolls, but you would rather make a sourdough version, you could swap it out. You could make the Olive Pesto Pull-Apart Bread (page 248) with the Sourdough Brioche, or the Lemon Marmalade and Vanilla Sourdough Maritozzi (page 202) with the Quickest Buttery Brioche instead of the sourdough version.

Creating a Danish dough that is flaky has been one of my biggest accomplishments. Use this dough to make Croissants (page 234), Cider-Roasted Apple and Vanilla Cream Danish (page 230), and more.

Sourdough Brioche

FOR THE SWEET STIFF SPONGE

75 grams Whole-Grain Brown Rice–Teff Sourdough Starter (page 48)

45 grams whole milk or oat milk, at around 80° to 85°F (27° to 29°C)

70 grams superfine brown rice flour

20 grams granulated sugar

FOR THE DOUGH

30 grams psyllium husk powder

250 grams whole milk or oat milk, at around 80° to 85°F (27° to 29°C)

160 grams potato starch

140 grams sweet white rice flour

120 grams tapioca starch, plus more for dusting

100 grams granulated sugar

2½ teaspoons (10 g) kosher salt

1 teaspoon (2 g) finely grated orange zest

3 large eggs, at room temperature

2 teaspoons (8 g) vanilla paste or extract

55 grams extra-virgin olive oil, unsalted butter, or vegan butter, at room temperature, plus more for greasing

This sourdough brioche is made with a sweet stiff starter sponge, which provides a very milky and buttery taste and not the sour one you might associate with sourdough. It is fermented for a long time—this is a two-day process—so plan ahead for it. I like to make the sweet stiff sponge the morning before I am going to bake the brioche. Let the sponge ferment during the day, then in the evening, mix the brioche and chill it in the refrigerator overnight. The following morning, I shape the dough, proof, and bake.

If this is your first time using a sweet stiff starter, read more on page 51. Finally, note that I list olive oil, unsalted butter, and vegan butter as options for the fat in this recipe and all work well. But I personally prefer olive oil, as it makes the dough slightly moister and more pliable.

MAKES 1 LOAF

Make the sweet stiff sponge. In a medium bowl, whisk together the starter and milk until smooth. Add the brown rice flour and sugar and mix with a spatula until you have a thick paste. Knead it a few times. Place the sponge in a wide-mouth 12-ounce (340 ml) mason jar or plastic container, gently pressing it down into the bottom. Place a rubber band around the jar right where the top of the sponge sits so you will be able to see how much it has grown. Loosely cover the jar with a small kitchen towel or the lid without sealing.

Ferment the sponge. Let the sponge sit until it has risen about 50 percent and the top feels very springy and soft to the touch, 8 to 12 hours. This stiff sponge does best at 80° to 85°F (27° to 29°C), so in the winter, I like to keep it in the oven with the light on and a small pot with boiling-hot water next to the pan that I reheat every hour to keep at a constant temperature.

Make the dough. Place the psyllium in a medium bowl and vigorously whisk while adding the milk. Let it gel for 5 minutes. In a stand mixer, stir together the potato starch, sweet white rice flour, tapioca starch, sugar, salt, and orange zest. Add the sweet stiff sponge, psyllium gel, eggs, and vanilla. Snap on the dough hook and mix on medium speed until the dough comes together, about 1 minute. Add the olive oil or soft butter and continue mixing until

FOR THE EGG WASH

1 large egg

15 grams coarse sugar, sesame seeds, poppy seeds, or any other topping you prefer

FOR BRUSHING

25 grams unsalted butter or vegan butter (optional), melted

you have a smooth dough, 2 to 3 minutes. The dough will feel soft and moist but should hold together.

Proof the dough. Grease a large bowl with a bit of butter or olive oil and place the dough in it. Cover the bowl with plastic wrap, proof at room temperature for an hour, then refrigerate for 10 to 20 hours.

Shape the dough. The following morning, remove the bowl from refrigerator. Grease an 8½-by-4½-inch (22 by 11 cm) loaf pan with some butter or olive oil and line with a strip of parchment paper, letting some hang over the sides. The dough will feel very cold and firm (not as firm if using olive oil). Place the dough on a work surface and knead a few times until it is smooth. Cut the dough into 6 equal pieces (about 190 g each). Lightly dust the work surface with some tapioca starch and shape each piece of dough into a tight ball. Place all the pieces of dough in the pan snugly pressing against one another.

Proof the brioche. Cover the pan with a kitchen towel or plastic wrap and proof until the dough feels marshmallow-like, 2 to 4 hours. Again, in the wintertime, I like to proof the dough in the oven with the light on and a small pot of boiling-hot water next to the pan. The dough will rise about 50 percent and feel light to the touch.

Preheat the oven. When the dough feels nearly done proofing, position a rack in the bottom third of the oven and preheat the oven to 350°F (180°C). (Remember to remove the pan from the oven first if you are using it for proofing.)

Make the egg wash. In a small bowl, lightly whisk the egg. Gently brush the top of the dough with the egg wash and sprinkle with coarse sugar or any other topping you are using.

Bake the brioche. Bake for 40 to 45 minutes, until the brioche is golden brown and puffed up. As soon as the brioche comes out of the oven, brush the top with the melted butter, if using.

Cool the brioche. Let the brioche cool in the pan for 15 minutes, then transfer to a wire rack. I like to pull it apart when it's still slightly warm, and it feels satisfying to see the crumb stretch, but you could let it cool completely and slice it. It is best eaten the same day.

Lemon Marmalade and Vanilla Sourdough Maritozzi

FOR THE DOUGH

Dough for Sourdough Brioche (page 198)

2 teaspoons (4 g) finely grated lemon zest

Tapioca starch, for dusting

FOR THE EGG WASH

1 large egg, lightly beaten

FOR THE FILLING

225 grams heavy cream, full-fat coconut cream, or vegan whipping cream

30 grams powdered sugar, plus more for dusting

½ vanilla bean, split lengthwise

150 grams Lemon and Vanilla Bean Marmalade (page 362)

Chopped pistachios, for topping

Maritozzi are brioche buns filled with whipped heavy cream. They are typical in Italy, but there is a similar brioche in Spain called cristinas o bombas de nata. At my family bakery, we make cristinas exclusively on Sundays. The brioche bun gets a small almond crumble on top and is filled with the lightest sweetened cream. You can find maritozzi that have a multitude of fillings and not just cream—a layer of flavored pastry cream buried under the heavy cream, ganache, or jam. In this case, I add a bit of the homemade lemon marmalade in the center and then cover the rest with heavy cream. Eating one is a delight as a midafternoon treat with some coffee or tea. You can also make this with the dough for Quickest Buttery Brioche (page 208).

MAKES 12 MARITOZZI

Make the dough. Make the brioche dough as directed, adding the lemon zest when you incorporate the dry ingredients. Proof the dough in the refrigerator for 10 to 20 hours.

Shape the dough. Line two sheet pans with parchment paper. Transfer the dough to a work surface and knead a few times to bring back the elasticity and smooth it out. Cut the dough into 12 equal pieces (about 100 g each). Lightly dust the work surface with tapioca starch. Shape the dough into tight balls and place them on the prepared sheet pans. Cover the pans loosely with plastic or wrap them in a large plastic bag. Proof until the dough feels soft and a little marshmallow-like, 2 to 4 hours. The dough won't rise much in volume and that is okay.

Preheat the oven. About 20 minutes before the dough is done proofing, position a rack in the bottom third of the oven and preheat the oven to 350°F (180°C).

Bake the buns. I like to bake one sheet pan at a time for even coloring. Gently brush the tops of the dough with the beaten egg. Place the sheet pan inside another empty sheet pan (this will protect

the bottoms from becoming too dark or thick, but it's optional). Bake for 25 minutes, or until golden brown.

Cool the buns. Let the brioche buns cool on the pan for a minute, then transfer them to a wire rack. Bake the second sheet pan. Cool all the buns completely before filling.

Make the whipped cream. In a stand mixer (or a large bowl with a hand mixer), combine the cream and powdered sugar. Scrape the vanilla seeds into the bowl. Beat the cream on high speed with the whisk until it forms firm peaks, about 1 minute.

Fill the maritozzi. Use a serrated knife to make a cut lengthwise down the center of each bun while keeping it intact at the base. Open each bun slightly and spoon in 2 teaspoons of the marmalade, then 2 to 3 tablespoons of whipped cream. Run a small offset spatula along the edge of the bun to smooth out the cream, making it flush with the edge of the bun. Wipe the cream that might have spilled out of the cavity onto the top of the bun to create a very clean finish. You can dust the tops with powdered sugar and sprinkle some chopped pistachios along the edge of the cream. Serve immediately.

Spiced Apple Streusel Brioche Crown

FOR THE DOUGH

Dough for Sourdough Brioche (page 198)

Tapioca starch, for dusting

FOR THE APPLE FILLING

80 grams unsalted butter or vegan butter, cut into large pieces

140 grams granulated sugar

4 medium Honeycrisp or other juicy and sweet apples (1 pound/455 g total), peeled, cored, quartered, and thinly sliced

1 teaspoon (2 g) finely grated lemon zest

2 teaspoons fresh lemon juice, plus more if needed

1 teaspoon (3 g) ground cinnamon

½ teaspoon (2 g) ground ginger

½ vanilla bean, split lengthwise

10 grams tapioca starch (optional)

FOR THE STREUSEL

35 grams almond flour

35 grams granulated sugar

(Ingredients continue)

This is one of my favorite brioches to make in the fall. The streusel adds crunch and the spiced apple filling becomes creamy and makes a delicious, moist brioche. Start by making the sourdough brioche the morning of the day before you are going to bake the crown. Make the filling and streusel ahead of time, then assemble, proof, and bake the morning you are going to serve it. You can also make this recipe using the dough for Quickest Buttery Brioche (page 208).

MAKES 1 CROWN

Make the dough. Make the brioche dough as directed, up through resting the dough in the refrigerator for 10 to 20 hours.

Make the apple filling. Heat a medium sauté pan over medium heat. Add the butter and swirl it around until melted. Add the sugar and stir with a wooden spoon until it melts into the butter and begins to caramelize, about 2 minutes. Add the apples, lemon zest, lemon juice, cinnamon, and ginger. Scrape in the vanilla seeds and add the pod, too. Stir so the apples are coated with the sugar and butter and cook until very soft and lightly caramelized, about 10 minutes. If the mixture seems dry, add more lemon juice. If it seems too wet, whisk the tapioca starch with a splash of lemon juice, add to the simmering apple mixture, and cook until it thickens. The filling should be creamy and not burned. Transfer the cooked apples to a large plate, discard the vanilla bean, and let them cool completely before assembling the crown. (You can make the apple filling a day in advance and keep refrigerated.)

Make the streusel. In a medium bowl, stir together the almond flour, sugar, and brown rice flour. Add the diced butter and work it between your fingers until you have a crumbly, moist dough. Keep refrigerated until ready to use. (You can make the streusel a day in advance.)

Roll and fill the dough. Grease the walls and center tube of a 9-inch (23 cm) tube pan with olive oil or butter. Remove the brioche dough from the refrigerator and knead it on a work surface a few times. Cut the dough into 3 equal pieces (about 380 g each). Work with one

10 grams superfine brown rice flour

35 grams unsalted butter or vegan butter, cut into ½-inch (1.3 cm) pieces

FOR THE EGG WASH

1 large egg, lightly whisked

FOR THE TOPPING (OPTIONAL)

Powdered sugar

Chopped pistachios

Finely grated orange zest

piece at a time and keep the remaining dough in the refrigerator. Dust the work surface with some tapioca starch. Flatten one piece of dough and roll it into a rectangle that is 16 by 5 inches (41 by 13 cm) and about ¼ inch (6 mm) thick. Move the dough around often to make sure it is not sticking to the work surface and gently stretch it at the corners to try to get a rectangle with square edges. It's okay if it's not perfect. Spread one-third of the cooled apple filling over it in a thin layer, leaving a ½-inch (1.3 cm) border around the edges. Starting from a long side, roll the dough as tightly as possible into a 16-inch (41 cm) log. Pinch the seam together so the apples don't fall out when you braid the crown. Place the log next to you. Repeat the rolling and filling with a second piece of dough and set that log next to the first one. Repeat with the last piece of dough. Place the 3 filled strands of dough vertically in front of you. Pinch them gently on the top and braid them together carefully so they don't tear too much and the filling remains inside. Bring the prepared tube pan next to you. Carefully lift the braid and place it inside the pan. Pinch together the ends. The braid might have torn in a couple of places or might appear a bit wonky, but that's okay. It will come together in the oven.

Proof the dough. Cover the pan with a kitchen towel or wrap it in a large plastic bag and proof at room temperature for 2 to 4 hours. It won't rise much but should feel slightly marshmallow-like to the touch.

Preheat the oven. Position a rack in the bottom third of the oven and preheat the oven to 350°F (180°C).

Bake the brioche. Brush the brioche braid with the egg wash and sprinkle the streusel on top. Bake for 35 to 40 minutes, until golden brown.

Cool the brioche. Let the brioche cool in the pan for 20 minutes, then release from the tube pan and transfer to a wire rack and cool for at least 30 minutes. If desired, dust the top with powdered sugar, chopped pistachios, and orange zest. It's best eaten while warm.

Quickest Buttery Brioche

2½ teaspoons (10 g) active dry yeast

245 to 260 grams (see Note) whole milk or oat milk, heated to 105°F (41°C)

1 teaspoon (4 g) plus 100 grams granulated sugar

30 grams psyllium husk powder

200 grams potato starch

180 grams tapioca starch, plus more for dusting

90 grams sorghum flour

2½ teaspoons (10 g) kosher salt

1 teaspoon (4 g) xanthan gum (optional; see Note)

1 teaspoon (2 g) finely grated orange zest

3 large eggs, at room temperature

2 teaspoons (8 g) vanilla paste or extract

100 grams very soft (but not melted) unsalted butter or vegan butter, plus more greasing

FOR THE EGG WASH

1 large egg, lightly beaten

If you don't have two days to make Sourdough Brioche (page 198), this is a great shortcut. There is no bulk fermentation either; only one proof and then straight into the oven it goes. The crumb is light and tender and really fluffy. It is high in starch, but you really need it for brioche. The xanthan gum is listed as optional, but it does help create a crumb that has a bit more layering and pull. If using this brioche recipe to make buns or any variation that requires the dough to be stretched, I highly recommend using the xanthan gum to help provide structure or the dough can be too soft to handle.

MAKES 1 LOAF

Prep the pan. Line an 8½-by-4½-inch (22 by 11 cm) metal loaf pan with a strip of parchment paper, leaving some hanging over the edges.

Make the yeast-psyllium mixture. Sprinkle the yeast into a medium bowl. Add the milk and 1 teaspoon of the sugar and whisk until dissolved. Let the mixture sit until frothy, about 10 minutes. Add the psyllium and whisk vigorously until smooth. Let it gel for 5 minutes.

Make the dough. In a stand mixer, stir together the potato starch, tapioca starch, remaining 100 grams sugar, the sorghum flour, salt, xanthan gum (if using), and orange zest. Add the yeast-psyllium mixture. Snap on the dough hook and mix the dough on low speed. Add the eggs and vanilla. Increase the speed to medium and keep mixing until the dough comes together, 2 to 3 minutes. It will look dry and clumpy for the majority of that mixing time, but by the end, it should come together (or nearly together) into a ball. Add the soft butter, 1 tablespoon at a time, while the mixer is running. Scrape the bowl as needed. Continue mixing for another minute until you have a soft and sticky dough that holds together.

Shape the dough. Lightly dust a work surface with tapioca starch. Scrape the dough onto the work surface and knead together a few times shaping it into a ball. It will be soft, but by this point should not be terribly sticky. Cut the dough into 6 equal pieces (about 190 g each). Shape all the pieces of dough into tight balls and place them inside the prepared loaf pan snugly next to each other. (Alternatively, if you want to create a bit of a swirl effect in the crumb, roll each piece of dough into an oval that is about

¼ inch/6 mm thick. Fold the dough in thirds, creating a letter fold, then roll the dough into a cylinder. Add these pieces of dough into the prepared loaf pan.)

Proof the dough. Cover the pan with a kitchen towel and proof until nearly doubled, 45 minutes to 1 hour.

Preheat the oven. Position a rack in the bottom third of the oven and preheat the oven to 350°F (180°C).

Bake the brioche. Brush the top of the dough with the egg wash and bake until golden brown and the dough has risen to the top of the pan, 30 to 35 minutes.

Cool the brioche. Let the brioche cool in the pan for 10 minutes, then transfer to a wire rack to cool for 20 minutes. The brioche is best eaten while warm.

Note: If you don't use the xanthan gum, use the smaller amount (245 grams) of milk.

Cinnamon Buns

FOR THE DOUGH

Dough for Quickest Buttery Brioche (page 208)

Tapioca starch, for dusting

FOR THE FILLING

110 grams very soft (but not melted) unsalted butter or vegan butter

125 grams dark brown sugar

1½ teaspoons (6 g) ground cinnamon

FOR THE CREAM CHEESE ICING

150 grams full-fat cream cheese or vegan cream cheese, at room temperature

50 grams very soft (but not melted) unsalted butter or vegan butter

200 grams powdered sugar

10 grams whole milk or oat milk

1 teaspoon (4 g) vanilla extract or vanilla paste

Cinnamon buns are the quintessential comfort breakfast. I make them for lazy weekend mornings, and they are my family's Christmas morning tradition. Make the dough the night before you are going to serve the buns and chill it in the refrigerator overnight. In the morning, fill, proof, and bake the buns.

MAKES 12 BUNS

Make the dough. Make the brioche dough as directed. Place in a lightly greased bowl, cover with plastic wrap, and refrigerate for 4 to 12 hours.

Roll the dough. The dough will have risen in the refrigerator. Knead to deflate it and bring back some elasticity. Dust a work surface with some tapioca starch and roll the dough into a rectangle that is about 12 by 18 inches (30 by 46 cm) and ¼ inch (6 mm) thick.

Fill the dough. Make sure your butter is very soft and spreadable or it can tear the dough. Warm in the microwave for 5 seconds, if needed. Spread the very soft butter all over the dough. In a medium bowl, mix together the brown sugar and cinnamon and sprinkle evenly over the butter. Starting from a long side, roll the dough into a log making sure you leave the seam on the bottom.

Cut the dough. Line a sheet pan with parchment paper. Cut the log into 12 buns that are 1½ inches (4 cm) wide. Place the buns, cut-sides down, on the prepared sheet pan.

Proof the buns. Cover the pan with a kitchen towel or plastic wrap and proof the buns until they are puffed up, 40 to 45 minutes.

Preheat the oven. While the buns are proofing, position a rack in the bottom third of the oven and preheat the oven to 375°F (190°C).

Bake the buns. Transfer the pan to the oven and bake until golden brown, about 30 minutes.

Make the cream cheese icing. While the buns are baking, in a large bowl, whisk together the softened cream cheese, butter, powdered sugar, milk, and vanilla until smooth.

Finish the buns. Once the buns come out of the oven, let them cool for 5 to 10 minutes. Spread the cream cheese icing all over the top. Serve the buns while warm.

Chocolate Swirl Brioche

FOR THE DOUGH

Dough for Quickest Buttery Brioche (page 208)

Softened butter, for the bowl

Tapioca starch, for dusting

FOR THE FILLING

60 grams chocolate (70% cacao), finely chopped

58 grams unsalted butter or vegan butter, at room temperature

15 grams unsweetened cacao powder

30 grams powdered sugar

1 teaspoon (4 g) vanilla paste or extract

FOR THE EGG WASH

1 large egg, lightly beaten

This makes a beautiful brioche with a chocolate swirl inside. It is essentially the same recipe as the Chocolate Babka Wreath (page 326), but shaped slightly differently. Here each piece of dough is filled with a creamy chocolate paste, then laminated to create a swirl effect.

MAKES 1 LOAF

Make the dough. Make the brioche dough as directed. Grease a large bowl with butter. Place the dough in the bowl, cover with a kitchen towel, and proof until nearly doubled in size, 45 minutes to 1 hour.

Make the chocolate filling. About 30 minutes before rolling and filling the dough, in a heatproof bowl combine the chopped chocolate, butter, and cacao powder and place over a pot of simmering water. Stir until everything has melted together and it's smooth. Remove the bowl from the heat and whisk in the powdered sugar and vanilla. Set aside for 30 minutes or until it thickens to the consistency of soft ganache. (You can make the filling a day in advance, but you will have to warm it up a bit to be able to spread it.)

Roll, fill, and shape the dough. Lightly grease an 8½-by-4½-inch (22 by 11 cm) loaf pan and line with a strip of parchment paper, leaving the ends to hang over the pan. Dust a work surface with a little bit of tapioca starch, turn the dough out onto the surface, and knead it back together to deflate it. Cut the dough into 6 equal pieces (about 190 g each). Knead each piece of dough until smooth and shape into a tight ball. Roll a piece of dough into an oval that is about 6 inches (15 cm) long and 4 inches (10 cm) wide. Spread a couple of tablespoons of the chocolate filling over the dough into a thin, even layer all the way to the edges. With a short side facing you, fold the top third of the dough over the middle and the bottom third over it, creating a letter fold. Rotate the dough 90 degrees and roll the dough into a tight cylinder. Set aside. Repeat with the remaining dough pieces. Place the filled dough pieces inside the loaf pan, seam-side down, snugly against each other. This can be a bit tricky at times and some pieces might stick up a little higher. That is okay.

Proof the dough. Cover the pan with a kitchen towel or plastic wrap and proof until the dough has risen above the rim of the pan, about 30 minutes.

Preheat the oven. Position a rack in the bottom third of the oven and preheat the oven to 350°F (180°C).

Bake the chocolate brioche. Brush the tops with the egg wash and bake until golden brown, 30 to 35 minutes.

Cool the brioche. Let the brioche cool for 10 minutes in the pan, then transfer to a wire rack and cool for 20 minutes before slicing. Serve while still warm.

Vanilla Cream and Strawberry Brioche Buns

PICTURED ON PAGES 216–217

Dough for Quickest Buttery Brioche (page 208)

Tapioca starch, for dusting

Pastry Cream (recipe follows)

225 grams sliced strawberries or other fruit (see Note)

10 grams granulated sugar, plus more for sprinkling

1 teaspoon (4 g) rose water (optional)

Powdered sugar, for dusting

Rose petals, for garnish (optional)

Brioche buns were often my breakfast before school when I was a kid. We call them bollos suizos in our family pastry shop—pillowy brioche buns with a tiny sprinkle of sugar on top. In this recipe, I take that idea but add a bit of pastry cream and fresh strawberries to the bun.

MAKES 12 BUNS

Make the dough. Make the brioche dough as directed.

Shape the dough. Line two sheet pans with parchment paper. Cut the dough into 12 equal pieces (about 90 g each). Dust a work surface with some tapioca starch. Shape each piece into a tight ball making sure to seal the seams well. Place 6 balls of dough on each sheet pan, leaving 3 to 4 inches (7.5 to 10 cm) between them.

Proof the buns. Cover the pans with kitchen towels and proof until the dough feels marshmallow-like, 40 to 45 minutes.

Make the pastry cream. While the buns are proofing, make the pastry cream as directed.

Preheat the oven. Position racks in the middle and lower third of the oven and preheat the oven to 375°F (190°C).

Macerate the strawberries. In a medium bowl, toss the strawberries, granulated sugar, and rose water (if using) together. Let them macerate for 20 minutes, or until they release some juices.

Fill the buns. Dip a ¼-cup (60 ml) measuring cup or another vessel of that diameter in some tapioca starch or flour you have on hand. Press the measuring cup into the center of each ball to create a well that is about ¾ inch (2 cm) deep. Fill with a heaping teaspoon of pastry cream and some of the macerated strawberries. Sprinkle the tops and edges with granulated sugar.

Bake the buns. Bake for 25 to 30 minutes, switching racks halfway through, until golden brown.

Cool the buns. Let the buns cool on the pan for 5 to 10 minutes. Dust them with powdered sugar and sprinkle with rose petals (if using). They are best eaten while warm. You can keep them refrigerated, tightly wrapped, for 2 days and warm them up before serving. See Storing and Refreshing Bread (page 33).

Note: You can make these with any fruit or fruit compote. Fresh apricots, peaches, raspberries, blueberries, apple compote, poached quince—there are so many possibilities.

Pastry Cream

450 grams whole milk or oat milk

100 grams granulated sugar

1 vanilla bean, split lengthwise

4 large egg yolks

30 grams cornstarch or tapioca starch

110 grams unsalted butter or vegan butter, cut into 1-inch (2.5 cm) pieces, at room temperature

MAKES APPROXIMATELY 3 CUPS (700 G)

Heat the milk. In a medium pot, combine the milk and 50 grams of the sugar. Scrape in the vanilla seeds and add the vanilla pod, too. Warm over medium heat until the milk begins to simmer.

Make the egg mixture. While the milk is heating, in a medium bowl, whisk together the egg yolks, remaining 50 grams sugar, and the cornstarch until smooth. When the milk has come to a simmer, slowly pour it over the egg mixture while constantly whisking until smooth.

Cook the custard. Strain this custard through a fine-mesh sieve back into the pot and continue cooking over medium heat while whisking until it thickens, about 1 minute. Immediately pour the cream into a clean medium bowl. Let the cream cool to lukewarm, 5 to 10 minutes, whisking it occasionally to help it release steam.

Add the butter. When the cream feels lukewarm, whisk in the butter, one piece at a time, until smooth and shiny. Cover with a piece of plastic wrap, pressing it down to touch the surface of the cream, and refrigerate for at least 4 hours. (You can make the pastry cream up to 2 days in advance and keep refrigerated.)

Vanilla-Glazed Doughnuts

FOR THE DOUGH

Dough for Quickest Buttery Brioche (page 208)

Tapioca starch, for dusting

FOR THE VANILLA GLAZE

240 grams powdered sugar

50 grams warm water

2 teaspoons (8 g) vanilla extract or vanilla paste

½ teaspoon (2 g) kosher salt

TO FINISH

Vegetable oil, for frying

Optional toppings: Edible flowers, calendula petals, rose petals, freeze-dried raspberries, chopped pistachios, passion fruit pulp

These brioche doughnuts have become the benchmark for all other doughnuts. They are so tender and fluffy that when people try them, they don't even know they are gluten-free. To fill them with pastry cream and jam, see the Sufganiyot on page 332.

MAKES ABOUT 18 DOUGHNUTS

Make the dough. Make the brioche dough as directed.

Shape the doughnuts. Line two sheet pans with eighteen 3-inch (7.5 cm) squares of parchment paper. Dust a work surface with some tapioca starch. Knead the dough a few times, then roll to ¾ inch (2 cm) thick. Dip a 2½-inch (6 cm) cookie cutter in some tapioca starch and cut the dough into rounds. Use a ¾-inch (2 cm) round cookie cutter to cut a center circle out of each round of dough. Place the cut doughnuts on the parchment squares. Cut all the dough and knead any remaining scraps together, then roll and cut the scraps the same way.

Proof the doughnuts. Loosely cover both sheet pans with a kitchen towel or plastic wrap and proof until the dough feels light and marshmallow-like, 40 to 45 minutes.

Make the vanilla glaze. In a medium bowl, whisk together the powdered sugar, warm water, vanilla, and salt. Set aside.

Fry the doughnuts. About 20 minutes before the dough is done proofing, pour 3 inches (7.5 cm) of oil into a medium saucepan or Dutch oven. Clip a deep-fry thermometer to the side of the pan and heat over medium-high heat to 350°F (180°C). Place a wire rack over a sheet pan next to your pan. Use the parchment ends to lift the dough and carefully invert onto the hot oil. Be careful not to drop the doughnuts in from high up or the oil will splatter and can burn you. Do not overcrowd the pan. The doughnuts will fall to the bottom and then rise again. Cook for 1 to 2 minutes on each side until golden brown. Use a spider or a perforated spatula to scoop the doughnuts out of the oil and place them on the wire rack. Continue with the remaining doughnuts.

Glaze the doughnuts. While the doughnuts are warm, dip them in the glaze. Return them to the rack. Do a second dip for a thicker coating. If using any toppings, sprinkle them on while the glaze is wet. Serve the doughnuts warm. They are best eaten the same day.

Vegan Brioche

- 12 grams active dry yeast
- 425 grams oat milk, heated to 105°F (41°C)
- 1 teaspoon (4 g) plus 100 grams granulated sugar
- 30 grams psyllium husk powder
- 140 grams millet flour
- 120 grams tapioca starch, plus more for dusting
- 120 grams potato starch
- 70 grams sorghum flour
- 2 teaspoons (8 g) kosher salt
- 1½ teaspoons (6 g) baking powder
- 1 teaspoon (2 g) finely grated orange zest
- 60 grams extra-virgin olive oil, plus more for greasing
- 2 teaspoons (8 g) vanilla extract, or 1 vanilla bean, split lengthwise
- 20 grams maple syrup, for brushing

It's not easy to make a gluten-free brioche that is also vegan—without eggs, we lose protein content and elasticity that is needed in gluten-free enriched doughs. But I've cracked the code. The shelf life for this bread is a bit shorter than the one with eggs, so after it's cooled for a couple of hours, it is probably best toasted before enjoying. You can use this vegan version in any recipe that calls for brioche dough, just remember that the lack of elasticity in the dough makes the stretching and twisting a bit more difficult and your final product will be denser.

MAKES 1 LOAF

Make the yeast-psyllium mixture. Sprinkle the yeast into a medium bowl. Add the milk and 1 teaspoon of the sugar and whisk until dissolved. Let the mixture sit until frothy, about 10 minutes. Whisk in the psyllium until completely dissolved. Let it gel for 5 minutes.

Make the dough. In a stand mixer, stir together the remaining 100 grams sugar, the millet flour, tapioca starch, potato starch, sorghum flour, salt, baking powder, and orange zest. Add the yeast-psyllium mixture. Snap on the dough hook and begin mixing on medium speed. Pour in the olive oil and vanilla (if using the vanilla bean, scrape in the seeds) and continue mixing until the dough comes together, 3 to 4 minutes. It should be moist and hold together nicely.

Proof the dough. Transfer the dough to a work surface and shape it into a ball. Grease a large bowl with a small amount of olive oil and add the dough to it. Cover with a kitchen towel and proof until nearly doubled in size, about 45 minutes.

Shape the dough. Grease an 8½-by-4½-inch (22 by 11 cm) loaf pan and line with a strip of parchment paper, letting some hang over the sides. Dust your work surface with a bit of tapioca starch. Transfer the dough to your work surface and knead the dough several times until smooth and deflated. Cut the dough into 6 equal pieces (about 190 g each) and knead them again a couple of times. Shape each piece of dough into a tight ball with a smooth seam. Arrange the pieces of dough in the prepared pan snugly next to each other.

Proof the brioche. Loosely cover the pan with a kitchen towel or plastic wrap. Proof until it has risen about 50 percent and the dough reaches the top of the pan, about 45 minutes.

Preheat the oven. Position a rack in the bottom third of the oven and preheat the oven to 375°F (190°C).

Bake the brioche. Once the dough is proofed, gently brush the top of the dough with the maple syrup, being careful not to deflate it and trying to reach all corners. Bake for 35 to 40 minutes, until golden brown.

Cool the brioche. Let the brioche cool in the pan for 15 minutes, then transfer to a wire rack and let it cool for 30 minutes more. It is best served warm.

Danish Dough

FOR THE DOUGH

2 teaspoons (8 g) active dry yeast

70 grams granulated sugar

130 grams whole milk or oat milk, heated to 105°F (41°C)

80 grams potato starch

70 grams sweet white rice flour

60 grams tapioca starch, plus more for dusting

60 grams sorghum flour

15 grams psyllium husk powder

1 teaspoon (4 g) baking powder

1 teaspoon (4 g) xanthan gum

½ teaspoon (2 g) kosher salt

2 large eggs (110 g; see Tips on page 226), at room temperature

45 grams unsalted butter or vegan butter, at room temperature

FOR THE BUTTER BLOCK

225 grams unsalted butter or vegan butter, at room temperature

10 grams superfine brown rice flour

Creating this gluten-free Danish dough, which can be used to make croissants and other layered pastries, feels like one of my greatest accomplishments. The trick to a successful Danish dough is having even layers of dough and butter without cracks, because any tear or crack will cause the butter to ooze out during baking. It is very important that the dough layer and butter layer be the same temperature and consistency, and it will take you a few tries to get to know what the dough is supposed to feel like. If the dough is too cold, it will crack when rolling and if the dough is too warm, the butter will melt. A dough that is fermented and then laminated requires a lot of elasticity, and that is why you can't omit the xanthan gum in this recipe.

You can double the dough mixture if you'd like, however, I don't recommend laminating the double amount of dough. Instead, cut the dough in half and laminate each piece as directed in the recipe. A large piece of dough will be difficult to handle, especially if you are new to laminating. For more tips, see page 226.

This dough is the base for Danish Morning Buns (page 227), Cider-Roasted Apple and Vanilla Cream Danish (page 230), Croissants (page 234), and Chocolatines (page 239).

MAKES A LITTLE SHY OF 900 GRAMS

Activate the yeast. Sprinkle the yeast into a medium bowl. Add 5 grams of the granulated sugar and the milk and whisk until dissolved. Let the mixture sit until frothy, about 10 minutes.

Mix the dough. In a stand mixer, stir together the potato starch, sweet white rice flour, tapioca starch, sorghum flour, psyllium, baking powder, xanthan gum, salt, and remaining 65 grams sugar. Add the yeast mixture to the flour mixture. Snap on the dough hook and begin mixing the dough on medium speed. Add the eggs and continue mixing until the dough comes together, about 2 minutes. Add the room-temperature butter 1 tablespoon at a time and continue mixing until you have a smooth dough. It should feel moist but not wet—the consistency of soft pasta or Play-Doh. The dough will be a bit softer than traditional gluten-containing dough and that is okay. Wrap the dough in plastic wrap, flatten it, and refrigerate overnight or up to 24 hours.

(Recipe continues)

Make the butter block. The following morning, lay a long piece of plastic wrap on a work surface. Set the butter on it and dust the top with the flour. Cover the top of the butter with one of the plastic wrap ends and pound it with a rolling pin to flatten it. Uncover the plastic wrap and fold the butter in half. Collect any of the flour that is around it and place on top. Cover with plastic wrap and flatten it again with the rolling pin. Repeat a few more times until the butter and flour are incorporated. Shape the butter block into a roughly 6-inch (15 cm) square. Wrap with plastic wrap and refrigerate for 10 minutes, until the butter has hardened slightly but is still pliable. You should be able to bend it over the edge of your counter without it cracking. If it cracks, it's too cold, so let it come to room temperature. If it's bending too much and feels very soft, refrigerate for another 5 to 10 minutes.

Lock in the butter. Remove the dough from the fridge. Unwrap it and knead it a few times to bring back some elasticity. Do not let it get too warm. Shape it into a rectangle. Dust the work surface and rolling pin with some tapioca starch and roll the dough into a rectangle roughly 7 by 16 inches (18 by 41 cm). Make sure to move your dough around so it doesn't stick to your surface or rolling pin. Use a pastry brush to brush off excess tapioca starch from the dough so it doesn't dry out and crack when folding. Orient the dough rectangle so a short side is facing you. Remove the butter block from the fridge. It should be pliable but chilled. Remove the butter from the plastic and place on the bottom half of the dough. Fold the top half of the dough over the butter and pinch the sides together to seal in the butter. The most important part of this step is that the dough and the butter block be the same consistency and pliability so they can be folded without cracking or the butter oozing out.

Laminate the dough. Make sure you keep the work surface and rolling pin dusted with tapioca starch so the dough doesn't stick. To laminate the dough, you are going to give the dough three letter folds.

First letter fold. Using gentle and even pressure, roll the dough to a rectangle that is roughly 7 by 21 inches (18 by 53 cm) and ¼ inch (6 mm) thick. It doesn't have to be precisely that size but you want a rectangle that you can fold into thirds. Dust excess starch off with a pastry brush. Fold one-third of the dough into the middle and then the other third over it. This is called a letter fold and this will be your first. Rotate the dough 90 degrees. Use your rolling pin to gently press down on the dough so the edge of the folded flap on top gets lightly pressed into the dough. If you are in a warm environment, you can chill the dough for 30 minutes between folds, but in the winter, you should be able to complete all three letter folds without any refrigeration. You will get used to the consistency, but for your first try, you should consider refrigerating the dough for at least 20 minutes in between rolling.

Second and third letter folds. Once again, roll the dough to a rectangle that is roughly 7 by 21 inches (18 by 53 cm) and ¼ inch (6 mm) thick. Brush off excess starch. Give it another letter fold. Repeat the process one more time.

Chill the dough. Wrap the dough in plastic wrap and refrigerate for 30 to 45 minutes before using. After that, you can use the dough as instructed in your recipe.

To freeze: If you'd like to freeze your dough, I recommend rolling it into a rectangle that is ½ inch (1.3 cm) thick. This will make rolling the dough easier after it's thawed. Slide the dough onto a sheet pan lined with parchment paper, then freeze it for 30 minutes, until frozen solid. Wrap the dough tightly in plastic wrap and store in the freezer for up to 1 month. To use, thaw out the dough in the refrigerator overnight and then shape as directed.

Tips for Working with Danish Dough

Start the process the night before you are going to bake the Danish. Make the dough and chill in the refrigerator overnight. The next morning roll, shape, proof, and bake.

European-style butter is best because it has a higher fat content and is much more pliable. In the winter, I leave the butter out on the kitchen counter overnight. It will soften but remain cold, which will be perfect to turn into the butter block the next morning. In the summer, take out the butter only a couple of hours before you are going to make the butter block so it doesn't get too soft.

I have tested many different vegan butters, and unfortunately not all perform the same. If you want to use vegan butter, use one that is specifically crafted for baking. You will likely have to try a couple of brands to see which one works best for you. Vegan butter tends to be less stable than cow's milk butter, which means it warms up quickly so you might need to chill your dough in between turns. Also, since the dough doesn't have the same elasticity, it can crack more easily when rolled. Be gentle with it.

Your 2 large eggs should weigh around 110 grams. This is important because if your eggs are much larger, your dough can turn softer.

Unfortunately, I have not been able to create an egg-free version of this recipe that is worth sharing. I have tried with aquafaba, but the needed elasticity wasn't there and butter oozed out every time.

Danish Morning Buns

Danish Dough (page 222)

FOR THE PAN

Unsalted butter or vegan butter, melted

Granulated sugar

FOR THE BUNS

75 grams granulated sugar, plus more for coating

75 grams dark brown sugar

1 tablespoon (9 g) ground cinnamon

1 tablespoon (6 g) finely grated orange zest

¼ teaspoon (1 g) kosher salt

Tapioca starch, for dusting

40 grams unsalted butter or vegan butter, melted and cooled

This is a take on cinnamon buns, but instead of brioche, they are made with Danish dough. The buns are very flaky and become deeply caramelized, almost like a sticky bun. You could bake these in 3-inch (7.5 cm) ring molds, if you have them, but the directions here are for a standard muffin tin.

MAKES 8 BUNS

Make the dough. Make the Danish dough as directed through the final refrigeration period of 30 to 45 minutes.

Prep the pan. Brush 8 cups of a standard muffin tin with melted butter. Add a teaspoon or two of granulated sugar to each cup and tilt the pan so the sugar coats all sides. Shake off the excess sugar.

Make the sugar filling. In a medium bowl, stir together the granulated sugar, dark brown sugar, cinnamon, orange zest, and salt.

Roll the dough. If your dough is very cold, let it sit on your counter for 10 minutes before rolling or it can crack. Lightly dust a work surface and rolling pin with tapioca starch. Place the dough on the work surface and roll it into to a rectangle that is roughly 14 by 10 inches (36 by 25 cm) and ¼ inch (6 mm) thick. Trim the edges of the dough with a very sharp knife so you have straight sides and right-angled corners. You will end up with a rectangle that is roughly 14 by 9½ inches (35 by 24 cm).

Fill and shape the dough. Brush the surface of the dough with a thin layer of melted butter. You only need enough for the sugar filling to stick so you might not use all of it. Spread an even layer of the sugar filling over the dough lightly pressing down and reaching all the edges. Starting on a long side, roll the dough into a tight log. Cut it crosswise into 8 equal pieces of dough, about 1½ inches (4 cm) wide, and place them in the prepared muffin tin, cut-side down. Lightly press the dough down into the cups.

Proof the buns. Use a large plastic bag to wrap the entire muffin tin. (Alternatively, you can loosely cover the tin with plastic.) Proof the buns until they feel light and marshmallow-like to the touch. You should be able to see distinct layers of dough and butter. This process can take from 1½ to 4 hours, and it might take you a couple

of tries to get it perfect in your kitchen. The most important thing is to not let your room temperature get over 82°F (28°C) or the butter will start to melt. In the winter, you could experiment with proofing inside your oven (turned off); turn the light on and add a small pot of boiling-hot water next to the tin. The steam and temperature will create a humid and warm environment for the buns to proof. I prefer to proof them slowly at room temperature.

Preheat the oven. Once the buns are done proofing, remove the plastic from the muffin tin and chill it in the refrigerator for 20 minutes while the oven is preheating. Position a rack in the bottom third of the oven and preheat the oven to 425°F (220°C).

Bake the buns. Place the muffin tin on a sheet pan to catch any butter that oozes out while baking. Bake for 5 minutes, reduce the oven temperature to 375°F (190°C), and bake until the buns are deeply golden brown, 25 minutes. Fill a shallow bowl with granulated sugar. As soon as the pan comes out of the oven, carefully remove the buns and roll them in the sugar to coat. The sugar will stick to the buns better when they are warm, but be careful not to burn yourself. Let them cool for 5 minutes if they are too hot too handle.

Cool the buns. Transfer the buns to a wire rack and let cool for 15 minutes before serving. They are best eaten warm.

Cider-Roasted Apple and Vanilla Cream Danish

You can make this recipe with any fruit you would like. If you're using soft and tender fresh fruit, such as peaches, apricots, berries, or plums, there is no need to roast the fruit. Simply slice it raw and place it on top of the pastry cream before baking. When the Danish comes out of the oven, glaze the fruit with a bit of warm apricot jam. Other fruits I love to substitute for the apples are pears, quince, or pineapple.

MAKES 9 DANISH

FOR THE DOUGH

Danish Dough (page 222)

Tapioca starch, for dusting

FOR THE FILLING

½ recipe Pastry Cream (page 215)

50 grams granulated sugar

15 grams unsalted butter or vegan butter

25 grams apple cider

2 teaspoons (8 g) vanilla extract or vanilla paste

2 medium firm, juicy apples (12 ounces/340 g total), such as Honeycrisp, peeled, cored, and cut into slices ¾ inch (2 cm) thick

FOR TOPPING

30 grams pistachios, finely chopped

Powdered sugar, for dusting

Make the dough. Make the Danish dough as directed through the final refrigeration period of 30 to 45 minutes.

Make the pastry cream. Prepare the pastry cream as directed and chill for at least 2 hours.

Roll and cut the dough. Line a sheet pan with parchment paper. If your dough is very cold, let it sit on the counter for 10 minutes before rolling or it can crack. Lightly dust a work surface and rolling pin with tapioca starch. Place the dough on the work surface and roll it into a rectangle roughly 12 by 13 inches (30 by 33 cm) and ¼ inch (6 mm) thick. Trim the edges of the dough with a very sharp knife so you have straight sides and right-angled corners. Using a 4-inch (10 cm) round cookie cutter, cut 9 disks of dough and transfer them to the prepared sheet pan. Place a 3-inch (7.5 cm) round cookie cutter over each disk, making sure it's centered on the dough, and use a very sharp paring knife to score a small indentation around the circumference of the smaller cookie cutter without cutting all the way through to the bottom of the dough. This will allow for the exterior border of the dough to rise independently of the center, where you will place the filling.

Proof the Danish. Use a large plastic bag to wrap the entire sheet pan. (Alternatively, you can loosely cover the pan with plastic wrap.) Proof the Danish until they feel light and marshmallow-like to the touch. You should be able to see distinct layers of dough and butter. Even though you created the semi-cut in the center, the dough should rise pretty evenly. This process can take from

1½ to 4 hours, and it might take you a couple of tries to get it perfect in your kitchen. The most important thing is to not let your room temperature get over 82°F (28°C) or the butter will start to melt. In the winter, you could experiment with proofing inside your oven (turned off); turn the light on and add a small pot of boiling-hot water next to the pan. The steam and temperature will create a humid and warm environment for the Danish to proof. I prefer to proof them slowly at room temperature.

Roast the apples. While the dough is proofing, pan-roast the apples. You want them to be cool when you fill the Danish. Heat a medium sauté pan over medium-high heat. Sprinkle the sugar evenly around the pan and cook until it turns a deep caramel color, about 2 minutes. Stir in the butter, cider, and vanilla. Add the apples in a single layer and reduce the heat to medium-low. Cook the apples until tender, 5 to 7 minutes. Set aside and let the apples cool.

Fill the Danish. When the dough is ready, add a tablespoon of pastry cream to the center of each dough disk and place a slice or two of pan-roasted apple on top, lightly pressing them down into the cream. Reserve the cider caramel in the sauté pan for glazing the Danish. Transfer the sheet pan to the refrigerator and chill for 25 minutes.

Preheat the oven. Position a rack in the bottom third of the oven and preheat the oven to 425°F (220°C). Set a cast-iron pan in the bottom of the oven.

Bake the Danish. Set the sheet pan with the Danish inside another sheet pan. This will protect the bottom of the dough from the high heat. Place the Danish in the oven and toss 3 ice cubes in the cast-iron pan in the bottom of the oven. Bake for 5 minutes. Reduce the oven temperature to 400°F (200°C) and bake for 10 minutes. Reduce the temperature to 375°F (190°C) and bake for 5 minutes, or until the Danish are deeply caramelized and golden. A little bit of butter oozing out is normal, but if a lot of butter is pooling on your sheet pan, see Troubleshooting Tips (page 236).

Glaze and cool the Danish. When the Danish come out of the oven, brush the tops with a little bit of the reserved cider caramel, sprinkle the tops with chopped pistachios, and dust with powdered sugar. Let the Danish cool on a wire rack for 5 minutes and enjoy while warm.

Croissants

Danish Dough (page 222)

Tapioca starch, for dusting

1 large egg

10 grams water

Gluten-free croissants can be a challenge; the lack of elasticity in the dough makes the fermentation and lamination extremely difficult, but this recipe will result in a pastry that is buttery, flaky, and well layered. Don't be disappointed if you don't get a perfect croissant on your first attempt. It takes a few tries to develop a sense for the consistency of the dough, how much pressure to apply when rolling, or when the dough is done proofing. Have a ruler and a very sharp paring knife nearby to help you cut even triangles and make sharp cuts to not blunt the layers.

MAKES 6 CROISSANTS

Make the dough. Make the Danish dough as directed through the final refrigeration period of 30 to 45 minutes.

Roll the dough. Lightly dust a work surface and rolling pin with tapioca starch. Place the dough on the work surface and roll it into a rectangle roughly 12 by 13 inches (30 by 33 cm) and ¼ inch (6 mm) thick. Trim the edges of the dough with a very sharp knife so you have straight sides and right-angled corners.

Shape the croissants. Line a sheet pan with parchment paper. With a long side facing you, cut the dough vertically into three rectangles 4 inches (10 cm) wide. Then cut each rectangle diagonally so you have 6 triangles total. Position the triangles so the points are facing away from you. Cut a 1-inch (2.5 cm) notch in the center of the base of each triangle. Using your thumb and forefinger, gently pull the notch away from center and roll up away from you, building a curved croissant shape as you roll the base of the dough toward the tip. Do not roll them up too tightly or they can crack when proofing and baking. Leave the croissant tail hanging down without tucking it under or it can crack in the middle when baking. Shape all the croissants. Place the croissants on the lined pan. They can wobble on the pan when you move it around, so be careful that the croissants don't unravel as you lift the pan. If they do, put them back in shape and leave the tail hanging so it nearly touches the pan.

Proof the croissants. Use a large plastic bag to wrap the entire sheet pan. (Alternatively, you can loosely cover the pan with plastic wrap.) Proof the croissants until they feel light and marshmallow-like

Troubleshooting Tips

Butter is oozing out of the croissants when baking. Some butter will inevitably ooze out of the croissants while baking. Some of it will quickly get reabsorbed once the croissants come of the oven and cool for a couple of minutes. If a lot of butter has leaked out and there aren't very distinct layers, it can be due to two things. One, your croissant dough is underproofed. Make sure that the dough feels light and marshmallow-like when it goes into the oven. Or, two, your lamination needs some work and your butter wasn't locked properly into the dough. Make sure your dough and butter block have a similar cold but pliable consistency so they can be laminated into even layers without cracking.

Butter is oozing out of the croissants during proofing. This means your proofing temperature is too warm. If this happens, transfer them to the refrigerator immediately and do a cold and long proof.

Your dough is cracking during rolling. If your dough is cracking when you roll it (before adding the butter block), it could be because your dough is too cold. Let the dough come to room temperature for 10 minutes while your butter block is chilling before locking it in and laminating it. Knead the dough a few times before locking in the butter to bring back some elasticity, but don't let it get too warm. You will learn to recognize exactly the right consistency. Your dough could also be cracking because it's too dry. It's normal if your dough cracks on the outer edges when rolling, but it shouldn't crack in the center. Make sure you are using finely milled flour so the dough is properly hydrated and not too coarse.

The inside of your croissant is dense. It should not be as airy as traditional croissants made with gluten flour, but it also shouldn't be brioche or scone-like. If it's dense, it could be because you laminated the dough too many times or your layers were not distinct enough. Practice your rolling and lamination process.

Your croissants didn't expand in the oven. Proof them longer next time or make sure your yeast isn't old.

to the touch. You should be able to see distinct layers of dough and butter. This process can take from 1½ to 4 hours, and it might take you a couple of tries to get it perfect in your kitchen. The most important thing is to not let your room temperature get over 82°F (28°C) or the butter will start to melt. In the winter, you could experiment with proofing inside your oven (turned off); turn the light on and add a small pot of boiling-hot water next to the pan. The steam and temperature will create a humid and warm environment for the croissants to proof. I prefer to proof them slowly at room temperature.

Make the egg wash. In a small bowl, lightly whisk the egg and water together. When your croissants are done proofing, gently brush the tops with the egg wash, being careful not to brush the exposed edges or the layers will stick together while baking and not rise properly. Transfer the pan, uncovered, to the refrigerator for 20 to 30 minutes.

Preheat the oven. Position an oven rack in the center of the oven and preheat the oven to 450°F (230°C). Set a cast-iron pan in the bottom of the oven.

Bake the croissants. Set the sheet pan with the croissants inside another sheet pan. This will protect the bottom of the dough from the high heat. Place the croissants in the oven and toss 3 ice cubes in the cast-iron pan in the bottom of the oven. Reduce the oven temperature to 425°F (220°C) and bake for 10 minutes. Reduce the temperature to 375°F (190°C) and bake 10 minutes, until deeply golden brown. A little bit of butter oozing out is normal, but if a lot of butter is pooling on your sheet pan, see Troubleshooting Tips (opposite).

Cool the croissants. Let the croissants cool on a wire rack for 5 minutes. Enjoy while warm.

Chocolatines

Danish Dough (page 222)

Tapioca starch, for dusting

80 grams good-quality semisweet chocolate baking batons (70% cacao)

1 large egg

10 grams water

The chocolatine is very similar to the traditional pain au chocolat, but made with a slightly sweeter dough. Make sure you use good-quality chocolate. I like to use batons that are specifically shaped for pain au chocolat, but you can chop a chocolate bar into long shards and use as you would batons.

MAKES 4 LARGE CHOCOLATINES

Make the dough. Make the Danish dough as directed through the final refrigeration period of 30 to 45 minutes.

Roll the dough. If your dough is very cold, let it sit on your counter for 10 minutes before rolling or it can crack. Lightly dust a work surface and rolling pin with tapioca starch. Place the dough on the work surface and roll it into a rectangle roughly 12 by 13 inches (30 by 33 cm) and ¼ inch (6 mm) thick. Trim the edges of the dough with a very sharp knife so you have straight sides and right-angled corners. With a short side facing you, cut the dough vertically into 4 strips 3 inches (7.5 cm) wide.

Fill and shape the chocolatines. Line a sheet pan with parchment paper. Take a rectangle of dough and place it on your work surface with a short side facing you. Place about 20 grams of the chocolate on the dough about ½ inch (1.3 cm) from the edge closest to you. Roll the dough into a log. Don't tuck the flap underneath the chocolatine or the top can tear when proofing. Transfer the dough to the prepared sheet pan. Repeat with the remaining dough.

Proof the chocolatines. Use a large plastic bag to wrap the entire sheet pan. (Alternatively, you can loosely cover the pan with plastic wrap, but the large bag really seals the air.) Proof the chocolatines until they feel light and marshmallow-like to the touch. You should be able to see distinct layers of dough and butter. This process can take from 1½ to 4 hours, and it might take you a couple of tries to get it perfect in your kitchen. The most important thing is to not let your room temperature get over 82°F (28°C) or the butter will start to melt. In the winter, you could experiment with proofing inside your oven (turned off); turn the light on and add a small pot of boiling-hot water next to the pan. The steam and temperature will create a humid and warm environment for the chocolatines to proof. I personally prefer to proof them slowly at room temperature.

Make the egg wash. In a small bowl, whisk together the egg and water. Gently brush the tops with the egg wash, being careful not to brush the exposed edges or the layers will stick together while baking and not rise properly. Do not cover the sheet pan. Transfer the pan to the refrigerator for 20 to 30 minutes.

Preheat the oven. Position a rack in the center of the oven and preheat the oven to 450°F (230°C). Set a cast-iron pan in the bottom of the oven.

Bake the chocolatines. Set the sheet pan with the chocolatines inside another sheet pan. This will protect the bottom of the dough from the high heat. Place the chocolatines in the oven and toss 3 ice cubes in the cast-iron pan in the bottom of the oven. Reduce the oven temperature to 425°F (220°C) and bake for 10 minutes. Reduce the temperature to 375°F(190°C) and bake for 10 to 12 minutes, until deep golden brown. A little bit of butter and chocolate oozing out is normal, but if a lot of butter is pooling on your sheet pan, see Troubleshooting Tips (page 236).

Cool the chocolatines. Let the chocolatines cool on a wire rack for 5 minutes. Enjoy while warm.

Note: To make 8 small chocolatines instead of 4 large ones, cut the 4 strips of dough in half crosswise so you have 8 pieces of dough that are approximately 3 inches (7.5 cm) wide and 7.5 inches (19 cm) long. Bake at 425°F (220°C) for 10 minutes, then reduce the temperature to 375°F (190°C) and bake for 8 to 10 minutes, until deep golden brown.

What to Do with Danish Dough Scraps

If you make any of the recipes using Danish dough, you will likely end up with some dough scraps. I like to collect the scraps and refrigerate them. You can even freeze them and gather a bunch after a while (in which case thaw them out in the fridge). Don't knead the scraps together. Simply arrange them next to each other, as well as on top, then use a rolling pin to press down to create a rectangle or square that is about ½ inch (1.3 cm) thick. Cut into squares, toss the squares in granulated sugar and cinnamon, and pile them in a muffin tin or English muffin ring. Proof and bake as you would with croissants.

Almond Croissants

Here's a great use for day-old croissants or those that have been in the freezer for a while. Split the croissants in half, soak them in an almond syrup, fill with frangipane, and bake with a sprinkle of sliced almonds on top. They are addictive!

MAKES 6 ALMOND CROISSANTS

FOR THE ALMOND SYRUP

50 grams granulated sugar

50 grams water

1 teaspoon (4 g) almond extract

FOR THE ALMOND FRANGIPANE

50 grams very soft (but not melted) unsalted butter or vegan butter

50 grams almond flour

50 grams granulated sugar

1 large egg

½ teaspoon (2 g) almond extract

½ teaspoon (2 g) vanilla extract

¼ teaspoon (1 g) kosher salt

TO ASSEMBLE

6 Croissants (page 234), sliced in half horizontally

30 grams sliced almonds

Powdered sugar, for dusting

Preheat the oven. Position a rack in the bottom third of the oven and preheat the oven to 350°F (180°C). Line a sheet pan with parchment paper.

Make the almond syrup. In a small saucepan, combine the sugar, water, and almond extract and heat over medium heat until the sugar is dissolved.

Make the almond frangipane. In a medium bowl, stir together the soft butter, almond flour, sugar, egg, almond extract, vanilla extract, and salt and stir until you have a spreadable paste. You will have more than you need. Store the rest in a container in the refrigerator for up to a week.

Assemble the almond croissants. Brush the cut sides of the croissants with some of the almond syrup (leave some for the tops). Spread a thin layer of the almond frangipane on the cut sides of the croissant halves and sandwich them back together. Brush the tops with a bit of syrup and a very thin layer of the almond frangipane. Sprinkle with sliced almonds. Place the croissants on the lined sheet pan.

Bake the almond croissants. Transfer the pan to the oven and bake for 10 to 15 minutes, until the frangipane and almonds are golden brown. Dust the croissants with powdered sugar and serve while warm.

Soft and Fluffy Potato Rolls

1 medium russet potato (12 ounces/340 g)

12 grams active dry yeast

1 teaspoon (4 g) plus 100 grams granulated sugar

300 grams whole milk or oat milk, heated to 105°F (41°C)

30 grams psyllium husk powder

120 grams tapioca starch

120 grams potato starch, plus more for dusting

90 grams sweet white rice flour

90 grams sorghum flour

1½ teaspoons (6 g) kosher salt

1 teaspoon (4 g) baking powder

55 grams extra-virgin olive oil, plus more for greasing

2 large eggs, at room temperature

Unsalted butter or vegan butter, melted, for brushing

Flaky sea salt, for sprinkling

Here is the dinner roll recipe you've been looking for. In the past, I have made rolls using the brioche recipe in my book *Cannelle et Vanille Bakes Simple*, but they felt slightly eggy. These rolls are soft and fluffy because of the addition of cooked potato. They make great hamburger buns, too, but cut the dough into 6 pieces for the larger rolls.

MAKES 12 ROLLS

Bake the potato. Preheat the oven to 400°F (200°C). Wrap the potato in foil and bake for 45 minutes to 1 hour, until it can be easily pierced with the tip of a knife all the way through. Let the potato cool completely. Peel the potato and mash the flesh with a fork or potato ricer. Measure 225 grams of mashed potato and set aside.

Make the yeast-psyllium mixture. Sprinkle the yeast and 1 teaspoon (4 g) of the sugar into a medium bowl. Add the milk and whisk until smooth. Let the mixture sit until frothy, about 10 minutes. Whisk in the psyllium until completely dissolved. Let it gel for 5 minutes.

Make the dough. In a stand mixer, stir together the tapioca starch, potato starch, remaining 100 grams sugar, the sweet white rice flour, sorghum flour, kosher salt, and baking powder. Add the olive oil, eggs, mashed potato, and the yeast-psyllium mixture. Snap on the dough hook and mix on medium speed until the dough comes together, about 3 minutes. The dough should be smooth and not very wet but feel moist and slightly sticky.

Proof the dough. Grease a large bowl with some olive oil and add the dough into it. Cover with a kitchen towel and proof until nearly doubled, about 30 minutes. Wrap the bowl in plastic wrap so it doesn't dry out and refrigerate for at least 4 hours and up to 8 hours.

Shape the rolls. Transfer the dough to a work surface and knead the dough back together until smooth. Cut the dough into 12 equal pieces (a little bit over 100 g each). Dust the work surface with some potato starch. Shape the dough pieces into tight balls.

Proof the rolls. Line a 13-by-9-inch (33 by 23 cm) sheet pan with parchment paper and place the rolls on it. Cover with a kitchen

towel or plastic wrap and ferment until the rolls have nearly doubled in size and touch each other, 30 to 45 minutes.

Preheat the oven. Position a rack in the bottom third of the oven and preheat the oven to 375°F (190°C).

Bake the rolls. Place the pan in the oven and bake for 20 to 25 minutes, until golden brown. As soon as the rolls are done, brush them with the melted butter and sprinkle with flaky salt.

Cool the rolls. Let the rolls cool on the pan for at least 20 minutes before serving. They are best eaten the same day or can be kept tightly wrapped for the next day.

VARIATION

Vegan Potato Rolls

Omit the eggs and increase the milk to 395 grams. The dough is not as elastic and will be a little clumpier when kneading, especially after the bulk ferment. Try to get it as smooth as possible when shaping into the rolls. This eggless version doesn't caramelize the same, so you can brush a little bit of oil on the rolls before they go in the oven to give them some color.

Olive Pesto Pull-Apart Bread

Dough for Soft and Fluffy Potato Rolls (page 244)

Olive oil, for greasing

Superfine brown rice flour, for dusting

Olive Pesto (recipe follows)

This bread is made with pieces of potato brioche dough and a green olive pesto. It is a soft and savory addition to any pasta dinner.

MAKES 1 LOAF

Make the dough. Make the potato roll dough as directed. Grease a large bowl with olive oil and place the dough inside. Cover tightly with plastic wrap and proof for 30 minutes at room temperature. Refrigerate the dough for at least 4 hours and up to 8 hours.

Roll the dough. When the dough is ready, dust a work surface with some brown rice flour. Place the dough on it and knead a few times to deflate it and bring some elasticity back. Pat the dough down and roll it into a rectangle roughly 18 by 12 inches (46 by 30 cm) and about ¼ inch (6 mm) thick. It doesn't have to be perfectly rectangular but try to get the corners as straight as possible. Move the dough around while rolling so it doesn't stick to your surface and dust the top with brown rice flour if needed, but be careful not to add too much flour.

Fill the dough. Measure out 1 tablespoon of the pesto and set aside. Spread the rest of the pesto over the dough. With a long side facing you, use a sharp knife to cut the dough vertically into 6 equal strips, each one about 3 inches (7.5 cm) wide. Cut each strip crosswise into 4 pieces for a total of twenty-four 3-inch (7.5 cm) squares.

Proof the bread. Grease an 8½-by-4½-inch (22 by 11 cm) loaf pan with some olive oil and line with a strip of parchment paper that hangs over the edges of the pan. Arrange the pieces of dough inside the prepared pan vertically so they sit tightly together. It's okay if you have to press the dough in slightly and if some pieces stick out more than others. Cover with a kitchen towel or plastic wrap and proof until the dough feels light to the touch, 30 to 45 minutes.

Preheat the oven. Position a rack in the bottom third of the oven and preheat the oven to 375°F (190°C).

(Recipe continues)

Bake the bread. Place the loaf pan on a sheet pan and bake for 30 to 35 minutes, until golden brown and puffed up. Brush the top of the bread with the reserved pesto.

Cool the bread. Let the bread cool in the pan for at least 30 minutes before serving. It's best eaten while warm.

Olive Pesto

MAKES ABOUT 1 CUP (235 G)

- 50 grams fresh basil leaves, tough stems removed
- 25 grams fresh Italian parsley, tough stems removed
- 35 grams pitted green olives
- 10 grams pine nuts
- 1 garlic clove, peeled
- 1 teaspoon (4 g) kosher salt
- ½ teaspoon (1 g) red pepper flakes
- 20 grams finely grated Parmesan or vegan Parmesan-style cheese
- 100 grams extra-virgin olive oil

In a food processor, combine the basil, parsley, olives, pine nuts, garlic, salt, and pepper flakes and pulse until all ingredients are finely chopped and begin to form a paste. Scrape the sides of the bowl. Add the Parmesan and pulse a couple of times to combine. Drizzle in the olive oil while the processor is running until you have a smooth paste. Use immediately or store in a sealed jar in the refrigerator for up to 1 day.

Potato Brioche Tart with Cabbage and Mushrooms

PICTURED ON PAGE 254

You can make tarts using any brioche dough as your base in place of pastry; it is especially good in savory options using the dough for fluffy potato rolls. The dough is rolled into the tart pan, then topped with pan-roasted mushrooms and cheese. It is a perfect brunch meal served alongside a generous green salad. See below for a roasted vegetable variation.

MAKES 1 TART

FOR THE DOUGH

½ recipe dough for Soft and Fluffy Potato Rolls (page 244)

Tapioca starch, for dusting

FOR THE CABBAGE

10 grams extra-virgin olive oil

1 garlic clove, thinly sliced

½ head purple napa cabbage (8 ounces/225 g), cored and thinly sliced

10 grams water

¼ teaspoon (1 g) kosher salt

2 teaspoons (10 g) Dijon mustard

FOR THE PAN-ROASTED MUSHROOMS

25 grams extra-virgin olive oil, plus more for brushing

1 medium shallot, thinly sliced

2 garlic cloves, thinly sliced

225 grams mushrooms (cremini, shiitake, oyster, trumpet), sliced

½ teaspoon (2 g) kosher salt

¼ teaspoon (1 g) freshly ground black pepper

FOR THE TOPPING

60 grams Fontina or mozzarella cheese, grated

Finely chopped fresh parsley

Make the dough. Make the potato roll dough as directed. Grease a large bowl and place the dough inside. Cover tightly with plastic wrap and proof for 30 minutes at room temperature. Refrigerate the dough for at least 4 hours and up to 8 hours.

Shape the dough. Dust a work surface with a bit of tapioca starch. Place the dough on it and knead a few times until smooth. Roll the dough into a 10-inch (25 cm) round. Gently lift the dough and place it inside a 9-inch (23 cm) tart pan with a removeable bottom. Fold the excess dough underneath itself to create a thick border all around the pan.

Proof the dough. Cover with plastic wrap or a kitchen towel and proof until the dough feels marshmallow-like, 30 to 45 minutes.

Cook the cabbage. Heat a medium sauté pan over medium-high heat. Add the olive oil and garlic and cook for 30 seconds. Add the cabbage and stir to coat it in the oil. Add the water and salt and stir to combine. Cover the pan, reduce the heat to medium, and cook for 10 minutes, until the cabbage is wilted. Add the mustard and increase the heat to medium-high. Stir to combine and cook, uncovered, stirring occasionally, until all the moisture has evaporated and the cabbage feels dry, about 5 minutes. Transfer the mixture to a plate to cool.

Cook the mushrooms. Dry any excess moisture from the sauté pan with a paper towel. Heat the pan over medium-high heat. Add the olive oil, shallots, garlic, mushrooms, salt, and pepper. Stir to combine and cook, stirring occasionally, until the mushrooms are soft and have begun to caramelize slightly, about 10 minutes. Let the mushrooms cool for 15 minutes.

Preheat the oven. Position a rack in the bottom third of the oven and preheat the oven to 375°F (190°C).

Fill the tart. When the dough is ready, scatter half of the cheese over the dough. Top with the cooked cabbage and mushrooms and sprinkle the top with the remaining cheese.

Bake the tart. Transfer the tart to the oven and bake for 30 minutes, or until the crust is golden brown. Brush the edges of the crust with some olive oil, if desired. Sprinkle the tart with parsley.

Cool the tart. Let the tart cool for 20 minutes before serving. It is best eaten the same day.

VARIATION

Roasted Vegetable Tart

- 2 medium carrots or 6 baby carrots, scrubbed and cut into bite-size pieces
- 115 grams mushrooms (trumpet, morels, cremini, oyster), sliced
- 90 grams baby potatoes, scrubbed and halved or quartered if large
- 90 grams radishes, tips removed, halved or quartered if large
- 1 medium shallot, cut into 1-inch (2.5 cm) pieces
- 35 grams extra-virgin olive oil
- 1 teaspoon (4 g) kosher salt
- ½ teaspoon (2 g) freshly ground black pepper
- 60 grams Fontina or mozzarella cheese, grated

Make, shape, and proof the dough as directed.

Preheat the oven to 400°F (200°C). On a sheet pan, toss together the carrots, mushrooms, potatoes, radishes, shallot, olive oil, salt, and pepper. Slide the pan into the oven and roast the vegetables until tender and lightly golden but not fully cooked, about 20 minutes. Set aside to cool.

Scatter half of the cheese over the proofed dough, then fill it with the roasted vegetables. Top with the remaining cheese and bake as directed.

Yogurt and Za'atar Twists

PICTURED ON PAGE 255

FOR THE DOUGH

½ recipe dough for Soft and Fluffy Potato Rolls (page 244)

Tapioca starch, for dusting

FOR THE FILLING

15 grams sesame seeds

15 grams za'atar

2 teaspoons (10 g) white (shiro) miso

115 grams very thick unsweetened plain Greek yogurt, labneh, or vegan yogurt

15 grams extra-virgin olive oil, plus more for brushing

Just like the Artichoke and Hummus Potato Buns (page 258), this is one of those recipes you can add to a breakfast buffet. They are soft and savory and stay moist for a while. Make sure to use yogurt that is very thick, Greek-style or even labneh. If using vegan yogurt, choose one that is very thick. If your yogurt is runny, it will make the dough wet and very difficult to shape.

MAKES 8 TWISTS

Make the dough. Make the potato roll dough as directed. Grease a large bowl and place the dough inside. Cover tightly with plastic wrap and proof for 30 minutes at room temperature. Refrigerate the dough for at least 4 hours and up to 8 hours.

Make the filling. Toast the sesame seeds in a medium sauté pan over medium heat until golden and beginning to smell nutty, about 2 minutes. Transfer to a bowl and let cool. Stir in the za'atar. Place the miso in a small bowl and loosen it slightly with a spatula. Whisk the yogurt and olive oil into the miso until smooth.

Roll the dough. Dust a work surface with tapioca starch. Transfer the chilled dough to it and knead a few times to deflate it and to bring back elasticity. Dust with more tapioca starch if needed. Roll the dough into a rectangle roughly 10 by 14 inches (25 by 36 cm). Try to keep the corners as square as possible. Trim the edges if needed.

Fill the dough. Line a sheet pan with parchment paper. With a short side of the dough facing you, spread a thin layer of the yogurt all over, reaching the top of the dough all the way to the edge. Sprinkle the za'atar mixture over the yogurt. Fold the dough in half so you have a rectangle that is 10 by 7 inches (25 by 18 cm).

Cut and shape the twists. With a long side facing you, cut the dough vertically into 8 equal strips each about 1¼ inches (3 cm) wide. Now, cut each strip in half lengthwise (you will have 16 strips). Take 2 strips of dough that are next to each other and gently twist them together. Taper the ends slightly. You should end up with 8 twists. Place them on the prepared sheet pan, leaving about 2 inches (5 cm) between them.

Proof the twists. Cover the pan with a kitchen towel and proof until the dough feels marshmallow-like, 30 to 45 minutes.

Preheat the oven. Position a rack in the bottom third of the oven and preheat the oven to 375°F (190°C).

Bake the twists. Transfer the pan to the oven and bake for 20 to 22 minutes, until golden brown. Brush the twists with olive oil when they come out of the oven.

Cool the twists. Let the twists cool on the pan for 20 minutes before serving. They are best eaten the same day but can be refrigerated, tightly wrapped, for 2 days.

Artichoke and Hummus Potato Buns

FOR THE DOUGH

Dough for Soft and Fluffy Potato Rolls (page 244)

Tapioca starch, for dusting

FOR THE FILLING

150 grams roasted cauliflower hummus (see page 367)

100 grams marinated artichokes, cut into small bite-size pieces

35 grams pine nuts

15 grams sesame seeds

30 grams Parmesan cheese or vegan Parmesan-style cheese, finely grated

Flaky sea salt

Freshly ground black pepper

Extra-virgin olive oil, for brushing

Next time you host a large breakfast gathering, make these little savory potato brioche buns filled with hummus and artichokes and you will thank me later. They are best served warm. If you make them ahead of time, you can reheat them by spraying with a bit of water and baking at 350°F (180°C) for 10 minutes right before serving.

MAKES 10 BUNS

Make the dough. Make the potato roll dough as directed. Grease a large bowl and place the dough inside. Cover tightly with plastic wrap and proof for 30 minutes at room temperature. Refrigerate the dough for at least 4 hours and up to 8 hours.

Cut and shape the buns. Line a sheet pan with parchment paper. Dust a work surface with tapioca starch. Place the dough on it and knead a few times until smooth. Cut the dough into 10 equal pieces (about 110 g each). Shape each piece of dough into a tight ball. Place the balls of dough on the prepared sheet pan. Dip the bottom of a ¼-cup measuring cup into the tapioca starch. Use the measuring cup to press the center of each dough ball down, creating a well in the center.

Proof the buns. Cover the pan with a kitchen towel or plastic wrap and proof until the buns feel slightly lighter, about 30 minutes.

Preheat the oven. Position a rack in the center of the oven and preheat the oven to 375°F (190°C).

Fill the buns. Lightly press down on the center of a bun. Add 1 tablespoon of hummus to the center. Top with 3 or 4 pieces of chopped artichokes and sprinkle with pine nuts, sesame seeds, Parmesan, flaky salt, and pepper. Repeat with the remaining buns.

Bake the buns. Transfer the pan to the oven and bake for 22 to 25 minutes, until golden brown. Brush the buns with olive oil when they come out of the oven.

Cool the buns. Let the buns cool on the pan for 10 minutes and serve warm.

No. 6

Flatbreads

Whisk-and-Pour Oat Roti

The history of flatbread can teach us a lot about the evolution of civilization. According to archeologists, the origin of flatbread can be traced back to ancient Egypt and Mesopotamia nearly thirty thousand years ago. Grain was crushed and ground using two stones, then this coarse flour was combined with water to form a dough. The dough was later cooked on a flat rock that had been heated by the sun. At some point, dough was left out for days and humans discovered fermentation. There are endless flatbread varieties from so many cuisines around the world; I include here recipes that are on heavy rotation in my baking repertoire.

There are sourdough flatbreads, such as Crispy Paper Dosa (page 288), Sourdough Focaccia (page 270), Turmeric and Cumin Sourdough Lavash (page 278), or Sourdough Pizza Margherita (page 294). There are also flatbreads that are made with baker's yeast, such as my childhood favorite Fennel Seed and Olive Oil Tortas (page 284), Rosemary Focaccia (page 266), or Pillowy Pita (page 272). You'll also find unleavened flatbreads, such as Matzo (page 283), Sourdough Naan (page 293), and Whisk-and-Pour Oat Roti (page 291).

Sourdough Focaccia

Rosemary Focaccia

PICTURED ON PAGES 268–269

FOR THE SPONGE

175 grams sorghum flour

45 grams millet flour

10 grams active dry yeast

280 grams water, heated to 105°F (41°C)

FOR THE DOUGH

170 grams water, at room temperature

35 grams extra-virgin olive oil, plus more for drizzling

10 grams apple cider vinegar

20 grams psyllium husk powder

160 grams tapioca starch

90 grams potato starch

15 grams granulated sugar

2½ teaspoons (10 g) kosher salt

FOR THE TOPPING

Fresh rosemary leaves

Fresh thyme leaves

Flaky sea salt

Freshly ground black pepper

My favorite focaccia has a very thin, slightly crispy, golden crust with a soft open crumb. This is achieved with a high-hydration dough that includes a lot of olive oil and millet flour to give the dough that golden color. This focaccia works really well for sandwiches when you cut it in half horizontally; a combination of mortadella, arugula, and Almond Aioli (page 372) is my favorite.

If you have ever worked with gluten-containing focaccia dough, you might expect this dough to be very bubbly and might even be tempted to aggressively dimple the dough with your fingers before it goes in the oven. This dough will not create those large air pockets, so try to be gentle with the dimpling. I don't recommend adding any heavy toppings, like a bunch of tomatoes, because they can weigh down the dough while baking and compress the crumb.

For a sourdough focaccia, turn to page 270. If you don't have a 9-inch (23 cm) square pan, you can use a 9-by-13-inch (23 by 33 cm) pan, but only stretch the dough to a 9-inch square.

MAKES ONE 9-INCH (23 CM) FOCACCIA

Make the sponge. In a medium bowl, stir together the sorghum flour, millet flour, and yeast. Pour in the water and whisk until smooth. Cover with a kitchen towel and proof until the sponge rises up creating a dome and it has a mousse-like texture, about 45 minutes.

Make the dough. Add the water, olive oil, and vinegar to the bowl with the sponge and whisk together. Whisk in the psyllium and let it gel for 5 minutes. In a stand mixer, stir together the tapioca starch, potato starch, sugar, and salt. Add the gelled sponge mixture. Snap on the dough hook and mix on medium speed until the dough comes together and is smooth, 3 to 4 minutes. Transfer the dough to a work surface and knead it a few times to smooth out the surface.

Proof the dough. Drizzle the bottom of a 9-inch (23 cm) square metal pan with 2 to 3 tablespoons of olive oil. Place the dough inside the pan and flatten it with your hands until it nearly reaches the edges and is about ¾ inch (2 cm) deep. Using your fingers, dimple the surface of the dough, making deep indentations. Cover the pan with a kitchen towel and proof until nearly doubled in size, 45 minutes to 1 hour.

Preheat the oven. Position a rack in the bottom third of the oven and preheat the oven to 425°F (220°C).

Top and bake the focaccia. Drizzle the top of the focaccia with more olive oil. Gently dimple the top of the focaccia with your fingertips. Sprinkle with rosemary, thyme, flaky salt, and black pepper. Bake the focaccia for 45 to 50 minutes, until the surface is a deep golden brown. If the surface becomes too dark after 35 minutes, tent it with aluminum foil. Drizzle the focaccia with a bit of olive oil for extra shine when it comes out of the oven.

Cool the focaccia. Let the focaccia cool in the pan for 10 minutes, then slide it onto a wire rack to cool completely before cutting. It is best eaten the same day.

VARIATION

Focaccia Crackers

Thinly slice any leftover focaccia. Arrange the slices on a sheet pan in a single layer. Bake at 300°F (150°C) until dry and crispy, about 20 minutes. Transfer to a wire rack to cool. Store the focaccia crackers in an airtight container for up to a week. Serve with dips and cheeses.

Sourdough Focaccia

PICTURED ON PAGES 8 AND 265

FOR THE SPONGE

250 grams filtered water, heated to 80°F (27°C)

225 grams Whole-Grain Brown Rice–Teff Sourdough Starter (page 48)

140 grams sorghum flour, plus more for dusting

80 grams millet flour

FOR THE DOUGH

260 to 280 grams filtered water, heated to 80°F (27°C)

30 grams extra-virgin olive oil, plus more for drizzling

30 grams psyllium husk powder

240 grams tapioca starch

25 grams granulated sugar

12 grams kosher salt

FOR THE TOPPING

Fresh thyme leaves

Fresh rosemary leaves

Freshly ground black pepper

Flaky sea salt

This high-hydration sourdough focaccia yields a beautiful open crumb and slightly acidic flavor. The amount of moisture is what creates that open crumb, but it also makes it very delicate. The first time you make the dough, start with the smallest amount of water listed. If the crumb is a bit tighter than shown in the photo, use more water next time. It is essential to let the focaccia cool completely before cutting into it, or those open air pockets can easily collapse. I don't recommend adding any toppings to this recipe besides some rosemary and thyme because any extra weight can result in a dense and gummy crumb. If the top crust of your focaccia separates from the crumb, try using a bit less water next time and reduce the fermentation time. This "flying crust" doesn't bother me unless the crumb is compressed.

This focaccia is one of my favorite breads for sandwiches. Slice it in half, slather Olive Pesto (page 251) on both sides, and top with burrata, thinly sliced cucumber, tomato, and flaky salt—a classic.

MAKES ONE 9-INCH (23 CM) FOCACCIA

Make the sponge. In a large bowl, whisk together the water, starter, sorghum flour, and millet flour until smooth. The sponge should have the consistency of yogurt; if it seems too wet, add another 10 grams of sorghum flour. Cover the bowl with a kitchen towel and proof at room temperature until the top is domed and the sponge has a mousse-like texture, 3 to 4 hours.

Make the dough. Add the water, olive oil, and psyllium to the sponge and whisk until smooth. Let it gel for 5 minutes. In a stand mixer, stir together the tapioca starch, sugar, and salt. Add the gelled sponge. Snap on the dough hook and mix over medium-high speed until the dough comes together, 3 to 4 minutes. The dough will be moist and soft but should hold together nicely.

Shape and proof the dough. Lightly dust a work surface with sorghum flour. Transfer the dough to the work surface, knead it a few times, and shape it into a ball. Line a 9-inch (23 cm) square metal pan with parchment paper. Place the dough in the pan and cover the pan with a kitchen towel or plastic wrap. Proof at room temperature for 2 to 3 hours. (Alternatively, proof at room temperature for

30 minutes and then in the refrigerator for 8 to 12 hours.) The dough won't rise significantly as it proofs but should feel slightly lighter to the touch. If doing a cold ferment, bake straight from the fridge.

Preheat the oven. Position a rack in the lower third of the oven and place a large pizza stone on the rack. The hot pizza stone will help cook the bottom of the focaccia, but if you don't have one, you can forgo it. Preheat the oven to 450°F (230°C). Continue heating for 15 minutes after the oven has reached temperature.

Top and bake the focaccia. When the focaccia is done proofing, drizzle it with olive oil and lightly dimple the surface with your fingers. Be gentle with the dough at this point. Sprinkle with thyme, rosemary, black pepper, and flaky salt. Place the pan on the hot pizza stone in the oven. Bake the focaccia for 30 minutes, then reduce the oven temperature to 425°F (220°C) and bake for 20 minutes. If the top is getting very dark, tent the pan with aluminum foil. It will need the full baking time, so don't be tempted to take it out of the oven early based on the color of the crust.

Cool the focaccia. Slide the focaccia from the pan onto a wire rack to cool completely before slicing, about 1 hour. The crumb is very moist, so it needs time to set or it will collapse and become gummy. The crust will soften as the focaccia cools. It's best eaten the same day, but can be kept tightly wrapped at room temperature for up to 2 days or in the freezer for up to a month.

Pillowy Pita

FOR THE SPONGE

210 grams superfine brown rice flour, plus more for dusting

2 teaspoons (8 g) active dry yeast

2 teaspoons (8 g) granulated sugar

310 grams water, heated to 105°F (41°C)

FOR THE DOUGH

200 grams water, at room temperature

20 grams psyllium husk powder

12 grams extra-virgin olive oil, plus more for greasing

60 grams tapioca starch

60 grams potato starch

2 teaspoons (8 g) kosher salt

Use these fluffy pita for sandwiches, such as the Charred Eggplant and Saffron Tomato Confit Stuffed Pita (page 389), or in the Fattoush with Fried Pita and Labneh (page 371), and to serve alongside dips, such as Muhammara (page 365) or Roasted Cauliflower Hummus with Fried Chickpeas (page 367). The pita is pillowy and soft, with a very open air pocket in the center. I love watching how the dough expands while baking. Note that the dough is very wet, so if your brown rice flour is stone-ground and/or your psyllium is not as pure, use 300 grams of water to start with and then add more as needed or you could end up with a batter rather than a dough. Finally, if you don't have a pizza stone, you could preheat a 12-inch (30 cm) cast-iron pan in the oven and slide the pita dough onto it to bake.

MAKES 8 PITA

Make the sponge. In a large bowl, stir together the brown rice flour, yeast, and sugar. Pour in the water and whisk until you have a very smooth and thin mixture (resembling runny yogurt). Cover with a kitchen towel and let it proof until puffed up, about 30 minutes.

Preheat the oven. Position a rack in the bottom third of the oven and place a pizza stone on the rack. Preheat the oven to 500°F (260°C). Continue heating for 15 minutes after the oven has reached temperature.

Make the dough. Whisk the water, psyllium, and olive oil into the sponge until completely smooth and dissolved. Let it gel for 5 minutes. In a stand mixer, stir together the tapioca starch, potato starch, and salt. Add the gelled sponge. Snap on the dough hook and mix the dough on medium speed until it comes together, 3 to 4 minutes. The dough will be wet and sticky but should hold together and feel bouncy.

Proof the dough. Grease a large bowl with olive oil and scrape the dough into it. Cover with a kitchen towel and proof until doubled, 30 to 40 minutes.

Shape the dough. Dust a work surface with brown rice flour and invert the dough onto it. Cut the dough into 8 equal pieces (about 110 g each). Knead each piece of dough a few times and shape into a tight ball. Lightly dust both sides of the dough with brown rice flour

and roll it into a disk that is 6 to 7 inches (15 to 18 cm) in diameter and ⅛ inch (3 mm) thick. Make sure there are no holes or tears in the dough or air will escape when baking and your dough won't puff up. If you do have a tear, knead the dough together and roll again.

Bake the pita. I use a pizza peel to slide the dough onto the pizza stone, but you can also use the back of a sheet pan. Slide 2 pieces of dough onto the pizza stone (more if your stone is big enough). Bake for 5 minutes. The dough will puff up significantly. Carefully flip the dough over with tongs (or your fingers, if you can take the heat) and bake for 4 minutes, or until it has some specks of golden brown on the surface. If you overbake the dough, it will end up being a little bit too crispy and won't deflate, but if you underbake it, it might be a little gummy and wet in the center. Transfer the baked pita to a wire rack. Bake the remaining dough.

Cool the pita. Let the pita cool for at least 20 minutes before eating. They will deflate a little as they cool, but remain fairly puffed. They should be hollow and mostly dry inside with a touch of moisture. They are best eaten the same day. They can be frozen for up to 3 months tightly wrapped. To refresh, spray with water and reheat in a cast-iron pan.

Sourdough Socca with Fennel, Chickpea, and Olive Salad

FOR THE SOCCA

270 grams filtered water, heated to 80°F (27°C)

180 grams chickpea flour

150 grams Whole-Grain Brown Rice–Teff Sourdough Starter (page 48) or Grain-Free Buckwheat-Chestnut Sourdough Starter (page 50)

55 grams extra-virgin olive oil, plus more for the skillet

1 teaspoon (4 g) kosher salt

1 rosemary sprig, leaves picked and finely chopped

¼ teaspoon (1 g) freshly ground black pepper

FOR THE DRESSING

30 grams extra-virgin olive oil

30 grams fresh lemon juice

1 teaspoon (4 g) Dijon mustard

½ teaspoon (5 g) maple syrup or honey

½ teaspoon (2 g) kosher salt

Pinch of red pepper flakes (optional)

Pinch of ground cumin (optional)

Socca, also called farinata, is a Mediterranean flatbread made with chickpea flour, water, and olive oil. It is one of the easiest things you can make, and I often use it as a base for pizza. It is naturally gluten- and grain-free. Here I take the traditional socca and add a bit of sourdough starter for extra tang. You can ferment the batter overnight, as written, or simply whisk and bake in the moment. It is a very versatile recipe that you can top with any vegetables you like, raw or roasted, or simply serve cut in wedges as a side to hummus or other spreads.

If you are using the buckwheat-chestnut sourdough starter, the socca will have a nuttier flavor profile and is suitable for those following a grain-free diet. In this case, you will need to add a couple extra tablespoons of water to the batter.

MAKES 2 LARGE SOCCA

Ferment the socca batter. In a large bowl, whisk together the water, chickpea flour, and starter. Cover with a kitchen towel and let the mixture ferment at room temperature overnight (see Note).

Preheat the oven. The next day, position a rack in the bottom third of the oven and place a 12-inch (30 cm) cast-iron skillet on the rack. Preheat the oven to 450°F (230°C).

Bake the socca. Whisk the olive oil and salt into the batter until smooth; it should feel like thin pancake batter. Add a little bit more water if the batter feels thick. Remove the skillet from the oven and drizzle about a tablespoon of olive oil over the bottom. Swirl the oil around. Pour in half of the batter and swirl so the entire bottom of the skillet is covered. Sprinkle the top with half of the chopped rosemary and black pepper. Bake for 12 to 15 minutes, until golden brown. Using a spatula, carefully lift the socca out of the pan onto a wire rack. Repeat the process with more oil and the remaining batter, rosemary, and pepper.

(Recipe continues)

FOR THE SALAD

One 15-ounce (425 g) can chickpeas, drained

½ medium fennel bulb, outer layers and core removed, very thinly sliced

100 grams pitted green olives, coarsely chopped

¼ medium red onion, thinly sliced

Large handfuls of arugula, washed

Small handful of Italian parsley, coarsely chopped

Leaves from a few tarragon sprigs (optional)

A few chives, roughly chopped (optional)

Make the dressing. In a medium screw-top jar, combine the olive oil, lemon juice, mustard, maple syrup, salt, pepper flakes (if using), and cumin (if using). Shake vigorously and set aside.

Make the salad. In a medium bowl, toss together the chickpeas, fennel, olives, red onion, arugula, parsley, tarragon (if using), and chives (if using). Pour the dressing over the salad and toss together.

Assemble the socca. Transfer the socca to a serving platter and top with the dressed salad. Serve immediately.

Note: If you would prefer to skip the fermentation stage and make the socca right away, whisk the water, chickpea flour, starter, olive oil, and salt together in a large bowl and it's ready to be baked.

Turmeric and Cumin Sourdough Lavash

FOR THE SPONGE

170 grams filtered water, heated to 80°F (27°C)

150 grams Whole-Grain Brown Rice–Teff Sourdough Starter (page 48)

140 grams superfine brown rice flour, plus more for dusting

FOR THE DOUGH

7 grams cumin seeds

20 grams psyllium husk powder

250 grams whole milk, oat milk, or water, heated to 80°F (27°C)

15 grams extra-virgin olive oil, plus more for greasing

60 grams oat flour

60 grams tapioca starch

60 grams potato starch

2 teaspoons (8 g) kosher salt

2 teaspoons (8 g) ground turmeric

1 teaspoon (4 g) xanthan gum

Lavash is a thin flatbread original to the areas surrounding the Caspian Sea. Traditionally, it is baked in a tandoor or on hot stones, but in this recipe, you can bake it in the oven on a very hot pizza stone. You can serve lavash alongside stews, soups, or mezze. It also makes a fantastic wrap for sandwiches. Some people say lavash shouldn't be made with milk, but I find the addition makes for a very tender flatbread. You can replace the milk with water if you prefer. Superfine brown rice flour will help this dough stretch a bit more, as it hydrates better. If you don't have superfine brown rice flour, stone-ground is okay, but use tapioca starch for dusting. Wrapping the baked lavash in a towel while it cools helps it retain moisture that would otherwise evaporate and keeps the bread soft. Finally, note that the dough needs to rest in the refrigerator for 6 to 12 hours, so start the process the day before you are going to bake the lavash.

MAKES 6 LAVASH

Make the sponge. In a medium bowl, whisk together the water, starter, and brown rice flour until smooth. You should have a thick yogurt-like paste. Cover the bowl with a towel and proof until the sponge has puffed up and has a mousse-like texture, 3 to 4 hours.

Toast and crush the cumin seeds. Toast the cumin seeds in a small sauté pan over medium heat until they are fragrant and lightly toasted, 2 to 3 minutes. Transfer to a mortar and pestle or spice grinder and crush them to a coarse powder. Set aside.

Make the dough. Place the psyllium in a medium bowl and whisk in the milk and olive oil until completely dissolved. Let it gel for 5 minutes. In a stand mixer, stir together the oat flour, tapioca starch, potato starch, salt, turmeric, cumin, and xanthan gum. Add the sponge and psyllium gel. Snap on the dough hook and mix on medium speed until the dough comes together, 3 to 4 minutes. The dough will be very sticky.

Proof the dough. Grease a large bowl with olive oil and scrape the dough into it. Turn it around to coat all sides with the olive oil. Cover the bowl tightly with plastic wrap. Proof at room temperature for

1 hour, then transfer to the refrigerator and chill for 6 to 12 hours. The dough will rise about 25 percent in the fridge.

Preheat the oven. About 45 minutes before you are going to bake the lavash, position a rack in the bottom third of the oven and place a pizza stone on the rack. Preheat the oven to 500°F (260°C). Let the oven continue heating for at least 30 minutes after it has reached temperature.

Shape and roll the lavash. Dust a work surface and rolling pin with brown rice flour. Transfer the dough to the work surface. The dough will continue to be sticky, but it should feel a bit more solid and bouncy. Cut the dough into 6 equal pieces (about 140 g each). Knead each piece of dough a few times and shape it into a tight ball. Have a bench knife nearby as you might need it to scrape the work surface and rolling pin. Take one piece of dough and flatten it. Begin rolling the dough into a rectangle (it doesn't have to be perfect or an exact size—it can even be a round if you prefer). Move the dough around and keep the rolling pin dusted with brown rice flour. Roll the lavash as thin as possible, about 1⁄16 inch (2 mm) or thinner. If your dough tears and sticks to your surface or rolling pin, scrape the work surface so you don't have sticky and dry pieces of dough; knead the dough back together and roll it again. Be patient. It might take a couple of times to get it as thin as possible. Cut a large piece of parchment paper and transfer the lavash onto it. You can do some final rolling on the parchment paper, too. Turn a sheet pan upside down and slide the parchment paper with the lavash onto it. This will help you slide the parchment onto your stone.

Bake the lavash. Slide the parchment paper with the lavash onto the heated stone. Close the oven and bake for 1 to 2 minutes until the lavash has puffed slightly and has only some small brown spots. Do not overbake the lavash or it will be too crispy and not soft and pliable. Gently turn the lavash over with tongs (or your fingers, if you can tolerate the heat) and bake for 1 to 2 minutes more. Immediately transfer the lavash to a large kitchen towel and fold one edge of the towel over so it is completely covered. The puffed-up pockets will deflate and that is okay. Continue rolling and baking the rest of the dough. You can reuse the parchment paper every time. Keeping the bread covered after baking is crucial to keeping it moist and pliable. As the lavash come out of the oven, I stack them and keep them tightly wrapped in the towel.

Cool the lavash. Let the lavash cool completely as they are wrapped in the kitchen towel. Stacking the baked breads together is important for the final texture. They are best eaten the same day, or freeze them tightly wrapped in plastic for up to 1 month. To refresh the lavash, spray them with water and reheat them on a cast-iron pan.

VARIATION

Crispy Lavash Crackers

For longer storage, it's best to dry out the lavash completely by putting it in a 325°F (160°C) oven for 25 to 30 minutes, which will transform it into a delicate, brittle cracker. You can brush the top with olive oil and sprinkle with seeds and spices before baking if you wish.

Matzo

60 grams tapioca starch

50 grams oat flour

50 grams sorghum flour

1 teaspoon (4 g) kosher salt

¼ teaspoon (1 g) xanthan gum

100 grams warm water

25 grams extra-virgin olive oil

Matzo is unleavened cracker that is traditionally eaten around Passover, although it is great for any time of year. The trick to crispy matzo is to roll the dough very thin so it snaps when baked. The dough is rolled, then blistered in a hot cast-iron pan, and finished in the oven. This recipe can easily be doubled.

MAKES 4 SHEETS

Preheat the oven. Position a rack in the bottom third of the oven and preheat the oven to 325°F (160°C).

Make the dough. In a medium bowl, stir together the tapioca starch, oat flour, sorghum flour, salt, and xanthan gum. Add the water and olive oil and stir together until you have a loose dough. Cover and let the dough rest for 5 to 10 minutes. The dough should feel similar to pasta dough.

Roll the dough. Cut the dough into 4 equal pieces (about 70 g each). Roll each piece of dough in between two pieces of parchment paper until it is very thin, about 1⁄16 inch (2 mm). Peel off the top layer of parchment. If you want a perfect square that resembles traditional matzo, trim the sides and save the trimmings to roll with another piece of dough. Prick holes all over the dough with a fork.

Preheat the pan. Heat a 12-inch (30 cm) cast-iron griddle or pan over high heat.

Cook the matzo. When your pan is very hot, almost smoking, grease it with a little bit of neutral oil or pan spray. Flip a piece of dough onto your hand and place it in the pan pricked-side down. Cook until you have some charred spots, about 1 minute. Flip the matzo and cook for another minute. Transfer to a sheet pan. Repeat with the remaining dough.

Bake the matzo. Place the sheet pan in the oven and bake for 10 to 15 minutes to dry out the matzo pieces and make them crispy.

Cool the matzo. Let the matzo cool completely on a wire rack. Store in an airtight container for up to 2 weeks.

Fennel Seed and Olive Oil Tortas (Tortas de Aceite y Anís)

FOR THE SPONGE

70 grams superfine brown rice flour, plus more for dusting

35 grams millet flour

2 teaspoons (8 g) active dry yeast

130 grams water, heated to 105°F (41°C)

FOR THE DOUGH

1 to 2 teaspoons (2 to 3 g) fennel seeds

35 grams extra-virgin olive oil

60 grams potato starch

15 grams granulated sugar, plus more for sprinkling

1 teaspoon (4 g) kosher salt

1 teaspoon (4 g) xanthan gum

1 teaspoon (3 g) psyllium husk powder

1 large egg white (optional), for brushing

Tortas de aceite are thin and crispy crackers made with olive oil, anise seeds, and a dusting of sugar. They are original to southern Spain and were traditionally made by nuns in convents. When I was a child, my family took many family trips through small rural towns, and it was always a treat to visit nuns, who were historically the greatest bakers in Spain.

The egg wash is used so the sugar sticks to the crackers, and it makes the crackers shiny. But if you need to omit the egg to make the recipe vegan, brush the top of the dough with a very small amount of water; just enough for the sugar to stick to the surface.

Serve these tortas as an aperitif with some wine and cheese, or as an afternoon snack with a cup of tea.

MAKES 6 OR 7 TORTAS

Preheat the oven. Position an oven rack in the bottom third of the oven and preheat the oven to 450°F (230°C).

Make the sponge. In a large bowl, whisk together the brown rice flour, millet flour, and yeast. Add the water and whisk until smooth and the consistency of yogurt. Cover the bowl with a kitchen towel and proof until the center has puffed up and the sponge has a mousse-like texture, about 30 minutes.

Infuse the oil. While the sponge is proofing, crush the fennel seeds in a spice grinder or mortar and pestle to a medium-coarse texture (4 to 5 pulses in a spice grinder). In a small saucepan, combine the olive oil and fennel seeds. Warm over medium heat for 1 minute. Do not let the oil begin to bubble. You are simply heating it to infuse the fennel flavors throughout the oil. Pour into a small bowl and set aside to cool.

Make the dough. In a medium bowl, stir together the potato starch, sugar, salt, xanthan gum, and psyllium. Add the dry ingredients to the sponge along with the fennel-infused olive oil. Stir everything together. It will initially feel like a wet batter but

will thicken rather quickly. Let the dough rest for 5 minutes, then knead it together a few times. The dough should feel moist and a little bouncy and hold together.

Roll the tortas. Lightly dust a work surface with some brown rice flour and transfer the dough to it. Knead a few times so the exterior of the dough is smooth but the dough still feels moist. Cut the dough into 6 equal pieces (a little under 60 g each). Knead each piece of dough a couple of times and shape into a tight ball. Dust a rolling pin with brown rice flour and roll each dough piece into a disk that is as thin as possible, almost translucent and a little over 6 inches (15 cm) in diameter. You can leave the edges as is, or if you prefer a perfectly round torta, place a 6-inch (15 cm) bowl upside down over the piece of rolled dough and cut a circle following the diameter of the bowl. It is very important that the dough be thin so it dries out in the oven and becomes a crispy cracker. If your disks are too thick, the final cracker will be a bit soft. If the dough tears, knead it back together and roll again. It is also important to keep the rolling pin dusted with brown rice flour. Roll 3 pieces of dough and place them on a sheet pan.

Bake the tortas. Brush the tops with a little bit of egg white (or water for a vegan version) and sprinkle with some sugar. Place the pan in the oven. (Roll the remaining 3 pieces of dough while the first 3 are baking. You can re-roll any scraps of dough you may have.) Bake the tortas for 7 to 9 minutes, until there are golden brown spots all over. Some might have small puffed-up pockets, which is desirable, but not all will have them. Transfer them to a wire rack immediately to dry completely. Repeat the process with the remaining 3 pieces of dough on a second sheet pan.

Cool the tortas. Let the tortas cool completely. Store them in an airtight container for up to 7 days.

Crispy Paper Dosa

400 grams short-grain rice

100 grams urad dal (split and peeled black lentils)

1 teaspoon (3 g) fenugreek seeds

1½ teaspoons (6 g) kosher salt

345 grams cold water

Vegetable oil, for cooking

Some of the best dosa I've ever had in Southern India were at tiny little roadway stops. It is mesmerizing to watch the cooks swirl large batches of batter onto a gigantic griddle. You can use a well-seasoned cast-iron pan, but traditionally dosa are cooked on tawas—flat nonstick pans that you can find in Indian supermarkets or specialty shops. The paper-thin dosa can be filled or eaten simply on its own.

Dosa is made by fermenting a batter made with rice and lentils. The ratio of rice to lentils might vary depending on who is making it, but 4 parts rice to 1 part lentils is my ideal. In India, most dosa batter contains a portion of parboiled rice, but because it can be difficult to find here, I use all raw rice. Urad dal, skinned split black lentils, are found commonly in specialty supermarkets.

The trickiest parts about cooking dosa are making sure that you have the right wrist movement while spreading the batter and that the pan is at the correct temperature. If your tawa is too warm, your batter will cook too quickly and you won't be able to spread it evenly; if your tawa is not warm enough, the dosa won't caramelize properly. It takes practice.

MAKES ABOUT 14 DOSA

Soak the rice and lentils. Place the rice in a large bowl and wash it under abundant cold water until the water is nearly clear (it's okay if it's slightly opaque). Cover the rice with abundant cold water and soak for 8 hours at room temperature. In a separate medium bowl, wash the urad dal under cold water until the water runs clean. Add the fenugreek seeds to the bowl. Cover with abundant cold water and soak for 8 hours at room temperature. In warmer climates, it might only take 4 to 6 hours for the rice and dal to soften, or you could soak them in the refrigerator overnight.

Make the batter. Drain the rice in a fine-mesh sieve and place half of it in a high-powered blender. Add 115 grams cold water and blend until you have a fine paste. Rice is a hard grain to grind, so you might have to stop the blender, stir the rice paste, and blend again several times. Transfer the rice paste to a large bowl. Blend the remaining rice with another 115 grams water. Add that paste to the bowl. Drain the dal and fenugreek in the fine-mesh sieve and add to the blender. Add the remaining 115 grams water and blend

until smooth. Add this paste to the bowl and whisk together. You should have a pourable, medium-thick batter.

Ferment the batter. Cover the bowl with a kitchen towel and ferment for 8 to 16 hours at room temperature. The length of time depends on the temperature of your kitchen. (For alternatives, see Notes.) The fermented batter should be bubbling and smell like yogurt. Whisk the salt into the batter. At this stage, decide if you are going to cook all the batter. If only cooking a portion of it, transfer your desired amount to a bowl and thin it out with water until you have a batter with the consistency of heavy cream or crêpe batter. Keep the dosa batter you are not going to cook right away in the refrigerator, in an airtight container, for up to 5 days.

Cook the dosa. Heat a tawa, crêpe pan, or nonstick skillet over medium heat. Consider the first dosa as a trial one, so don't worry if it doesn't turn out. It will allow you to see how hot the pan really is. The pan is ready when a sprinkle of water sizzles gently on the surface. Drizzle a small amount of oil on the pan and use a piece of paper towel to rub the whole pan with it. Add about ⅓ cup (85 g) of dosa batter to the center of the pan. Use a measuring cup with a flat bottom or the bottom of a ladle to spread the batter outward, counterclockwise in a circular motion, until it forms a very thin crêpe. This takes some practice. If the batter sticks to the pan as you do this, it might mean the batter is too thick (thin it out with a bit of water) or the pan is too hot (reduce the heat). Cook the dosa until the top has dried out, about 1 minute, and brush with a small amount of oil. Cook until the edges begin to come off the pan and the bottom is crispy and golden, 1 to 2 minutes. With a spatula, carefully loosen the dosa, lift from the pan, and serve immediately. Repeat with the rest of the batter (see Notes). Dosa are best eaten right away.

Notes: To ferment the batter in an Instant Pot, pour the batter directly into the Instant Pot bowl (or you can even transfer the batter into two 1-quart/1 L mason jars and place these in the Instant Pot). Ferment on the yogurt setting for 8 to 10 hours.

You can also ferment the batter in the oven with the light on and add a small pot of boiling-hot water next to your bowl.

I like to splash the pan with a few drops of water in between dosa so it's not too hot while spreading the batter. You will have to keep adjusting the heat throughout cooking. Reduce the heat when you are about to spread the batter and increase it when the dosa is cooking.

Whisk-and-Pour Oat Roti

PICTURED ON PAGE 263

- 90 grams oat flour
- 30 grams tapioca starch
- 1 teaspoon (4 g) granulated sugar
- 1 teaspoon (4 g) kosher salt
- ⅛ teaspoon (0.5 g) baking powder
- 225 grams water, at room temperature
- 15 grams extra-virgin olive oil or melted ghee
- Melted ghee, for frying

Roti is a round flatbread traditional in India. It is served as an accompaniment for curries and stews. Making them is as simple as can be. No rolling involved; simply whisk all the ingredients together and pour into a pan. The recipe may be basic, but you can dress it up by stirring a bunch of finely chopped parsley and green onions, and a pinch of crushed toasted mustard seeds into the batter.

MAKES SIX 7-INCH (18 CM) ROTI

Make the batter. In a medium bowl, stir together the oat flour, tapioca starch, sugar, salt, and baking powder. Whisk in the water and olive oil until smooth. The batter will be very thin and watery. Let the batter rest for 15 to 20 minutes. At this point, the batter will have thickened slightly, but still be very thin.

Cook the roti. Heat a cast-iron skillet or tawa (a flat nonstick pan) over medium-high heat. Remove the skillet from the heat and brush with some ghee. Pour ¼ cup (45 g) of batter in the center of the skillet and use the back of a spoon or soup ladle to spread the batter in a circular motion to roughly 7 inches (18 cm) in diameter. Return the skillet to the heat and cook the roti until it is no longer translucent and has golden brown spots, 2 to 3 minutes. Flip the roti over with a spatula and cook for 2 to 3 minutes. Transfer to a plate. Repeat with the remaining batter, removing the skillet from the heat every time you are going to cook another roti. If the skillet is too hot when you add the batter, it will be hard to spread it without it sticking. Brush the pan with some more ghee, pour in the batter, spread it, and cook as before.

Store the roti. Keep the roti tightly wrapped for up to 3 days. They can also be frozen tightly wrapped up to 3 months and simply thawed out at room temperature. To refresh them, spray with water and reheat in a cast-iron pan.

Sourdough Naan

1 teaspoon (4 g) active dry yeast

140 grams whole milk or oat milk, heated to 105°F (41°C)

1 teaspoon (4 g) granulated sugar

2 teaspoons (7 g) psyllium husk powder

90 grams sorghum flour

60 grams cassava flour

1½ teaspoons (6 g) kosher salt

½ teaspoon (2 g) baking powder

150 grams Whole-Grain Brown Rice–Teff Sourdough Starter (page 48)

55 grams whole-milk yogurt or vegan yogurt

Tapioca starch, for dusting

Olive oil or ghee, for frying

Naan is a yeast-leavened flatbread original to western and southern Asia and probably most known as part of Indian cuisine. This naan is made with a mixture of baker's yeast and sourdough starter, which adds a distinct tang in addition to the yogurt. Serve naan alongside curries and stews.

MAKES 6 NAAN

Make the yeast-psyllium mixture. Sprinkle the yeast into a medium bowl. Add the milk and sugar and whisk until the yeast is dissolved. Let the mixture sit until frothy, about 10 minutes. Whisk in the psyllium. Let it gel for 5 minutes.

Make the dough. In a large bowl, stir together the sorghum flour, cassava flour, salt, and baking powder. Add the sourdough starter, yogurt, and yeast-psyllium mixture. Stir everything together with a fork and then knead with your hands until you have a smooth dough. It will be tacky but not very wet; it should feel similar to soft pasta dough. Shape into a ball and leave in the bowl, covered with a kitchen towel, to proof for 3 to 4 hours until the dough rises about 50 percent.

Shape the naan. Divide the dough into 6 equal pieces (about 80 g each). Lightly dust a work surface with some tapioca starch. Roll each piece of dough into an oval that is ⅛-inch (3 mm) thick. The shape doesn't really matter, but roll them evenly. If the edges crack, use the palms of your hands to round them.

Cook the naan. Heat a 12-inch (30 cm) cast-iron skillet over medium heat for 2 to 3 minutes. It's important to keep a steady heat on the skillet. If it's too hot, the naan will burn and if not hot enough, it won't get the desired blistered surface. Adjust the heat as needed, especially once you begin cooking the naan. Brush one side of the naan with olive oil or ghee and add to pan. Cook until it has golden brown spots and some bubbles rise on the dough, 2 to 3 minutes. Brush the side facing up with olive oil or ghee, flip the naan over, and cook for 2 to 3 minutes.

Cool the naan. Transfer the naan to a wire rack to cool completely. Repeat with the remaining pieces of dough. Store the naan tightly wrapped at room temperature for up to 3 days or in the freezer for up to 3 months.

Sourdough Pizza Margherita

If you are looking for gluten-free pizza dough that is chewy and crispy, you've found it. This is a high-hydration dough (120% to 122%), which makes it bouncy and a pleasure to work with. Make sure you use finely milled and pure psyllium so it can absorb all the water perfectly, otherwise you will end up with dough that is too wet and gummy (see Note). If baking this dough in a wood-fired pizza oven (the type that reaches 700°F/371°C or more), the baking time will be much shorter. You might have to experiment a bit with the specifics of your wood-fired oven, but in general, I like to parbake the dough for 5 minutes, rotating it around as it begins to blister in spots, then add toppings and finish baking for 2 to 3 minutes, until the cheese is melted.

MAKES TWO 11-INCH (28 CM) PIZZAS

FOR THE SPONGE

150 grams Whole-Grain Brown Rice–Teff Sourdough Starter (page 48)

140 grams superfine brown rice flour or sorghum flour

170 grams filtered water, heated to 80°F (27°C)

FOR THE DOUGH

20 grams psyllium husk powder

225 to 250 grams (see Note) filtered water, heated to 80°F (27°C)

120 grams tapioca starch

80 grams potato starch

2 teaspoons (8 g) granulated sugar

2 teaspoons (8 g) kosher salt

15 grams extra-virgin olive oil, plus more for brushing

White rice flour, for dusting

FOR THE TOPPINGS

1 cup (240 g) tomato sauce or pizza sauce

8 ounces (220 g) fresh mozzarella cheese, torn or sliced

Handful of fresh basil leaves

Make the sponge. In a medium bowl, whisk together the starter, brown rice flour, and water until smooth. Cover with a kitchen towel and ferment at room temperature until the sponge is mousse-like when you run a spoon through it, 3 to 5 hours.

Make the dough. Sprinkle the psyllium into a medium bowl. Whisk in the water vigorously until you have a thick gel. In a stand mixer, stir together the tapioca starch, potato starch, sugar, and salt. Add the psyllium gel, sponge, and olive oil. Snap on the dough hook and mix the dough until it is smooth, bouncy, and holds together nicely, 2 to 3 minutes. The dough will be moist but shouldn't be terribly sticky.

Shape the dough. Cut the dough into 2 equal pieces. Shape each piece of dough into a tight ball and place on a sheet pan lightly floured with white rice flour. Cover with a kitchen towel and ferment at room temperature until the dough feels light, 2 to 3 hours. It won't increase significantly in volume but should feel lighter. (Alternatively, wrap the pan in a large plastic bag, ferment at room temperature for 1 hour, then transfer to the refrigerator for 8 to 24 hours.) At this point, you can freeze any dough you will not be using right away. Wrap it tightly in plastic wrap and freeze. Thaw in the refrigerator overnight and proceed as directed.

Preheat the oven. Position a rack in the bottom third of the oven and place a pizza stone on the rack. Preheat the oven to 500°F (260°C). Let the stone continue heating for at least 15 minutes after the oven has come to temperature.

Roll the dough. If you have fermented the dough in the refrigerator, let it come to room temperature for 30 minutes. Lightly dust a work surface with white rice flour. Press down in the center of one dough ball and gently stretch it (make sure it doesn't tear). You can use a rolling pin to roll the center. Leave a thicker border around the edges of the pizza. You should have a pizza that is roughly 10 to 11 inches (25 to 28 cm) in diameter, ⅛ to ¼ inch (3 to 6 mm) thick in the center, and ½ inch (1.3 cm) thick around the edges. Dust a pizza peel with white rice flour and transfer the dough onto it. Roll out the second piece of dough and cover it with a kitchen towel while the first pizza cooks.

Parbake the pizzas. Slide the first pizza onto the preheated stone and bake for 5 minutes. The dough will bubble up and that is okay. Don't try to press it down too hard, let it deflate on its own. Parbaking allows for the center of the dough to get a head start before adding the moist toppings.

Top and bake the pizzas. Slide the first pizza out of the oven and add half of the sauce and cheese (or any toppings you prefer). Brush the exposed dough with a little bit of olive oil. Slide it back onto the pizza stone and bake for 15 minutes, or until the crust is golden brown and the cheese is bubbling. Top with fresh basil. Let the pizza cool for 5 minutes before serving. Repeat the parbaking, topping, and baking steps with the second pizza.

Note: When you make this for the first time, especially if you're not sure if your psyllium can absorb all the water, hold off on 25 grams (about 2 tablespoons) of the water; wait until your dough is mixed and then add more as needed.

Melted Cauliflower, Tomato, and Olive Sourdough Pizza

The idea of melted cauliflower comes from Carla Lalli Music's book *That Sounds So Good* where cauliflower is cooked down and caramelized to a sauce that she then tosses with pasta. As soon as I made it, I was smitten. I am borrowing her idea here as the cauliflower makes a lovely creamy sauce for pizza, too.

MAKES ONE 11-INCH (28 CM) PIZZA

FOR THE DOUGH

½ recipe dough for Sourdough Pizza Margherita (page 294)

White rice flour, for dusting

FOR THE MELTED CAULIFLOWER

55 grams extra-virgin olive oil, plus more for brushing

3 garlic cloves, thinly sliced

½ medium head cauliflower (14 ounces/400 g), cut into ½-inch (1.3 cm) or smaller pieces

1 teaspoon (4 g) kosher salt

⅛ teaspoon red pepper flakes

FOR THE TOPPINGS

40 grams pizza sauce or marinara

90 grams fresh mozzarella cheese, sliced into ¼-inch (6 mm) rounds, or shredded vegan mozzarella-style cheese

20 grams black olives, sliced

Dried oregano

Fresh basil leaves

Freshly grated Parmesan cheese

Make the dough. Make the pizza dough as directed.

Cook the cauliflower. Heat a medium sauté pan over medium heat. Add the olive oil and garlic and cook until the garlic softens slightly and the edges begin to turn golden, about a minute. Add the cauliflower, salt, and pepper flakes. Stir everything together and cook until some of the cauliflower begins to caramelize around the edges, about 5 minutes. Reduce the heat to medium-low, cover the pan, and cook, stirring occasionally, until the cauliflower is completely soft and has a light golden color, about 20 minutes.

Preheat the oven. Position a rack in the bottom third of the oven and place a pizza stone on the rack. Preheat the oven to 500°F (260°C). Let the stone continue heating for at least 15 minutes after the oven has come to temperature.

Roll the dough. Lightly dust a work surface with white rice flour. Press down in the center of the dough and gently stretch it (make sure it doesn't tear). You can use a rolling pin to roll the center. Leave a thicker border around the edges of the pizza. You should have a pizza that is roughly 10 to 11 inches (25 to 28 cm) in diameter and ⅛ to ¼ inch (3 to 6 mm) thick in the center and ½ inch (1.3 cm) thick around the edges. Dust a pizza peel with white rice flour and transfer the dough onto it.

Bake the pizza. Slide the dough onto the preheated stone. Bake for 5 minutes.

Top the pizza. Slide the pizza out of the oven and spread with the pizza sauce. Top with the melted cauliflower, mozzarella, olives, and dried oregano. Brush the exposed dough with a little bit of olive oil. Return the pizza to the oven and bake for 15 minutes, or until the bottom of the crust is golden brown and the cheese is melted and golden.

Serve the pizza. Remove the pizza from the oven and top with fresh basil and Parmesan cheese. Let the pizza cool for 5 minutes before serving.

Pear and Balsamic Shallot Sourdough Pizza Bianca

FOR THE DOUGH

½ recipe dough for Sourdough Pizza Margherita (page 294)

White rice flour, for dusting

FOR THE ALMOND RICOTTA

150 grams sliced blanched almonds

110 grams water, at room temperature

20 grams white (shiro) miso

15 grams fresh lemon juice

15 grams extra-virgin olive oil

½ teaspoon (2 g) garlic powder

FOR THE BALSAMIC SHALLOTS

15 grams extra-virgin olive oil, plus more for drizzling

110 grams small shallots (3 or 4), peeled and halved

25 grams water

½ teaspoon (2 g) kosher salt

15 grams balsamic vinegar

FOR THE TOPPINGS

½ medium pear, cored and thinly sliced

2 tablespoons Olive Pesto (page 251; optional)

Fruit on pizza might not be everyone's cup of tea, but I love the little bit of sweetness in this instance. The pear complements the savory almond ricotta and balsamic shallots. You can most certainly make this pizza using cow's milk ricotta and skip the homemade almond version.

MAKES ONE 11-INCH (28 CM) PIZZA

Make the dough. Make the pizza dough as directed.

Make the almond ricotta. Place the almonds in a medium bowl and cover them with boiling water. Cover the bowl with a plate and let the almonds soften for 30 minutes. Drain the almonds. In a high-powered blender, combine the almonds, water, miso, lemon juice, olive oil, and garlic powder. Blend until you have a smooth cream. You might have to stop, scrape, and blend again several times to get it going. Add a tablespoon of water if needed to create a spreadable, smooth cream. Set aside.

Make the balsamic shallots. Heat a small sauté pan over medium-high heat. Add the olive oil, shallots, water, and salt and cook until the shallots begin to soften, 2 or 3 minutes. Cover the pan, reduce the heat to medium-low, and cook the shallots until tender and lightly caramelized, 5 minutes. Remove the pan from the heat and stir in the balsamic.

Preheat the oven. Position a rack in the bottom third of the oven and place a pizza stone on the rack. Preheat the oven to 500°F (260°C). Let the stone continue heating for at least 15 minutes after the oven has come to temperature.

Roll the dough. Lightly dust a work surface with white rice flour. Press down in the center of the dough and gently stretch it (make sure it doesn't tear). You can use a rolling pin to roll the center. Leave a thicker border around the edges of the pizza. You should have a pizza that is roughly 11 inches (28 cm) in diameter and ⅛ to ¼ inch (3 to 6 mm) thick in the center and ½ inch (1.3 cm) thick around the edges. Dust a pizza peel with white rice flour and transfer the dough onto it.

- 90 grams fresh mozzarella cheese, sliced into ¼-inch (6 mm) rounds, or shredded vegan mozzarella-style cheese
- Handful of tender baby greens or herbs (spinach, arugula, watercress, dill, basil, chervil, etc.)
- Freshly grated Parmesan cheese
- Freshly ground black pepper

Bake the pizza. Slide the dough onto the preheated stone. Bake for 5 minutes.

Top the pizza. Slide the pizza out of the oven and spread with a generous amount of almond ricotta leaving a 1-inch (2.5 cm) border around the edges. Top with the pear, olive pesto (if using), balsamic shallots, and mozzarella. Drizzle the top and exposed edges of dough with olive oil. Slide the pizza back onto the pizza stone and bake for 15 minutes, or until bubbling and golden brown.

Serve the pizza. Let the pizza cool for 5 minutes. Top with tender greens, Parmesan, black pepper, and extra olive oil, if desired. Serve immediately.

No. 7

Holiday Breads

Marzipan-Filled Semlor

Chocolate Babka Wreath

The holidays can be a bittersweet time for those who must avoid gluten; it's a season filled with tempting treats that are off-limits. So it's no surprise that every fall, I receive requests from readers hoping to convert their beloved family heirloom bread recipes to be gluten-free. Few aromas evoke more warm, festive feelings than that of freshly baked bread wafting through the kitchen.

The recipes in this chapter are special-occasion breads perfect for celebratory gatherings. Many of these breads are enriched doughs, made luxuriously rich with butter and eggs and fragrant with warm spices. Some, like the Roscón de Reyes (page 328) and Sourdough Panettone (page 350), are bakes I grew up with, evoking cherished childhood memories. Others, such as the Sourdough Stollen (page 316), Marzipan-Filled Semlor (page 334), and Challah (page 336), are treasured recipes I've gathered over the years. I hope these holiday breads will become part of your traditions. Share them with your family and community and create heirlooms to pass along to those you love.

Buckwheat and Cardamom Buns

FOR THE DOUGH

2 teaspoons (8 g) active dry yeast

200 grams whole milk or oat milk, heated to 105°F (41°C)

80 grams granulated sugar

20 grams psyllium husk powder

120 grams potato starch

105 grams light buckwheat flour

90 grams tapioca starch, plus more for dusting

2 teaspoons (8 g) kosher salt

1½ teaspoons (6 g) xanthan gum

1 teaspoon (3 g) freshly ground cardamom

2 large eggs, at room temperature

1 large egg white, at room temperature

55 grams soft (but not melted) unsalted butter or vegan butter

FOR THE FILLING

75 grams light brown sugar

70 grams soft (but not melted) unsalted butter or vegan butter

2 teaspoons (6 g) freshly ground cardamom

(Ingredients continue)

In Scandinavian countries, cardamom buns are an everyday affair and not reserved for holidays, but I make them mostly for special occasions; something about cardamom says holiday to me. For this recipe, I encourage you to buy green cardamom pods and grind the interior black seeds in a spice grinder or mortar and pestle immediately before using. Preground cardamom loses a lot of the strong spicy aroma that the buns need. It is also important that you use light buckwheat flour in this recipe, because very dark buckwheat will be dense and might overpower the cardamom. The dough needs to chill in the refrigerator overnight, so plan on starting the process the night before.

MAKES 8 BUNS

Make the yeast-psyllium mixture. Sprinkle the yeast into a medium bowl. Add the milk and 5 grams of the sugar and whisk until dissolved. Let the mixture sit until frothy, about 10 minutes. Whisk in the psyllium vigorously. Let it gel for 5 minutes.

Make the dough. In a stand mixer, stir together the remaining 75 grams sugar, the potato starch, buckwheat flour, tapioca starch, salt, xanthan gum, and cardamom. Add the yeast-psyllium mixture. Snap on the dough hook and begin mixing the dough on medium speed. Add the eggs and egg white and continue mixing for 2 minutes until the dough comes together. Add the soft butter 1 tablespoon at a time and continue mixing for another minute. The dough will be soft, moist, and sticky but should hold together.

Chill the dough. Lay a large sheet of plastic wrap on a work surface and scrape the dough onto it. Shape the dough into a rectangle that is roughly 6 by 7 inches (15 by 18 cm). The exact size is not important at this stage. Wrap the dough and place it in the refrigerator to chill overnight.

Make the filling. In a medium bowl, stir together the brown sugar, soft butter, cardamom, and cinnamon until it is easy to spread and very creamy. You can also do this in a stand mixer with the paddle, but it should work well with a wooden spoon if your butter is soft. It

2 teaspoons (6 g) ground cinnamon

FOR THE CARDAMOM SUGAR

25 grams granulated sugar

1 teaspoon (3 g) freshly ground cardamom

1 large egg, lightly beaten

FOR THE GLAZE

50 grams granulated sugar

35 grams water

is important that the butter be soft so it is easy to spread and doesn't tear the dough. If your room is cold, microwave the butter for 5 seconds to warm it up. Set aside.

Roll the dough. Lightly dust a work surface and a rolling pin with tapioca starch. Remove your dough from the refrigerator, unwrap, and place it on the work surface. Knead the dough a few times to bring back some elasticity and then let it sit for 10 minutes to take the chill off. If the dough is too cold, it will crack while rolling. Gently roll the dough to a rectangle that is roughly 16 by 11 inches (41 by 28 cm). Move the dough around and dust with tapioca starch as needed so it doesn't stick to your surface. It's okay if the edges crack a little. Gently pull the corners out to create more of a rectangle than an oval, but don't pull too hard or the dough may crack. There is little elasticity, so you must work gingerly.

Add the filling and roll. Line a sheet pan with parchment paper. Spread the filling all over the surface of the dough, trying not to tear it. With a short side facing you, fold the top third onto the middle and the lower third up over it, creating a letter fold. Rotate the dough 90 degrees. Dust the dough and rolling pin with tapioca starch, if needed, and roll the dough to a rectangle that is roughly 15 by 8½ inches (38 by 22 cm). Transfer the dough to the lined sheet pan and refrigerate for 20 to 30 minutes.

Cut the dough. Remove the dough from the refrigerator and place it on your work surface with a short side facing you. Trim the edges to create sharp corners. Make 7 small marks 1 inch (2.5 cm) apart, at both ends. Use a long ruler to help you line up the top and bottom marks and cut the dough vertically into 8 strips that are roughly 1 inch (2.5 cm) wide and 15 inches (38 cm) long.

Shape the cardamom buns. Take one strip of dough and place it in front of you. Start twisting the dough in the middle toward one end and then twist toward the other end. Loosely coil the twisted dough into a spiral or a snail, tucking only the tip underneath at the end. Using both hands or a spatula, carefully transfer each spiral onto the lined sheet pan. Repeat with the remaining strips of dough until all the buns are shaped.

Proof the cardamom buns. Cover the pan with a kitchen towel or wrap it in a large plastic bag. Proof at room temperature until the buns feel lighter to the touch, about 40 to 45 minutes.

Preheat the oven and make the cardamom sugar. While the buns are proofing, position a rack in the bottom third of the oven and preheat the oven to 450°F (230°C). In a small bowl, stir together the sugar and cardamom. Set aside along with the lightly beaten egg, which will be used to brush the tops.

Make the glaze. In a small saucepan, cook the sugar and water together over medium heat until the sugar is completely dissolved. Set aside.

Bake the cardamom buns. When the buns are proofed, lightly brush the tops with the beaten egg and sprinkle some cardamom sugar on top. Transfer the pan to the oven and reduce the oven temperature to 425°F (220°C). Bake for 15 minutes, or until the buns are a deep golden brown. Don't worry if your buns crack in spots. There is not a lot of elasticity in the dough, so this can happen if you twist the buns too tightly.

Glaze the buns. When the buns come out of the oven, brush them with the sugar syrup. Serve the buns while they are still warm. They can be reheated in the microwave for 20 seconds.

Note: If you have English muffin rings, you can place them around the shaped buns and let them proof in them. This gives a nice round shape to the buns and helps them rise up rather than sideways in the oven, but free-form buns will also work very well.

Spiced Star Bread

FOR THE DOUGH

2 teaspoons (8 g) active dry yeast

225 grams whole milk or oat milk, heated to 105°F (41°C)

55 grams granulated sugar

120 grams potato starch

105 grams sweet white rice flour

90 grams tapioca starch, plus more for dusting

45 grams sorghum flour

20 grams psyllium husk powder

2 teaspoons (8 g) kosher salt

1 teaspoon (4 g) xanthan gum

2 teaspoons (4 g) finely grated orange zest

2 large eggs, at room temperature

40 grams soft (but not melted) vegan butter or unsalted butter

Olive oil, for greasing

FOR THE FILLING

75 grams granulated sugar

½ teaspoon (2 g) ground cinnamon

½ teaspoon (2 g) ground cardamom

40 grams soft (but not melted) vegan butter or unsalted butter

This bread, which can be served for afternoon tea or as a sweet treat in the morning, also makes a beautiful centerpiece for your holiday table. The dough is scented with orange and filled with cinnamon and cardamom butter, but you could fill it with Nutella or raspberry jam for beautiful contrast and flavor. If you are trying to serve this bread in the morning and you would like to save some time, you can make the dough the night before, proof it for 30 minutes at room temperature, then cover the bowl with plastic wrap and refrigerate overnight. Roll and fill the dough in the morning and add 10 minutes of proofing time.

MAKES ONE 10-INCH (25 CM) BREAD; SERVES 6 TO 8

Activate the yeast. Sprinkle the yeast into a medium bowl. Add the milk and 5 grams of the granulated sugar and whisk until dissolved. Let the mixture sit until frothy, about 10 minutes.

Mix the dough. In a stand mixer, stir together the remaining 50 grams sugar, the potato starch, sweet white rice flour, tapioca starch, sorghum flour, psyllium, salt, xanthan gum, and orange zest. Add the proofed yeast. Snap on the dough hook and begin mixing the dough on medium speed. Add the eggs one at a time and continue mixing for another minute or until the dough comes together. Add the soft butter, 1 tablespoon at a time, mixing after each addition so the butter is fully incorporated. The dough will be moist and a little sticky but should hold together nicely.

Proof the dough. Grease a medium bowl with a little olive oil or cooking spray and add the dough to it. Roll the dough around so all sides are coated. Cover the bowl with a kitchen towel and proof until nearly doubled in size, 45 minutes to 1 hour.

Make the filling. In a small bowl, stir together the sugar, cinnamon, and cardamom. Set aside.

Cut the dough. When the dough is done proofing, transfer it to a work surface. Knead the dough a few times to deflate and add back some elasticity. Cut the dough into 4 equal pieces (about 200 g each). Knead each piece of dough a few times and shape into a tight ball.

(Recipe continues)

FOR THE EGG WASH

1 large egg

1 tablespoon (12 g) water, at room temperature

FOR SPRINKLING

Powdered sugar

Roll and fill the dough. Cut a long piece of parchment paper and set it aside. Dust a work surface and a rolling pin with some tapioca starch. Take one piece of dough and place it on the work surface. Gently roll it to a disk that is roughly 10 inches (25 cm) in diameter. Place this disk on the sheet of parchment right next to you. Spread one-third of the butter for the filling over the dough and sprinkle the top with one-third of the cinnamon-cardamom sugar. Roll a second piece of dough to a disk that is also 10 inches (25 cm) in diameter. Place this on top of the other rolled piece of dough. Repeat with the butter and sugar layer and the remaining dough. You will have a total of 4 layers of dough with 3 layers of filling. Using a pizza cutter, cut any scraps around the edges so you have an even round.

Shape the star bread. Place a 3- to 4-inch (7.5 to 10 cm) ramekin in the center of the dough to make a light indent, which will be the center of the star. To create the star, you will use a pizza cutter to make cuts from the edge of the center circle to the edge of the large circle (the center circle that you created the indentation for will stay intact). To do this, envisioning the round as a clock, first make cuts at 3 o'clock, 6 o'clock, 9 o'clock, and 12 o'clock. Then cut each quarter in half (for a total of 8 strips), then cut each of those in half so you end up with 16 strips connected to the middle circle. Using both hands, grab two strips that are next to each other and twist them away from each other twice, then press the two ends together to make a point. Gently press the ends to seal well or they might separate while baking. Your star bread will end up with 8 points. Gently slide the parchment paper with the dough on it onto a sheet pan.

Proof the star bread. Cover the pan with a kitchen towel and proof for 25 minutes. Make sure not to overproof the dough or your bread will crack when baking.

Preheat the oven. Position a rack in the bottom third of the oven and preheat the oven to 375°F (190°C).

Make the egg wash and bake the star bread. In a small bowl, whisk together the egg and water. Brush the top of the dough with the egg wash. Transfer the pan to the oven and bake for 20 minutes, or until golden brown. Dust the top of the star bread with powdered sugar when it comes out of the oven.

Cool the star bread. Let the star bread cool on the pan for 10 minutes and serve warm. To refresh it, spray the bread with water and bake at 350°F (180°C) for 10 minutes.

Oat and Honey Sourdough Hot Cross Buns

FOR THE SWEET STIFF SPONGE

115 grams Whole-Grain Brown Rice–Teff Sourdough Starter (page 48)

65 grams oat milk or whole milk, heated to 80°F (27°C)

30 grams granulated sugar

115 grams oat flour

FOR THE DOUGH

25 grams psyllium husk powder

200 grams oat milk or whole milk, heated to 80°F (27°C)

120 grams tapioca starch, plus more for dusting

120 grams potato starch

40 grams oat flour

50 grams granulated sugar

2 teaspoons (8 g) kosher salt

2 teaspoons (4 g) finely grated orange zest

2 teaspoons (4 g) finely grated lemon zest

1 teaspoon (4 g) baking powder

1 teaspoon (4 g) ground cinnamon

½ teaspoon (2 g) ground cardamom

(Ingredients continue)

Hot cross buns are sweet and spiced yeast rolls, studded with dried currants or raisins, served before and during Easter. They are traditional in the UK as well as Ireland and other parts of the world. Made with a stiff oat sourdough starter and honey, this dough is one of my favorites to work with. It's denser and less eggy than brioche but still light and tender. I love watching the oat starter grow as it is filled with beautiful air pockets. Start the process the day before you are going to bake the buns. You will make the sponge, then the dough, and let it refrigerate overnight. The next morning, shape the buns, proof, and bake.

MAKES 12 BUNS

Make the sweet stiff sponge. In a medium bowl, stir together the starter, milk, and sugar. Add the oat flour and stir together vigorously until you have a thick paste. Transfer to a 1 quart (1 L) mason jar. Loosely cover with a lid (no need to seal it, simply set the lid on top). Proof until nearly doubled in size, 4 to 8 hours, ideally in an environment that is around 75° to 85°F (24° to 29°C); I like to put mine in the oven with the light on and a small pot of boiling-hot water next to it.

Make the dough. Sprinkle the psyllium husk into a medium bowl. Add the milk and whisk until dissolved. Let it gel for 5 minutes. In a stand mixer, stir together the tapioca starch, potato starch, oat flour, sugar, salt, orange zest, lemon zest, baking powder, cinnamon, and cardamom. Add the proofed sponge, psyllium gel, eggs, and honey. Snap on the dough hook and mix on medium speed until the dough comes together, about 2 minutes. Add the soft butter, 1 tablespoon at a time, and continue mixing until incorporated, about 1 minute. Add the currants and mix until they are thoroughly mixed. The dough will be soft and sticky.

Chill the dough. Lightly grease a large bowl with some butter and transfer the dough to it. Cover with plastic wrap and let it proof for 1 hour. Transfer the dough to the refrigerator and chill for 8 to 12 hours.

(Recipe continues)

2 large eggs, at room temperature

50 grams honey

55 grams soft (but not melted) unsalted butter or vegan butter, plus more for greasing

50 grams plump dried currants or small raisins

FOR THE FLOUR PASTE

55 grams water

45 grams superfine brown rice flour

FOR THE EGG WASH

1 large egg, lightly beaten

Small pinch of salt

FOR THE GLAZE

50 grams granulated sugar

35 grams freshly squeezed orange juice

Shape the buns. Line a 9-by-13-inch (23 by 33 cm) sheet pan with parchment paper. Dust a work surface with tapioca starch and transfer the chilled dough onto it. Cut the dough into 12 equal pieces (about 90 g each) and shape each piece of dough into a tight ball. Place the balls of dough on the prepared sheet pan in 4 rows of 3.

Proof the buns. Cover the pan with plastic wrap or a kitchen towel or place it in a large plastic bag. Proof at room temperature (or in the oven with the light on and a small pot of boiling-hot water next to it) until the buns feel lighter to the touch, 2 to 4 hours. They won't necessarily be much larger.

Preheat the oven. Position a rack in the bottom third of the oven and preheat the oven to 375°F (190°C).

Make the flour paste. In a small bowl, whisk the water and brown rice flour until you have a smooth paste. Place the paste in a piping bag and cut a very small opening in the tip, just enough to be able to pipe a ⅛-inch (3 mm) line.

Make the egg wash and decorate the buns. In a small bowl, whisk together the egg and salt. Brush all sides of the buns with the egg wash. Pipe the flour paste over the tops, creating crosses.

Make the glaze. In a small saucepan, heat the sugar and orange juice together over low heat until the sugar has dissolved. Set aside.

Bake the buns. Bake for 30 to 35 minutes, until golden brown.

Glaze the buns. As soon as the buns come out of the oven, brush the tops with the glaze. Let the buns cool for 15 minutes before eating. Serve warm or at room temperature.

VARIATION

Vegan Hot Cross Buns

For the dough: Increase the oat milk to 300 grams and add 15 grams fine flaxseed meal to the milk along with the psyllium. Omit the eggs. Use maple syrup or brown rice syrup in place of the honey. Omit the egg wash and use maple syrup to brush the top of the dough before baking.

Sourdough Stollen

Stollen is a traditional German spiced fruit-and-nut Christmas bread. It is dense, buttery, sweet, and filled with candied fruits and marzipan. When I was working as a pastry cook at the Ritz-Carlton Palm Beach many years ago, our German executive chef was obsessed with the perfect stollen. We started making them right after Thanksgiving and they sat covered in powdered sugar and butter for days before we finally served them for Christmas brunch. When kept tightly wrapped, stollen stays moist for a long time. Start the brioche dough the morning before you are going to bake the stollen because you will need to proof the sponge during the day, make the dough in the evening, and let it chill in the fridge overnight. Then the next day, shape, proof, and bake.

MAKES 2 STOLLEN

FOR THE DOUGH

Dough for Sourdough Brioche (page 198), made with butter or vegan butter

Unsalted butter or vegan butter, for greasing

FOR THE SOAKED FRUIT

250 grams mixture of currants, raisins, and dried cherries

90 grams finely chopped candied orange peel

115 grams dark rum or orange juice

FOR THE MARZIPAN

180 grams powdered sugar

150 grams almond flour

1 large egg white

2 teaspoons (8 g) almond extract

¼ teaspoon (1 g) kosher salt

FOR THE MIX-INS

50 grams slivered almonds or pistachios

1 teaspoon (3 g) ground cinnamon

1 teaspoon (3 g) ground cardamom

1 teaspoon (3 g) ground mace or nutmeg

Superfine brown rice flour, for dusting

(Ingredients continue)

Make and proof the dough. Make the sourdough brioche dough as directed, using butter or vegan butter instead of olive oil. Grease a large bowl with a bit of butter and place the dough in it. Cover the bowl with plastic wrap and refrigerate overnight.

Soak the dried fruit. Combine the dried fruit, candied orange peel, and rum in a medium bowl. Let sit at room temperature overnight.

Make the marzipan. In a food processor, combine the powdered sugar and almond flour and pulse a few times to mix. Add the egg white, almond extract, and salt and process until it forms a dough. Transfer to a work surface and knead the dough a few times. It will be sticky but firm. Cut the dough in half and roll into 2 logs about 7 inches (18 cm) long and 1 inch (2.5 cm) in diameter. Wrap them in plastic wrap and store in the fridge overnight. (The marzipan can be made a couple of days in advance and kept in the refrigerator.)

Add the mix-ins to the dough. In the morning, remove the dough from the fridge and place on a lightly floured surface. Flatten the dough to a round that is about 1 inch (2.5 cm) thick. It doesn't matter if it's not perfect. Drain the dried fruit and place on top of the dough along with the almonds, cinnamon, cardamom, and mace. Fold the dough in thirds to encase the mix-ins, then knead together to incorporate them into the dough. The dough will rip and the dried fruit will fall out. That is okay. Reincorporate any fruit that falls

FOR THE EGG WASH

1 large egg

1 teaspoon water

Small pinch of kosher salt

FOR FINISHING

100 grams unsalted butter or vegan butter, melted

240 grams powdered sugar

out. The added moisture from the soaked fruit will make the dough sticky. Dust the dough lightly with brown rice flour, if needed. Knead until the fruit is well mixed in. Use a bench knife to clean your surface if it becomes too messy.

Shape the dough. Line a sheet pan with parchment paper. Cut the dough in half. Set one of the dough pieces aside. Lightly dust a work surface with brown rice flour. Pat down the dough and roll it into an oval that is roughly 8 by 9 inches (20 by 23 cm) and ½ inch (1.3 cm) thick. Unwrap one of the marzipan logs and place it lengthwise down the center of the dough. Take the left side of the dough and fold it over the marzipan. Use the side of your palm or your fingers to press down on the dough to seal the marzipan in. Take the right side of the dough and fold it to where it meets the marzipan log. Again, use the side of your palm or fingers to seal the marzipan in. Pinch the top and bottom of the oval to seal the marzipan in on that side as well. Repeat with the other piece of dough and marzipan. Place both stollen on the prepared sheet pan.

Proof the dough. Wrap the pan in a large plastic bag or loosely cover with plastic wrap. Proof at room temperature until the dough has risen about 25 percent and feels lighter to the touch, 2 to 4 hours. It might not seem like it has risen much, but it will rise in the oven. The length of time will depend on how cold the dough was and your room temperature. I like to proof mine in the oven with the light on and a small pot of boiling-hot water next to it so it's about 80°F (27°C).

Preheat the oven and make the egg wash. Position a rack in the bottom third of the oven and preheat the oven to 375°F (190°C). In a small bowl, lightly whisk the egg, water, and salt.

Bake the stollen. When the dough is ready, brush the top with the egg wash. Bake for 30 to 35 minutes, until golden brown.

Finish the stollen. Let the stollen cool on the pan for 15 minutes. Brush the top of the stollen generously with the melted butter. Place the powdered sugar on a sheet pan and coat all sides of the stollen in it. This will be a bit messy. Make sure the stollen is well coated—this is what will keep it moist for days.

Rest the stollen. When nearly fully cooled, wrap the stollen in plastic wrap and let it rest at room temperature for at least a day and up to 1 week. Slice and serve.

Chestnut and Cranberry Sourdough Batard

Large chunks of roasted chestnuts, sweet cranberries, pumpkin seeds, and flaxseeds give this tender sourdough bread lots of texture. If you can get roasted and peeled whole chestnuts, you can save yourself some time, but if you can't, see How to Roast Whole Chestnuts (page 322). You can also bake this bread in a boule shape.

MAKES 1 BATARD

FOR THE SPONGE

170 grams filtered water, at around 75° to 80°F (24° to 29°C)

150 grams Whole-Grain Brown Rice–Teff Sourdough Starter (page 48)

140 grams sorghum flour or superfine brown rice flour

FOR THE DOUGH

25 grams psyllium husk powder

370 grams filtered water, at around 75° to 80°F (24° to 29°C)

20 grams maple syrup

12 grams extra-virgin olive oil

105 grams sorghum flour, plus more for dusting

90 grams chestnut flour

90 grams tapioca starch

10 grams kosher salt

90 grams roasted and peeled whole chestnuts, cut in half

60 grams dried sweetened cranberries

40 grams pumpkin seeds

20 grams flaxseeds

White rice flour, for dusting

Make the sponge. In a medium bowl, whisk together the water, starter, and sorghum flour until smooth. Cover with a kitchen towel or plate and proof for 3 to 4 hours, until the sponge feels mousse-like when you run a spoon through it.

Make the dough. In a medium bowl, whisk together the psyllium, water, maple syrup, and olive oil until smooth. Let it gel for 5 minutes. In a stand mixer, stir together the sorghum flour, chestnut flour, tapioca starch, and salt. Add the sponge and the psyllium gel. Snap on the dough hook and mix on medium speed until the dough comes together, 3 to 4 minutes. The dough should be moist and hold together nicely. Add the chestnuts, cranberries, pumpkin seeds, and flaxseeds and mix to combine. Dust a work surface with some sorghum flour. Transfer the dough to your work surface and knead it a few times. Shape the dough into a tight ball and then into an oval. Lightly dust an oval banneton with some white rice flour and place the dough in it seam-side up.

Proof the dough. Cover the banneton with plastic wrap and proof at room temperature for 30 minutes. Transfer the banneton to the refrigerator and proof for 12 hours. The dough will rise only about 25 percent, and don't worry if it doesn't seem much lighter. It will rise in the oven.

Preheat the oven. Position a rack in the bottom third of the oven and place a cast-iron Dutch oven on the rack. Preheat the oven to 500°F (260°C). Once the oven has reached temperature, let the Dutch oven continue heating for 15 minutes.

(Recipe continues)

Bake the bread. Cut an 8-inch (20 cm) square piece of parchment paper and place it on a work surface. Invert the dough onto the parchment. Dust the top with a little bit of white rice flour and score the top of the dough. Lift the dough with the parchment into the Dutch oven. Add 2 or 3 ice cubes next to the dough, cover with the lid, and bake for 45 minutes. Remove the lid, reduce the oven temperature to 450°F (230°C), and bake for 15 minutes or until golden brown.

Cool the bread. Place the bread on a wire rack to cool for at least 1 hour before cutting it. Store the bread at room temperature wrapped in a paper bag for up to 2 days.

How to Roast Whole Chestnuts

Place the flat side of a chestnut down on a cutting board. Using a sharp paring knife, cut an X across the rounded side of the chestnut. Try not to score the inner skin, if possible. Repeat with the remaining chestnuts.

Place the cut chestnuts in a large bowl and cover with cold water. Soak the chestnuts for 30 minutes, then drain.

Preheat the oven to 400°F (200°C). Scatter the chestnuts on a sheet pan and bake for 25 to 30 minutes, until the skins pull back and the flesh feels tender. If some chestnuts need a bit more time, let them continue baking until the skins pull back.

As soon as the roasted chestnuts come out of the oven, wrap them in a thick kitchen towel and keep them tightly wrapped for 15 minutes. The steam they release will make them much easier to peel. Once the chestnuts are fully cooled, peel the skin.

Peeled chestnuts can be stored in an airtight container in the refrigerator for up to a week or in the freezer for up to 3 months.

Baklava Babka

FOR THE DOUGH

Dough for Sourdough Brioche (page 198), made with butter or vegan butter

Unsalted butter or vegan butter, for greasing

Tapioca starch, for dusting

FOR THE FILLING

120 grams pistachios

90 grams walnuts

Finely grated zest of 1 lemon

½ teaspoon (2 g) kosher salt

100 grams granulated sugar

2 teaspoons (6 g) ground cinnamon

55 grams unsalted butter or vegan butter, melted and cooled

FOR THE HONEY SYRUP

150 grams honey

100 grams water

¼ teaspoon (1 g) kosher salt

Babka is one of my favorite sweet yeast breads because of how adaptable it is. You can create a multitude of fillings for it and the braiding, although it might seem like it requires perfectionism, is quite forgiving. All babkas, no matter how messy they might seem during the braiding process, turn out beautiful once baked in the pan. This one is filled with pistachios, walnuts, and honey, creating a gooey and sticky interior. Start the process the day before you are going to bake the babka as you will need to create the sweet stiff sponge for the brioche dough in the morning, then make the dough in the evening and chill in the refrigerator overnight. The following morning, fill, proof, and bake your babka. If you are pressed for time, you could make it with the Quickest Buttery Brioche (page 208) instead of the sourdough brioche.

MAKES ONE 9-INCH (23 CM) ROUND BABKA OR 2 LOAVES

Make the dough. Make the brioche dough as directed, using butter or vegan butter instead of olive oil. Grease a large bowl with a bit of butter and place the dough in it. Cover the bowl with plastic wrap and refrigerate for 10 to 20 hours.

Make the filling. In a food processor, combine the pistachios, walnuts, lemon zest, and salt and pulse until you have finely chopped nuts (not fully pulverized but fairly small pieces). Set aside. In a small bowl, stir together the sugar and cinnamon. Set aside.

Prepare the pan. Grease a 9-inch (23 cm) tube pan or Bundt pan with melted butter, olive oil, or pan spray. Cut a round of parchment paper that fits the bottom of the pan and cut a center circle to make room for the tube. (Alternatively, grease two 8½-by-4½-inch/22 by 11 cm loaf pans and line with a strip of parchment paper that hangs over the edges of the pan.)

Fill the babka. Remove the dough from the refrigerator. It won't have risen much. Dust a work surface with some tapioca starch. Transfer the dough onto it and knead a few times to bring back some elasticity. Shape the dough into a ball, flatten it, and roll it into a rectangle roughly 20 by 15 inches (51 by 38 cm) and ¼ inch (6 mm) thick. Make sure you move the dough so it doesn't stick to your surface, and gently stretch the edges to create square corners

as much as possible. I like to run my hands over the surface of the dough to make sure I'm rolling it evenly. Place the dough with a long side facing you. Brush the edge of the long side farthest from you with some water (this will act as glue for when you roll the dough into a log). Brush the remaining dough with the melted butter. Sprinkle the cinnamon sugar all over the dough, then sprinkle the pistachio-walnut mixture so it covers the entire surface except the area brushed with water.

Shape the babka. Starting from the long side closest to you, begin rolling the dough into a log, making sure you keep the seam-side down. Trim off ½ inch (1.3 cm) or so from each end. Cut the dough in half crosswise so you have 2 logs that are roughly 9½ inches (24 cm) long. If your dough feels soft, place the logs on a sheet pan and transfer to the freezer for 10 to 15 minutes to firm up. Cut each log in half lengthwise, leaving the top 1 inch (2.5 cm) uncut. Twist the two halves together, trying to keep the cut sides facing up, and place in the prepared pan. Don't worry if this step feels messy. Transfer the twist as best as you can into one side of the prepared pan (or one of the loaf pans). Collect any of the nuts that spill out and sprinkle them back on top once the babka is in the pan. Repeat with the second log, transferring it to the other side of the pan (or the other loaf pan).

Proof the babka. Cover the pan(s) with a kitchen towel and proof at room temperature until the dough feels slightly lighter, 2 to 4 hours. It won't be significantly larger, but don't worry, it will rise in the oven.

Make the honey syrup. In a deep medium saucepan, combine the honey, water, and salt and cook over high heat until bubbling and reduced by nearly half into a runny and slightly thickened syrup, about 5 minutes. Set aside.

Bake the babka. Position a rack in the bottom third of the oven and preheat the oven to 350°F (180°C). When the babka has proofed, bake for 35 to 40 minutes, until golden brown.

Brush the babka. As soon as the babka comes out of the oven, brush with the honey syrup, getting it into all the crevices.

Cool the babka. Let the babka cool in the pan(s) for 30 minutes. If you baked the babka in a tube pan, run a metal spatula around the edges to release it. Remove the babka from the pan and serve lukewarm or at room temperature. Store the babka at room temperature, tightly wrapped, for up to 3 days.

Chocolate Babka Wreath

PICTURED ON PAGE 303

FOR THE DOUGH

Dough for Quickest Buttery Brioche (page 208)

Tapioca starch, for dusting

FOR THE FILLING

120 grams chocolate (70% cacao), finely chopped

115 grams unsalted butter or vegan butter, at room temperature

30 grams unsweetened cacao powder

60 grams powdered sugar

2 teaspoons (8 g) vanilla paste or extract

FOR THE GLAZE

50 grams granulated sugar

50 grams water

This chocolate babka is made with a less sticky dough than the Baklava Babka (page 323). It uses the Quickest Buttery Brioche dough, but again, you can make it with the Sourdough Brioche (page 198), too. The wreath shape is similar to the baklava babka, but it is baked free-form. It makes a beautiful centerpiece for any holiday gathering.

MAKES 1 WREATH

Make the dough. Make the brioche dough as directed. If you make it with the optional xanthan gum, it will help when twisting the dough. Place the dough in a lightly greased large bowl and cover it with plastic wrap. Proof for 15 minutes, then transfer to the refrigerator and chill for 4 to 12 hours.

Make the filling. About 30 minutes before you are going to shape the babka, combine the chopped chocolate, butter, and cacao powder in a heatproof bowl and place over a pot with simmering water. Stir until everything has melted together and is smooth. Remove the bowl from the heat and whisk in the powdered sugar and vanilla. Set aside for 30 minutes or until it thickens to the consistency of soft ganache.

Assemble the babka. Line a sheet pan with parchment paper. Remove the dough from the refrigerator and knead a few times to deflate it. Cut the dough in half and shape each half into a tight ball. Work with one piece of dough at a time. Lightly dust a work surface with tapioca starch and roll the dough into a rectangle roughly 15 by 11 inches (38 by 28 cm). Move the dough around so it doesn't stick to your surface while you are rolling. Trim any edges that might have ripped slightly. With a long side facing you, spread half of the chocolate filling over the dough leaving a ¼-inch (6 mm) border on all sides. Brush the long side farthest from you where the seam will be with a bit of water to seal it. Starting from a long side, roll the dough into a log and lightly press the edge to seal. Set the log aside making sure it is seam-side down. Repeat the same rolling and filling process with the second piece of dough. Trim about ½ inch (1.3 cm) off each end of the log using a very sharp knife, then cut each log in half lengthwise, making sure you cut all the way through. A clean, sharp cut will ensure clean, sharp layers when you twist the babka. With the cut sides facing up, take two halves of dough and gently twist them to create a two-strand braid. Repeat with the other two strands. Lift the two braids and transfer them to the prepared sheet pan. Shape them into one large circle, resembling a wreath, braiding and pinching the ends together. Don't worry if the dough looks a little messy at this point—it will come together when baking.

Proof the babka. Cover the babka with a kitchen towel and proof until it feels soft to the touch and slightly marshmallow-like, 45 minutes to 1 hour.

Bake the babka. While the babka is proofing, position a rack in the bottom third of the oven and preheat the oven to 350°F (180°C). Bake the babka for 30 minutes, or until golden brown.

Make the glaze. While the babka is in the oven, in a small saucepan, combine the sugar and water and simmer until the sugar is dissolved.

Glaze the babka. As soon as the babka comes out of the oven, glaze the entire surface with the sugar syrup. This will give the surface shine and also help sweeten and preserve the babka. Let it cool for 20 minutes on the pan and serve while it is still warm and soft. The babka is best eaten the same day, but can be kept in the refrigerator tightly wrapped for up to 3 days.

Roscón de Reyes

FOR THE DOUGH

2 teaspoons (8 g) active dry yeast

80 grams granulated sugar

225 grams whole milk or oat milk, heated to 105°F (41°C)

25 grams psyllium husk powder

160 grams potato starch

120 grams tapioca starch, plus more for dusting

70 grams sorghum flour

2 teaspoons (8 g) kosher salt

2 teaspoons (4 g) finely grated orange zest

2 teaspoons (4 g) finely grated lemon zest

40 grams extra-virgin olive oil

2 large eggs, at room temperature

1 teaspoon (4 g) orange flower water (optional)

FOR THE TOPPINGS

1 large egg

Small pinch of kosher salt

25 grams granulated sugar

¼ teaspoon (1 g) orange flower water or water

3 or 4 whole Candied Orange Slices (recipe follows)

20 grams sliced almonds

Roscón de reyes, also known as king cake, is a brioche-style bread served to celebrate Epiphany Day. The dough is scented with orange flower water and decorated with candied fruits and almonds. Most roscones de reyes are filled with whipped cream, but you can also find unfilled ones. The cake is served with coffee at breakfast or as a dessert after a big lunch. Basically, you eat it throughout the day on January 5 and 6. Traditionally, a small token, a dried bean, or a baby Jesus figurine is inserted in the dough before baking and whoever finds it while eating is king or queen for the day. My family's tradition was a bit more cynical and whoever got the token had to do the dishes that day.

MAKES 1 ROSCÓN; SERVES 8 TO 10

Make the yeast-psyllium mixture. In a medium bowl, combine the yeast and 5 grams of the sugar. Add the milk and whisk until dissolved. Let the mixture sit until frothy, about 10 minutes. Whisk in the psyllium vigorously until there are no lumps. Let it gel for 5 minutes.

Make the dough. In a stand mixer, stir together the remaining 75 grams sugar, the potato starch, tapioca starch, sorghum flour, salt, orange zest, and lemon zest. Add the yeast-psyllium mixture. Snap on the dough hook and begin mixing on medium speed. Add the olive oil, eggs, and orange flower water (if using) and continue mixing until the dough comes together and sticks slightly to the bottom of the bowl, 2 to 3 minutes. The dough will be sticky but should hold together nicely and not be too soft.

Proof the dough. Grease a large bowl. Scrape the dough into the bowl and cover it with plastic wrap. Proof the dough for 30 minutes, then transfer it to the refrigerator to chill for 4 to 12 hours. If you don't want to chill the dough and make it right away, proof the dough until nearly doubled, about 45 minutes. It will be soft and harder to shape but will work well.

Shape the roscón. Line a sheet pan with parchment paper. Dust a work surface with a little bit of tapioca starch, if needed. Remove the dough from the refrigerator and transfer to the work surface. The dough will have risen and cracked slightly. That's normal. Knead it a

FOR THE FILLING

450 grams heavy cream or vegan whipping cream

25 grams granulated sugar

2 teaspoons (8 g) vanilla extract

few times to deflate it and bring back elasticity. Shape the dough into a tight ball. Using your fingers or the end of a wooden spoon dipped in tapioca starch, make a hole in the center of the dough and use your fingers to stretch it. Shape the dough into an oval ring that is roughly 9 inches (23 cm) long and 8 inches (20 cm) wide. The center hole should be about 6 inches (15 cm) in diameter. You don't have to be super precise with the measurements. Gently transfer the dough to the lined sheet pan. Reshape into an oval if needed.

Preheat the oven. Position a rack in the bottom third of the oven and preheat the oven to 375°F (190°C).

Proof the roscón. Cover the pan with a kitchen towel and proof until the dough feels soft and marshmallow-like to the touch, 40 to 45 minutes. If you didn't refrigerate it, reduce the proofing time to 30 minutes.

Prepare the toppings. While the dough is proofing, in a small bowl, whisk together the egg and salt for an egg wash. In another small bowl, stir together the sugar and orange flower water until you have a sandy mixture. Cut the candied orange slices in half. Weigh out the sliced almonds.

Bake the roscón. When the roscón has proofed, brush the entire surface with the egg wash. Top with the candied oranges and sliced almonds and sprinkle with the orange flower–sugar mixture. Bake for 25 to 30 minutes, until lightly golden brown.

Cool the roscón. Transfer the roscón to a wire rack to cool completely, then using a serrated knife, cut it in half horizontally.

Make the filling. In a stand mixer fitted with the whisk (or by hand), combine the heavy cream, sugar, and vanilla and whip until you have soft peaks. Fit a large pastry bag with a star tip and fill with the whipped cream. Pipe rosettes of cream onto the bottom half of the roscón. If you don't have a pastry bag, simply spread the whipped cream with a spoon or spatula. Top with the other roscón half and serve immediately. It is best eaten right away while the roscón is tender and soft, but can be assembled and kept in the refrigerator for a few hours before serving.

Candied Orange Slices

1 medium navel orange, thinly sliced

450 grams water

175 grams granulated sugar

MAKES ABOUT 8 TO 10 SLICES

Bring a small pot of water to a boil. Add the orange slices, boil them for 30 seconds, and drain. Repeat this process two more times. This will remove any bitterness from the oranges and soften them.

Line a sheet pan with parchment paper and set it near the stove. In a medium saucepan, combine the water and the sugar and bring to a boil over medium-high heat. When the mixture comes to a boil and the sugar is dissolved, add the orange slices and continue cooking until the sugar syrup reaches 230°F (110°C). Use a candy thermometer for this. The syrup will have thickened.

Transfer the candied orange slices to the lined sheet pan and let them cool completely. Be careful not to burn yourself with the sugar. Store the candied orange slices in an airtight container for up to 5 days.

Sufganiyot (Cream and Jelly Doughnuts)

FOR THE DOUGH

Dough for Quickest Buttery Brioche (page 208)

Tapioca starch, for dusting

TO FINISH

Vegetable oil, for frying (about 1 gallon/3.8 L, depending on pot)

Granulated sugar, for rolling

Powdered sugar, for dusting

FOR THE CREAM FILLING

Pastry Cream (page 215)

300 grams raspberry jelly

Sufganiyot are Israeli doughnuts that are beloved all around the world and eaten during Hannukah. They're made with brioche dough, fried in oil, coated in sugar, and filled with jelly. For this recipe, I added a bit of custard to go along with the jelly. If you want to make a sourdough version, use the Sourdough Brioche dough (page 198).

MAKES 16 DOUGHNUTS

Prep the parchment. Cut sixteen 3-inch (7.5 cm) squares of parchment paper and divide them between two sheet pans.

Make the dough. Make the brioche dough as directed.

Shape the doughnuts. Dust a work surface with a small amount of tapioca starch and roll the dough into a rectangle that is ½ to ¾ inch (1.3 to 2 cm) thick. Using a 2½-inch (6 cm) round cookie cutter, cut out dough rounds as close to each other as possible to maximize surface area. Place each round of dough on a piece of parchment paper. Once you are done cutting all the dough, you can lightly knead the scraps again, roll, and cut until you have cut all the dough. You should have 16 rounds.

Proof the doughnuts. Loosely cover the pans with plastic wrap or wrap in large plastic bag. Proof the dough until it feels light to the touch and marshmallow-like, 40 to 45 minutes.

Heat the oil. While the doughnuts are proofing, pour 4 inches (10 cm) vegetable oil into a pot that is about 6 inches (15 cm) deep (I use a Dutch oven for this). Set over medium-high heat and clip on a deep-fry thermometer to keep track of the temperature. Place a wire rack over a sheet pan and line the rack with paper towels. Fill a medium bowl with granulated sugar. Set both near the stove.

Fry the doughnuts. When the oil has reached 350°F (180°C) and the dough is done proofing, work in batches of about 4 doughnuts (or however many will fit in your pot without crowding). Carefully lift each piece of parchment with the dough on it and invert it into the oil. Peel off the parchment. Be careful not to touch the hot oil with your fingers or to splash oil by dropping the dough in from too high up. Cook the dough until golden brown, 2 to 3 minutes, then flip over and cook for 2 to 3 minutes more. Using a perforated spatula or spider, scoop the doughnuts out of the oil and onto the paper towels. Let the doughnuts cool for 5 minutes, then roll them in the bowl with sugar to coat all sides.

Fill the doughnuts. Fit 2 pastry bags with medium plain tips. Fill one bag with the chilled cream and the other with the raspberry jelly. Pick up a doughnut in one hand and the pastry bag in the other. Make a small indentation on the side of the doughnut with the pastry tip and fill with jelly and then add some cream. Dust the doughnuts with powdered sugar and serve. They are best eaten the same day while slightly warm.

Marzipan-Filled Semlor

PICTURED ON PAGES 300–301

A semla is a cream-filled and cardamom-scented sweet bun traditional in Scandinavian countries that is very popular during Lent and Fat Tuesday celebrations. After the buns are baked, a little triangle is cut out of each bun. The crumb is hollowed out to fill with marzipan cream and topped with a nice rosette of whipped cream. The little triangle is placed back on top of the cream and the entire thing is dusted with powdered sugar. Make sure you are using freshly ground cardamom pods and not store-bought preground cardamom. It makes a big difference.

MAKES 8 SEMLOR

FOR THE DOUGH

2¼ teaspoons (10 g) active dry yeast

80 grams granulated sugar

280 grams whole milk or oat milk, heated to 105°F (41°C)

20 grams psyllium husk powder

120 grams potato starch

105 grams sweet white rice flour

90 grams tapioca starch

50 grams sorghum flour

2 teaspoons (8 g) kosher salt

1 teaspoon (2 g) cardamom seeds, finely ground

1 large egg, at room temperature

55 grams soft (but not melted) unsalted butter or vegan butter, plus more for greasing

FOR THE EGG WASH

1 large egg, lightly beaten

FOR THE MARZIPAN FILLING

100 grams almond flour

35 grams granulated sugar

1 teaspoon (4 g) almond extract

¼ teaspoon (1 g) kosher salt

70 grams whole milk or oat milk

Make the yeast-psyllium mixture. In a medium bowl, combine the yeast and 5 grams of the sugar. Pour in the milk and whisk until the yeast is dissolved. Let the mixture sit until frothy, about 10 minutes. Whisk in the psyllium vigorously until dissolved. Let it gel for 5 minutes.

Make and proof the dough. In a stand mixer, stir together the remaining 75 grams sugar, the potato starch, sweet white rice flour, tapioca starch, sorghum flour, salt, and cardamom. Add the yeast-psyllium mixture. Snap on the dough hook and begin mixing the dough on medium speed. Add the egg while the mixer is running and continue mixing for 2 minutes. Add the soft butter 1 tablespoon at a time and continue mixing for 2 to 3 minutes more, scraping down the bowl as necessary, until the dough comes together and begins to stick to the sides of the bowl. Grease the inside of a large bowl with some butter. Scrape the dough out of the mixer and shape it into a ball. Place it in the greased bowl, cover with a kitchen towel, and proof until doubled in size, 45 minutes to 1 hour.

Shape the dough. Line a sheet pan with parchment paper. Transfer the dough to a work surface and knead it a few times to deflate it and bring back elasticity. Cut the dough into 8 equal pieces (about 105 g each). Shape each piece of dough into a tight ball and place on the lined sheet pan, leaving 3 inches (7.5 cm) between them. Cover with a kitchen towel and proof until nearly doubled, 30 to 45 minutes.

Preheat the oven. Position a rack in the bottom third of the oven and preheat the oven to 375°F (190°C).

FOR THE CREAM FILLING

225 grams heavy cream, canned full-fat coconut cream, or vegan whipping cream

10 grams powdered sugar, plus more for dusting

1 teaspoon (4 g) vanilla paste or extract

Bake the dough. Brush the dough with the egg wash. Bake for 20 to 22 minutes, until golden brown. Transfer the buns to a wire rack to cool completely before filling or the cream will melt.

Prep the buns. Cut a circular or triangular lid off the top of each bun. Scoop the inside crumb (using your fingertips or a small spoon), leaving about ¼ inch (6 mm) of the bun wall intact. Set aside the crumbs.

Make the marzipan filling. In a food processor, combine the almond flour, sugar, almond extract, salt, and crumbs from the insides of the buns and process until the mixture starts to form a paste. Add the milk and process until smooth. The filling should be spreadable and creamy but not too soft or liquid. Add more milk if needed. Transfer the filling to a pastry bag fitted with a medium round tip.

Make the cream filling. In a stand mixer fitted with the whisk, combine the heavy cream, powdered sugar, and vanilla and whip to stiff peaks on medium-high speed. (You can also do this by hand with some elbow power.)

Assemble the semlor. Pipe the marzipan filling inside each bun until it reaches the top. Transfer the whipped cream to a pastry bag fitted with a star tip and pipe a large rosette of cream on top of the marzipan filling. Top with the lid and dust with powdered sugar. Serve immediately. They are best eaten the same day.

Challah

Challah is a traditional enriched and braided bread that is served for Shabbat and other Jewish holidays. I've made many versions of challah over the years, some milky and some slightly sweeter. This updated challah recipe is lighter and less brioche-like, which is the way I prefer it. The trick for getting the extra shine on the challah is to brush the dough with the egg wash twice: once while proofing and then again before putting it in the oven.

MAKES 1 CHALLAH; SERVES 8

FOR THE SPONGE

140 grams sorghum flour

2 teaspoons (8 g) active dry yeast

225 grams water, heated to 105°F (41°C)

FOR THE DOUGH

145 grams water, at room temperature

30 grams psyllium husk powder

160 grams potato starch

120 grams tapioca starch, plus more for dusting

75 grams granulated sugar

70 grams sweet white rice flour

2½ teaspoons (10 g) kosher salt

55 grams extra-virgin olive oil, grapeseed oil, or another vegetable oil, plus more for greasing

2 large eggs, at room temperature

FOR THE EGG WASH AND TOPPING

1 large egg

Pinch of salt

Sesame seeds (optional)

Make the sponge. In a medium bowl, whisk together the sorghum flour and yeast. Whisk in the water. Cover the bowl with a kitchen towel and proof until the sponge puffs up and has a mousse-like texture, 45 minutes to 1 hour.

Make the gelled sponge. Whisk the 145 grams water into the sponge until smooth. Then vigorously whisk in the psyllium until you have a thick gel. The mixture will set quickly, so don't wait.

Make the dough: In a stand mixer, stir together the potato starch, tapioca starch, sugar, sweet white rice flour, and salt. Add the gelled sponge. Snap on the dough hook and begin to mix on medium speed. Add the olive oil and eggs and continue mixing for 3 to 4 minutes, until the dough comes together. The dough will be moist and sticky, but will hold together nicely. Add a tablespoon of water if the dough seems dry or a touch of flour if it seems a bit too sticky.

Chill the dough. Grease a large bowl with some olive oil. Scrape in the dough, cover the bowl tightly with plastic wrap, and refrigerate for 4 to 12 hours.

Braid the dough. Lightly dust a work surface with tapioca starch. Knead the dough a few times to deflate it and bring back elasticity. Divide the dough into 4 equal pieces (about 250 g each). Knead each piece of dough a few times to make it smooth and shape into a tight ball. Roll each piece of dough into a strand that is roughly 14 inches (35 cm) long and has tapered ends. Dust the surface with more tapioca starch if needed. Arrange the strands of dough vertically in front of you and pinch the top ends together. Take the topmost left strand, place it on the opposite side, and weave the third strand over it. Reposition the strands, separating the left strand from the

other three. Take the left strand and bring it to the right, weaving the third strand over it. Repeat until all the strands are braided. Pinch the ends together and tuck them underneath the dough. If you are having a tough time braiding the dough and need to start over, don't worry. You can knead the dough back together and start again.

Make the egg wash. In a small bowl, whisk the egg and salt together.

Proof the braided challah. Line a sheet pan with parchment paper and place the braided challah on it. Brush the challah with the egg wash. I like to create a little proofing vessel for the challah (see Note) to support it, but you can skip this step and simply let the challah proof as is. Cover loosely with a kitchen towel and proof at room temperature until nearly doubled and the dough feels marshmallow-like, about 45 minutes.

Preheat the oven. Position a rack in the bottom third of the oven and preheat the oven to 400°F (200°C).

Bake the challah. Brush the top of the challah with a second layer of the egg wash. Sprinkle with sesame seeds, if desired. Bake for 25 to 30 minutes, until golden brown.

Cool the challah. Transfer the challah to a wire rack to cool for at least 30 minutes before cutting into it. It is best eaten the same day.

Note: To make a proofing vessel for the challah, fold the long edges of the parchment paper until you get close to the challah. Pinch the ends of the parchment paper and tie them with some string. Adjust the parchment so the dough has even support around it, yet with enough space to rise. This step is optional but helps the challah rise better.

VARIATIONS

Vegan Challah

Increase the water in the dough to 250 grams. (Leave the sponge as is.) Replace the white rice flour with millet flour. Add 2 teaspoons (8 g) baking powder to the dry ingredients in the dough. Since the dough is quite pale, you can add ¼ teaspoon (1 g) ground turmeric to enhance the color. Omit the eggs. Brush the top of the dough with 20 grams maple syrup before baking. Bake at 400°F (200°C) for 35 to

40 minutes. When the challah comes out of the oven, brush the top with 20 grams extra-virgin olive oil to add shine and soften the crust.

Four-Braid Challah Crown

Cut the dough into 4 equal pieces. Dust a work surface with tapioca starch and roll each piece into a strand 14 inches (35 cm) long. Lay two strands next to each other vertically. Weave one of the remaining strands horizontally under the center of the first vertical one and then over the second vertical one. Weave the remaining strand horizontally under the center of the first vertical one and then over the second vertical one. Push all the strands tightly together in the middle and separate the ends so you'll have room to start weaving.

Place the lower left vertical strand over the strand next to it on the right. Repeat around the circle, going counterclockwise. Now, do the same thing starting with the lower right vertical strand, placing the strand over its neighbor on the left, going around the circle clockwise. Repeat this pattern until you have braided all the strands and you have a crown-like challah. Tuck in the ends under the dough.

Place a 9- or 10-inch (23 to 25 cm) springform ring or cake ring around the dough. This will help the dough rise upward in the oven versus spreading more to the sides. Proof and bake as directed.

Three-Braid Loaf

Grease an 8½-by-4½-inch (22 by 11 cm) loaf pan with olive oil.

Cut the dough into 3 equal pieces (about 330 g each) and roll each piece into a strand that is 12 inches (30 cm) long and about 1½ inches (4 cm) thick. Braid the strands together and place in the prepared loaf pan. Proof and bake as directed, but add 5 to 10 minutes to the baking time. Tent the pan with foil if the top becomes too dark during baking. Let the challah cool in the pan for 15 minutes, then invert onto a wire rack to cool completely.

Hamburger Buns

Cut the dough into 8 equal pieces (about 130 g each). Knead each piece of dough a few times and shape into a tight ball. Proof as directed, then brush the tops with the egg wash and sprinkle with sesame seeds. Bake for 22 to 25 minutes, until golden brown.

Tahini-Marzipan Challah

FOR THE DOUGH

Dough for Challah (page 336)

1 teaspoon (4 g) xanthan gum (optional)

Olive oil, for greasing

Tapioca starch, for dusting

FOR THE TAHINI-MARZIPAN FILLING

120 grams powdered sugar

100 grams almond flour

½ teaspoon (2 g) kosher salt

100 grams well-stirred tahini

1 large egg white

25 to 50 grams freshly squeezed orange juice

2 teaspoons (8 g) almond extract

¼ teaspoon (1 g) ground cinnamon

FOR THE EGG WASH AND TOPPING

1 large egg, lightly beaten

Pinch of kosher salt

25 grams sesame seeds

This idea of stuffing challah came from Uri Scheft's book *Breaking Breads*. When I read that Uri fills his challah dough with a marzipan and butter mixture, I thought, "Why not use tahini?!" The xanthan gum is listed as optional, but it does help with lamination. If using, you might need to add a tablespoon of water to the dough.

MAKES 2 MEDIUM BRAIDED CHALLAH

Make the dough. Make the challah dough as directed, preferably adding the optional xanthan gum to the dry ingredients. If the dough feels dry, add 10 to 15 grams more water to the dough. Grease a large bowl with some olive oil. Place the dough in it. Cover the bowl tightly with plastic wrap and chill in the refrigerator for 4 to 12 hours.

Make the tahini-marzipan filling. In a food processor, combine the powdered sugar, almond flour, and salt and pulse a few times to aerate. Add the tahini, egg white, 25 grams orange juice, the almond extract, and the cinnamon and process until you have a sticky, thick spreadable paste. If your filling is too stiff to spread, add a touch more orange juice. (The filling makes more than you need; see Notes.)

Fill the challah. Line a sheet pan with parchment paper. Lightly dust a work surface with some tapioca starch. Place the chilled dough on the work surface and knead a few times to deflate it and bring back elasticity. Cut the dough in half (about 565 g per piece). Tightly wrap one portion in plastic wrap and chill it in the refrigerator while shaping the first challah. Cut the other portion into 3 equal pieces (about 185 g each). Shape the pieces of dough into tight balls and then roll each one into an oval that is roughly 7 by 5 inches (18 by 13 cm). Spread 2 to 3 tablespoons of filling over the dough, leaving a ½-inch (1.3 cm) border all around. Starting from a long side, roll the dough into a log. Roll the log into a 14-inch (35 cm) rope with a thick center and tapered ends. If the dough feels sticky, lightly dust it with tapioca starch while rolling. Set the log aside and repeat with the remaining 2 pieces of dough.

Braid the challah. Place the 3 filled strands in front of you vertically. Braid the strands and pinch the ends together. Transfer the braided challah onto the prepared sheet pan. Repeat the entire process of filling and shaping with the second portion of dough.

(Recipe continues)

Make the egg wash. In a small bowl, whisk together the egg and salt. Brush the challah with half of the egg wash.

Proof the challah. I like to create a little proofing vessel for the challah (see Notes), but you can skip this step and simply let the challah proof as is, sitting on top of the parchment. Cover both challahs with a kitchen towel or plastic wrap and proof until nearly doubled, 40 to 45 minutes at room temperature.

Preheat the oven. Position a rack in the bottom third of the oven and preheat the oven to 375°F (190°C).

Bake the challah. Brush the challah with the remaining half of the egg wash. Sprinkle the sesame seeds on top. Bake the challah for 30 minutes, or until golden brown.

Cool the challah. Let the challah cool on the pan for 10 minutes, then remove the parchment paper and cool for 20 minutes more before slicing. Serve warm. The challah is best eaten the same day.

Notes: To make a proofing vessel for the challah, fold the long edges of the parchment paper until you get close to the challah. Pinch the ends of the parchment paper and tie them with some string. Adjust the parchment so the dough has even support around it yet enough space to rise. This step is optional but helps the challah rise better.

The leftover filling makes delicious Bostock French toast. To make it, spread the filling over a slice of old challah or brioche and bake at 350°F (180°C) for 15 to 20 minutes, until set and golden brown. Top with fresh fruit and powdered sugar.

Spinach and Feta Pull-Apart Challah

A spinach-feta filling keeps this challah moist for a couple of days. Serve it as a centerpiece for your holiday meals.

SERVES 8

FOR THE DOUGH

Dough for Challah (page 336)

Tapioca starch, for dusting

Olive oil, for greasing

FOR THE SPINACH-FETA FILLING

300 grams frozen spinach, thawed and squeezed dry

110 grams feta cheese, drained

1 large egg

1 teaspoon (2 g) finely grated lemon zest

1 teaspoon (4 g) fresh lemon juice

1 teaspoon (2 g) dried oregano

½ teaspoon (2 g) garlic powder

FOR THE EGG WASH AND TOPPING

1 large egg, lightly beaten

2 tablespoons (25 g) grated Parmesan cheese

Flaky sea salt

Make the dough. Make the challah dough as directed. Grease a large bowl with some olive oil. Place the dough in it. Cover the bowl tightly with plastic wrap and chill it in the refrigerator for 4 to 10 hours.

Make the spinach-feta filling. In a food processor, combine the spinach, feta, egg, lemon zest, lemon juice, oregano, and garlic and pulse until it becomes a spreadable paste. Set aside.

Roll and fill the challah. The chilled dough should have risen slightly in the fridge. Line a sheet pan with parchment paper. Lightly dust a work surface with tapioca starch and knead the chilled dough to deflate it. Roll the dough into a roughly 12-inch (30 cm) square. Spread the filling over the dough to the edges. Roll the dough gently and seal the bottom seam. Transfer the challah to the prepared pan.

Cut the challah. Hold a sharp pair of kitchen scissors at a 45-degree angle and make deep cuts into the log (cut almost all the way to the bottom but leave about 1 inch/2.5 cm uncut). Make cuts at even intervals (about every 2 inches/5 cm), alternating sides. Pull the cuts outward in opposite directions to reveal the spiral inside.

Proof the challah. Brush the surface of the challah with half of the beaten egg. Cover the challah with a kitchen towel and proof until it feels light and marshmallow-like, 40 to 45 minutes.

Preheat the oven. Position a rack in the bottom third of the oven and preheat the oven to 350°F (180°C).

Bake the challah. Brush the entire surface of the dough with the remaining beaten egg. Sprinkle the top with Parmesan and flaky salt. Bake for 25 to 30 minutes, until golden brown.

Cool the challah. Let the challah cool on the pan for 20 to 30 minutes, then serve warm. It is best eaten the same day, but you can store it tightly wrapped for up to 3 days.

Challah French Toast

6 large eggs

340 grams half-and-half or canned full-fat coconut milk

20 grams maple syrup, plus more for serving

1 teaspoon (4 g) vanilla extract

1 teaspoon (2 g) finely grated orange zest

½ teaspoon (2 g) kosher salt

6 (¾-inch/2 cm) slices day-old Challah (page 336)

Unsalted butter or vegan butter, plus more for serving

Making French toast is a good way to use up any day-old bread, especially challah. I make this recipe for holiday brunches or slow weekend mornings.

MAKES 6 TOASTS

Soak the bread. In a large shallow bowl, whisk together the eggs, half-and-half, maple syrup, vanilla, orange zest, and salt until smooth. Soak as many challah slices as you can in the custard on each side until drenched but not soggy (if it's too soggy the bread could fall apart), 3 to 5 minutes.

Cook the French toast. Heat a large nonstick skillet over medium heat. Melt 2 tablespoons butter in the skillet and add the challah pieces without crowding the pan. Cook for 2 minutes on each side, adjusting the heat if needed (make sure they are not browning too quickly). Cook the remaining challah slices, adding more butter for each batch. Serve immediately with more butter and maple syrup.

Sourdough Panettone

FOR THE SWEET STIFF SPONGE

110 grams Whole-Grain Brown Rice–Teff Sourdough Starter (page 48)

60 grams filtered water, heated to 80°F (27°C)

30 grams granulated sugar

55 grams superfine brown rice flour

55 grams sorghum flour

FOR THE DOUGH

30 grams psyllium husk powder

150 grams whole milk or oat milk, heated to 80°F (27°C)

150 grams filtered water, heated to 80°F (27°C)

320 grams potato starch

150 grams tapioca starch, plus more for dusting

105 grams sweet white rice flour

Panettone is the ultimate Christmastime bread in my eye: pillowy sweet crumb with strands that pull apart, studded with liqueur-soaked candied fruit. It's a dough that can be intimidating to tackle but incredibly rewarding when accomplished. Traditional gluten-containing panettone has the tender crumb of a brioche with the pull and strands of a very hydrated and long-fermented dough. Traditional panettone is made with a very stiff sourdough starter called lievito madre that is fermented over the course of several days and incorporated into a high-hydration and enriched dough in stages. Because there is no gluten in this recipe, the crumb in the panettone is spongier with less pulling strands, but it is tender and soft.

This recipe makes a lot of dough. If you have a stand mixer on the smaller side, use a paddle attachment to mix in the butter, as a small dough hook might not get everything mixed evenly. I like to use a 7-inch (18 cm) panettone paper mold for this, but you can make two smaller ones (5 inches/13 cm). Because of its high hydration, the panettone must be hung upside down after it comes out of the oven. This ensures that the crumb dries out and doesn't collapse under its own weight.

MAKES 1 LARGE OR 2 SMALL PANETTONE

Make the sweet stiff sponge. In a medium bowl, stir together the starter, water, and sugar until dissolved. Add the brown rice flour and sorghum flour and stir until it forms a dough. It should be moist and slightly soft. Knead it several times until it is smooth. Transfer

Panettone Schedule

This recipe takes nearly 3 days to complete because each step of fermentation takes a long time, but the process itself is fairly easy. Here is my preferred schedule:

Day 1 morning: Feed the sourdough starter if it's not very active.

Day 1 evening: Mix the sweet stiff starter and ferment overnight.

Day 2 morning: Mix the dough. Soak the dried fruit.

Day 3 morning: Mix the soaked fruit into the dough. Proof and bake the panettone.

- 75 grams granulated sugar
- 2 teaspoons (8 g) baking powder
- 2 teaspoons (8 g) kosher salt
- 2 teaspoons (8 g) xanthan gum
- 2 teaspoons (4 g) finely grated orange zest
- 2 teaspoons (4 g) finely grated lemon zest
- 2 teaspoons (8 g) vanilla paste or extract
- 40 grams honey
- 3 large eggs, at room temperature
- 2 large egg yolks, at room temperature
- 150 grams very soft unsalted butter or vegan butter, cut into 1-inch (2.5 cm) pieces

FOR THE SOAKED FRUIT

- 150 grams raisins
- 70 grams chopped candied orange peel
- 35 grams chopped candied lemon peel
- 15 grams freshly squeezed orange juice
- 15 grams dark rum or brandy
- 1 teaspoon (2 g) finely grated orange zest

FOR THE EGG WASH

- 1 large egg
- 1 tablespoon water
- 1 tablespoon (12 g) cold unsalted butter or vegan butter
- Pearl sugar (optional)

the sponge to a 12-ounce (340 ml) mason jar or container and cover with a lid. Let it proof for 8 to 10 hours at around 75° to 85°F (24° to 29°C). If your room temperature is cool, place it in the oven with the light on and a small pot of boiling-hot water next to it. The sponge won't rise much because there isn't much water in it, but you should see some small bubbles and some expansion.

Make the dough. Sprinkle the psyllium into a medium bowl. Add the milk and water and whisk vigorously until smooth. Let it gel for 5 minutes. In a stand mixer, stir together the potato starch, tapioca starch, white rice flour, sugar, baking powder, salt, and xanthan gum. Add the sponge, psyllium gel, orange zest, lemon zest, and vanilla. Snap on the dough hook and begin mixing on medium-low speed. Add the honey, eggs, and egg yolks and continue mixing until you have a nice stiff dough, 2 to 3 minutes. Add the butter, one piece at a time, and continue mixing until you have a very sticky dough that almost feels like thick cake batter, 2 to 3 minutes.

Proof the dough. Grease a large bowl and scrape the batter into it. Smooth out the top slightly. Cover the bowl with plastic wrap and let it proof for 1 hour at room temperature, then transfer to the refrigerator for 10 to 20 hours.

Make the soaked fruit. In a medium bowl, toss together the raisins, candied orange peel, candied lemon peel, orange juice, rum, and orange zest. Cover the bowl and let the fruit soak at room temperature while the dough rests in the refrigerator.

Add the soaked fruit to the dough. Remove the dough from the refrigerator and place it in the stand mixer. The dough won't appear to have risen much and by now it will feel sticky but firmer. Snap on the dough hook, add the soaked fruit, and mix until thoroughly incorporated, about 1 minute.

Shape the panettone. Generously dust a work surface with tapioca starch. Transfer the dough to it and dust the top with tapioca starch. Knead the dough together a few times and shape into a tight ball. Place the dough inside a 7-inch (18 cm) paper panettone mold. Cover with a kitchen towel or plastic wrap and proof, preferably at around 75° to 85°F (24° to 29°C), until the dough has risen approximately 50 percent, 4 to 6 hours. If your room temperature is cool, place the mold in the oven with the light on and a small pot of boiling-hot water next to it.

(Recipe continues)

PALLARES
SOLSONA

Preheat the oven. If you proofed the dough in the oven, remove it. Position a rack in the lowest position and preheat the oven to 400°F (200°C). The panettone needs enough room in the oven to rise and not burn.

Make the egg wash. In a small bowl, whisk together the egg and water. When the panettone is ready, brush the top with the egg wash. Using a sharp paring knife or lame, cut 2 slashes 4 inches (10 cm) long in a cross shape in the center top of the panettone. Place the butter on top of the cross and sprinkle with pearl sugar, if desired.

Bake the panettone. Carefully place the mold on a sheet pan and transfer to the oven. Bake for 15 minutes. Reduce the oven temperature to 350°F (180°C) and bake until an instant-read thermometer inserted in the center reads about 190°F (88°C), about 1 hour. Tent the panettone with aluminum foil in the last 20 minutes of baking if the top is getting too brown.

Hang the panettone upside down. Get 2 large flour containers or mason jars set up on your kitchen counter. As soon as the panettone comes out of the oven, pierce 2 long wooden or metal skewers, in parallel, through the bottom of the mold. Turn the panettone upside down and rest the skewers on top of the jars so the panettone sits suspended upside down. Let the panettone cool completely, 1 to 2 hours, before turning it right-side up or cutting into it. Store it tightly wrapped in plastic so it retains its moisture for up to 2 days. After that, it is best toasted.

No. 8

Sandwiches, Soups, Salads, and a Hunk of Bread

Muhammara

It is rare for me to plan a sandwich. Usually I just raid my refrigerator in ravenous urgency and throw whatever I find together. *But*, I do think about balance. The perfect sandwich must have, first and foremost, incredible bread. What is its texture? Is it supposed to be soft so the filling and the bread can become one? Perhaps a juicy filling requires sturdy bread? And then there is dressing. This is where I make decisions on acidity and sweetness and what is going to complement both the bread and the filling. All these thoughts cross my mind when I craft the recipes I eat with bread. The Mediterranean Artichoke and Spinach Omelet Sandwiches (page 378) or the Melty Beet and Sauerkraut Reubens (page 381) are probably on heaviest rotation in my house.

Your homemade breads are also the perfect canvas for dips, such as Olive and Herb Dipping Oil (page 361), and spreads like Muhammara (page 365) and Roasted Cauliflower Hummus with Fried Chickpeas (page 367). Enjoy them with salads like the Fattoush with Fried Pita and Labneh (page 371) or Roasted Delicata Squash, Apple, and Bread Salad with Almond Aioli (page 372), and soup like the Caramelized Carrot, Sourdough, and Miso Soup (page 377). All of these recipes highlight and complement bread.

Olive and Herb Dipping Oil

½ cup (70 g) pitted mixed Kalamata, Niçoise, and green olives, finely chopped

1 medium garlic clove, peeled

2 tablespoons finely chopped shallots

2 tablespoons finely chopped fresh Italian parsley

½ teaspoon finely chopped preserved lemon or finely grated lemon zest

½ teaspoon dried oregano

½ teaspoon dried thyme

½ teaspoon kosher salt

⅛ teaspoon red pepper flakes

½ cup (100 g) extra-virgin olive oil

1 tablespoon (12 g) balsamic vinegar

Chive blossoms (optional)

The one thing that always goes with bread is olive and herb dipping oil. It's the simplest thing you can make, but it really makes eating warm, freshly baked bread even better.

MAKES A SCANT 1 CUP (240 G)

Put the finely chopped olives into a medium bowl. Using a Microplane, finely grate the garlic into the bowl. Stir in the shallots, parsley, preserved lemon, oregano, thyme, salt, and pepper flakes. In a small bowl, whisk together the olive oil and balsamic and pour over the olives. Stir everything together, top with chive blossoms (if using), and serve. Store the mixture in an airtight container in the refrigerator for up to 2 weeks. The oil will solidify in the fridge, so let it come to room temperature and stir before serving.

Lemon and Vanilla Bean Marmalade

2 pounds (900 g) lemons, washed and button where stem attaches removed

2 teaspoons (8 g) kosher salt

2½ pounds (1.14 kg) granulated sugar

2 vanilla beans, split lengthwise

Living in northern latitudes means short winter days and lots of darkness. The arrival of citrus on the supermarket shelves and the citrus-filled care packages that arrive from friends in warm climates light up my days. I clear my calendar on a Sunday afternoon to dedicate myself to marmalade making.

I like my marmalade a little bit jammy. I cook it somewhere around 218°F (103°C). Many recipes suggest cooking it to 220°F (105°C), but I find that yields a firmer marmalade. This recipe uses the whole-fruit method where the lemons are cooked intact, then thinly sliced.

MAKES ABOUT SEVEN 8-OUNCE (225 ML) JARS

Place 2 small plates in the freezer, which you will later use to test if the marmalade has set.

Place the lemons in a pot large enough to hold them all. Add the salt and cold water to cover the lemons (about 2½ quarts/2.36 L). Bring to a simmer over high heat. Reduce the heat to a gentle simmer, cover the pot, and cook the lemons until they are very tender, 1½ to 2 hours, depending on the thickness of the skin. The lemons will shrink while cooking. You want to be able to pierce the skin without much effort. As the lemons cook, they release natural pectin so you will see how the water changes color and slightly thickens.

Using a slotted spoon, transfer the whole lemons to a large bowl. Measure the remaining cooking liquid. You should have about 1½ quarts (1.4 L). If you have more than that, cook the poaching liquid over high heat to reduce it. It's okay if you have a little bit more than 1½ quarts, but be as close to it as possible.

Lay a large piece of cheesecloth or muslin fabric in a small bowl next to you. When the lemons are cool enough to handle, cut them in half lengthwise. Spoon out all the flesh and seeds from the lemons and place them in the bowl with the cheesecloth. Tie the ends of the cloth to create a sachet. This is where much of your natural pectin is, so don't discard any of those thick juices. Cut the lemon rinds into very thin strips. Collect any of the juices that are at the bottom of the bowl where the cooked lemons were resting.

Add the sugar, lemon strips, cheesecloth sachet, and any of the reserved juices to the pot with the poaching liquid. Scrape the vanilla seeds in and add the pods, too. Cook over high heat for 25 to 30 minutes, stirring occasionally with a wooden spoon to make sure the sugar doesn't burn at the bottom of the pan and using the back of the spoon to squeeze the sachet with the seeds so all the pectin inside goes into the marmalade, until a candy or instant-read thermometer reaches 218° to 220°F (103° to 105°C). As the marmalade cooks, the sugar syrup and the lemon pieces will turn into a deeper color—almost orange. The marmalade will thicken, but it might still look loose and not thick enough. Don't worry about the thickness in the pot as it will set once it cools.

Test the setting point by dropping a little marmalade onto a chilled plate, allowing it to cool for 1 minute, then pushing it gently with your finger. If the marmalade wrinkles, the setting point has been reached; if not, continue to boil and check again in a few minutes on the second plate.

When the desired consistency is reached, remove the pot from the heat and allow the marmalade to rest in the pot for 10 minutes. When the syrup in the marmalade is hot, the rinds will tend to sink a bit. After it has had a chance to cool for a few minutes, the syrup will thicken. Giving it a stir after it has thickened redistributes the rinds. Discard the cheesecloth bag and vanilla pods. Stir one more time so the lemon strips float and get evenly suspended in the marmalade and to disperse the foam and bubbles. Pour the marmalade into sterilized jars, let cool, then seal with the lids and store in the refrigerator. They keep for 2 to 3 weeks, but I've stored them for longer.

Canning Instructions

Set a wire rack in the bottom of a large pot. Fill the pot with water and bring to a simmer. Meanwhile, wash seven 8-ounce (225 ml) jars, lids, and screw bands in very hot soapy water. Rinse them well and place them on the rack in the pot using canning tongs. When the marmalade is done cooking (no need to rest it), carefully remove the jars from the water with the tongs, lightly dry them, and fill them to about ¼ inch (6 mm) from the top. Wipe the rim of each jar clean, place the lid seal-side down, and screw on the band. Return the jars to the rack in the hot water and boil gently for 10 minutes. Remove the jars with the tongs and let cool. The lids will be sucked down, which indicates a tight seal.

Muhammara

PICTURED ON PAGE 357

- 1 cup (130 g) walnuts
- 3 large red bell peppers
- 1 to 2 slices (about 2 ounces/60 g) your favorite leftover bread, torn into pieces
- 2 tablespoons extra-virgin olive oil, plus more for drizzling
- 2 tablespoons Aleppo pepper (see Note)
- 2 tablespoons pomegranate molasses, plus more for drizzling
- 1 tablespoon tahini
- 1 teaspoon fresh lemon juice
- ½ teaspoon kosher salt

Muhammara is a Middle Eastern dip made with walnuts, roasted red pepper, bread, and pomegranate molasses. I first tried it at Seattle's Mamnoon restaurant and have been hooked since. Use leftover Sourdough Salted Miso Baguettes (page 81), Pain de Mie (page 159), or Country White Sourdough Bread (page 86). You could use a seeded bread, too, but I prefer something simple. Serve alongside flatbreads, vegetables, grilled fish, or meats.

MAKES A LITTLE SHY OF 2½ CUPS (625 G)

Preheat the oven to 350°F (180°C).

Place the walnuts on a sheet pan and roast until lightly browned and very nutty smelling, about 10 minutes. Set aside.

Position an oven rack in the upper third of the oven. Increase the oven temperature to broil at 500°F (260°C).

Place the whole bell peppers on a sheet pan and roast, turning occasionally, until the skins are blistered and the peppers soften, 12 to 15 minutes. Transfer the peppers to a large bowl and cover with a plate. The steam trapped in the bowl will soften the peppers even further. Let the peppers sit until cool enough to handle, then peel them and remove and discard the seeds. (Alternatively, you can char and broil the peppers outside on a grill.)

In a food processor, combine the toasted walnuts (reserve a few for topping) and bread and pulse until coarsely chopped. Add the roasted peppers, olive oil, Aleppo pepper, pomegranate molasses, tahini, lemon juice, and salt. Pulse until it forms a smooth paste. Taste and adjust the seasoning, if needed. If the muhammara feels a bit runny, add a little bit more bread. If it feels too thick, add a teaspoon of water.

Transfer the muhammara to a bowl and drizzle with some pomegranate molasses and olive oil. Coarsely chop the reserved walnuts and sprinkle on top. Store leftovers in a mason jar in the refrigerator for up to 1 week.

Note: If you cannot find Aleppo pepper, use 1 tablespoon sweet paprika (you can even add a touch of smoked paprika) plus 1 teaspoon cayenne pepper.

Roasted Cauliflower Hummus with Fried Chickpeas

1 medium head cauliflower (1 pound 5 ounces/600 g), cored and cut into small florets

¼ cup (50 g) extra-virgin olive oil, plus more for frying and drizzling

1 teaspoon kosher salt, plus more to taste

1 teaspoon cumin seeds

One 15-ounce (425 g) can chickpeas, drained

1 garlic clove, peeled but whole

⅓ cup (90 g) well-stirred tahini

2 tablespoons fresh lemon juice, plus more to taste

1 teaspoon harissa powder or smoked paprika, plus more for garnish

2 tablespoons toasted sesame seeds, for garnish

I love the versatility of hummus. Sometimes I make it with canned chickpeas and other times with cooked red lentils. I also add other roasted vegetables in place of cauliflower, such as carrots, celery root, beets, or even marinated artichokes. You can serve it as a dip alongside pita, spread it on toasted bread topped with roasted vegetables and greens, or use it as a base and sauce for roasted chicken or fish.

MAKES ABOUT 3 CUPS (750 G)

Preheat the oven to 400°F (200°C).

On a sheet pan, toss the cauliflower with the olive oil, salt, and cumin seeds and spread evenly. Bake until tender and the edges of the cauliflower are caramelized, about 35 minutes. Let the cauliflower cool for 10 minutes.

In a food processor, combine about 1 cup (165 g) of the chickpeas (reserve the rest for frying) and the garlic and process for 1 minute, or until the chickpeas are broken down. Add the tahini and blend for another minute until it forms a dry paste. Scrape the edges and add the roasted cauliflower. Puree the mixture for 2 minutes. Stop and scrape the sides of the bowl. Add the lemon juice and puree for 3 minutes, or until the hummus is very smooth and creamy. If it appears dry, add warm water 1 tablespoon at a time until you have the desired consistency. Taste and adjust with salt and lemon juice. Store the hummus in the refrigerator, in an airtight container, for up to 7 days.

Pat dry the remaining chickpeas with a paper towel. Heat 1 tablespoon olive oil in a small sauté pan over medium heat. Add the dried chickpeas, a sprinkle of salt, and the harissa powder. Cook the chickpeas, tossing them around, until the exteriors are toasted and lightly golden, about 2 minutes.

To serve the hummus, spread it in a shallow bowl and create some swirls with the back of a spoon. Top with the fried chickpeas, a drizzle of olive oil, toasted sesame seeds, and a sprinkle of harissa powder.

Caponata with Pine Nuts and Fried Bread

½ cup (70 g) pine nuts

¾ cup (165 g) extra-virgin olive oil, plus more for frying the bread

1 large globe eggplant (1½ pounds/680 g), peeled and cut into ½-inch (1.3 cm) pieces

1 teaspoon kosher salt, plus more to taste

½ teaspoon freshly ground black pepper, plus more to taste

1 medium yellow onion, medium diced

1 medium red bell pepper, medium diced

2 celery stalks, thinly sliced

3 garlic cloves, thinly sliced

1 fresh bay leaf (optional)

One 14.5-ounce (411 g) can whole peeled tomatoes and their juices, roughly crushed

¾ cup (90 g) large green olives, pitted and roughly chopped

3 tablespoons salt-packed capers, rinsed

2 tablespoons granulated sugar, plus more to taste

¼ cup (55 g) red or white wine vinegar, plus more to taste

Handful of parsley, finely chopped

Caponata is a Sicilian sweet-and-sour stew of summer's star, the eggplant, augmented with onions, celery, tomatoes, olives, and capers. It is widely adaptable with the addition of peppers, fennel, carrots, or raisins. Caponata is usually served as a salad or relish to accompany grilled fish or meat, or on bread as a starter.

The eggplant can be cooked many different ways. It can be roasted, stewed with the rest of the vegetables, or fried like I do in this recipe. When fried, it will have a bit more of a bite and not become mushy. I find the key to a great caponata is the balance of salt, sugar, and acid. There is a bit of sugar and vinegar in the recipe, but taste your vegetables, because their own sweetness will alter the balance of the entire dish. Caponata is supposed to be a little saucy, although not soupy, so adjust the amount of liquid if it feels dry or if your tomatoes are very watery. You can use fresh Roma tomatoes, but make sure they are very ripe and peeled.

SERVES 6

Warm a medium sauté pan over medium heat. Add the pine nuts and toss them around until they smell nutty and toasted, 1 to 2 minutes. Set aside.

Heat a large sauté pan over medium-high heat. Add ¼ cup (55 g) of the olive oil and about half of the eggplant so it can be in a single layer. Do not overcrowd the pan or the eggplant will steam instead of fry. Cook the eggplant until lightly browned, about 2 minutes. Turn the pieces so they brown on the other side. Transfer the fried eggplant to a large plate. Add another ¼ cup (55 g) olive oil to the pan and cook the rest of the eggplant. Season the eggplant with ½ teaspoon of the salt and ¼ teaspoon of the black pepper. Set aside.

Heat the pan you used for the eggplant over medium heat. Add the remaining ¼ cup (55 g) olive oil, the onion, bell pepper, celery, garlic, bay leaf, and the remaining ½ teaspoon salt and ¼ teaspoon black pepper. Stir everything together and cook until tender, about 7 minutes.

Add the fried eggplant, tomatoes, olives, capers, sugar, and vinegar to the pan and cook until the vegetables fall apart and the liquid is

6 slices crusty bread, preferably Seeded Whole-Grain Teff Sourdough Boule (page 61) or Country White Sourdough Bread (page 86)

reduced slightly, about 7 minutes. Remember that caponata should be a little saucy, so add a little bit of water if it appears dry. Adjust the seasoning with salt, pepper, sugar, and vinegar, if needed.

Toss in the parsley and toasted pine nuts and set aside for 30 minutes so it mellows out a little bit. Caponata can be served lukewarm, at room temperature, or cold. It will keep in the refrigerator for up to 1 week. I like mine lukewarm or at room temperature, so if refrigerated, I allow it to come to temperature before serving.

When ready to serve, fry the bread. Heat a cast-iron skillet or sauté pan over medium-high heat. Add enough olive oil to coat the bottom of the pan and place the slices of bread in it. You might have to fry the bread in batches depending on the size of your pan. Cook the bread until golden brown on both sides, 3 to 4 minutes per side.

Top the fried bread with spoonfuls of caponata and serve immediately.

Fattoush with Fried Pita and Labneh

Fattoush, which is a traditional Lebanese salad, is the perfect fresh and crisp salad to serve on a warm summer day. Ripe tomatoes, cucumbers, and greens are tossed with a garlicky sour vinaigrette made with lemon juice, sumac, and pomegranate molasses, then all topped with freshly fried day-old pita bread. Purslane is a traditional green used in fattoush, but it is not readily available in most US supermarkets, so I didn't include it in the recipe. (I can find it only at the farmers market in the spring, though, of course, it can be foraged.) The vinaigrette is supposed to be sour, but different brands of pomegranate molasses vary in acidity, so balance it out with a touch of honey, if needed.

SERVES 6

FOR THE PITA CHIPS

2 Pillowy Pita (page 272)

2 tablespoons extra-virgin olive oil

¼ teaspoon kosher salt

FOR THE VINAIGRETTE

⅓ cup (70 g) extra-virgin olive oil

2 tablespoons fresh lemon juice

2 tablespoons pomegranate molasses

1 garlic clove, finely minced

2 teaspoons sumac

1 teaspoon kosher salt, plus more to taste

¼ teaspoon freshly ground black pepper

FOR THE SALAD

1 head romaine or butter lettuce, washed and cut into large pieces

2 medium tomatoes, cut into large pieces, or 2 cups (300 g) cherry tomatoes, halved

1 medium cucumber, peeled and cut into large pieces

6 radishes, greens trimmed, thinly sliced

2 scallions, sliced

¼ red onion, thinly sliced

Handful of fresh Italian parsley leaves

Handful of fresh mint leaves

¾ cup (170 g) labneh, Greek yogurt, or vegan Greek-style yogurt

Make the pita chips. Line a plate with paper towels and set near the stove. Break the pita bread into bite-size pieces. Heat a medium sauté pan over medium heat. Add the olive oil, pita, and salt and fry the pita, tossing frequently, until browned, about 2 minutes. Transfer the pita chips to the paper towels. Set aside.

Make the vinaigrette. In a medium bowl, whisk together the olive oil, lemon juice, pomegranate molasses, garlic, sumac, salt, and pepper until emulsified. (Alternatively, pour the ingredients into a screw-top jar, seal, and shake until emulsified.) Adjust the salt if needed and set aside.

Make the salad. In a large bowl, toss together the lettuce, tomatoes, cucumber, radishes, scallions, red onion, parsley, and mint. Add the vinaigrette and toss until well coated. Add half of the fried pita chips and toss together.

Spread the labneh on the bottom of a serving platter and top with the fattoush. Top with the remaining pita chips and serve immediately.

Roasted Delicata Squash, Apple, and Bread Salad with Almond Aioli

FOR THE CROUTONS

¼ cup (50 g) extra-virgin olive oil

2 teaspoons Dijon mustard

2 teaspoons honey

1½ teaspoons (6 g) kosher salt

½ teaspoon ground coriander

½ teaspoon freshly ground black pepper

1 medium delicata squash (1½ pounds/680 g), peeled, seeded, and cut into ¼- to ½-inch (6 mm to 1.3 cm) rounds

8 ounces (225 g) day-old bread, cut or torn in 1-inch (2.5 cm) pieces

FOR THE SALAD

Almond Aioli (recipe follows)

2 tablespoons fresh lemon juice, plus more as needed

4 cups (260 g) thinly sliced kale or thinly shaved Brussels sprouts

1 medium sweet, juicy apple, thinly sliced

A large handful of fresh dill fronds

FOR THE AIOLI

1 cup (100 g) sliced almonds

6 tablespoons (75 g) extra-virgin olive oil

6 tablespoons (90 g) water

2 tablespoons Dijon mustard

1 large garlic clove, peeled

¾ teaspoon kosher salt

Delicata squash has thin and edible skin and the flesh is extraordinarily sweet and creamy when roasted. Good choices for the croutons would be a Seeded Whole-Grain Teff Sourdough Boule (page 61) or Country White Sourdough Bread (page 86). The salad is tossed with an almond aioli that would also make a great dressing as a substitute for a Caesar salad or spread for a sandwich.

SERVES 4 TO 6

Preheat the oven to 400°F (200°C).

Roast the squash and bread croutons. In a medium bowl, whisk together the olive oil, mustard, honey, salt, coriander, and pepper. On a sheet pan, toss together the squash and bread pieces with the olive oil mixture until well coated. Try to keep everything in a single layer even if the pan is a little crowded. Bake until the squash is tender and golden brown and the bread is crispy and well toasted, 25 to 30 minutes.

Assemble the salad. In a large serving bowl, whisk together ½ cup (120 g) of the almond aioli and the lemon juice. Add a bit more lemon juice if the dressing feels too thick. Toss in the kale, apple, and dill and massage all the ingredients together until well coated. Top with the roasted squash and croutons and give it one light toss. Serve with the remaining aioli on the side.

Almond Aioli

MAKES ABOUT 1 CUP (240 G)

In a high-powered blender or food processor, combine the almonds, olive oil, water, mustard, garlic, and salt and puree until creamy and smooth. Add 1 tablespoon more water if needed. Stop the blender and scrape the sides, then puree again until light in color. Keep the almond aioli in an airtight container in the refrigerator for up to 3 days.

Mustard Mushroom and Lemony Swiss Chard Wraps

This is one of my favorite savory breakfasts during the cold months. I eat two of these before I am out the door and sometimes add fried eggs on top to keep me satisfied until lunchtime. It takes 10 minutes to cook, and you can use any other green you might have in your fridge, like spinach, mustard greens, beet greens, and even kale.

SERVES 2 TO 4

FOR THE MUSHROOMS

2 tablespoons extra-virgin olive oil

2 garlic cloves, thinly sliced

10 ounces (300 g) oyster or chanterelle mushrooms, torn into bite-size pieces

Small pinch of red pepper flakes

A couple of thyme sprigs

Pinch of kosher salt

1 tablespoon whole-grain mustard

1 tablespoon Dijon mustard

FOR THE SWISS CHARD

1 tablespoon extra-virgin olive oil

8 medium Swiss chard leaves, tough stems removed and chopped

Pinch of kosher salt

Grated zest and juice of 1 medium lemon

FOR ASSEMBLY

4 Whisk-and-Pour Oat Roti (page 291)

3½ ounces (100 g) soft cheese (goat, ricotta, cream cheese, or a vegan soft cheese)

⅓ cup (50 g) toasted walnuts, coarsely chopped

A few mint leaves, torn (optional)

Cook the mushrooms. Heat a large sauté pan over medium-high heat. Add the olive oil and garlic and cook for a few seconds. Add the mushrooms, pepper flakes, and thyme and stir and cook until the mushrooms are lightly caramelized and browned, 4 to 5 minutes. Add the salt, whole-grain mustard, and Dijon mustard. Stir everything together, then transfer the mushrooms to a plate.

Cook the Swiss chard. Return the pan to medium-high heat. Add the olive oil, Swiss chard, and salt. Stir together for a minute until the chard is wilted. Add the lemon zest and juice and cook for another 1 to 2 minutes, until the chard is completely wilted. Set aside.

Assemble the wraps. Heat the roti in a skillet. Spread the soft cheese on the roti. Top with the mushrooms, Swiss chard, toasted walnuts, and some mint (if using). Serve immediately.

Caramelized Carrot, Sourdough, and Miso Soup

2 tablespoons extra-virgin olive oil

2 pounds (900 g) carrots, peeled and cut into 1-inch (2.5 cm) pieces

1 large onion, finely chopped

4 garlic cloves, peeled

¾ teaspoon kosher salt

1 large slice (3 ounces/90 g) Seeded Whole-Grain Teff Sourdough Boule (page 61) or any other whole-grain sourdough bread, toasted and torn into pieces, plus more for serving

¼ cup (75 g) white (shiro) miso

6 cups (1.35 L) vegetable or chicken stock, plus more as needed

2 tablespoons fresh lime juice

Toasted sesame seeds, for sprinkling

Harissa powder, for sprinkling

Sesame oil, for drizzling

This sweet, tangy, and a little smoky soup is made by lightly blackening carrots in the pot before adding the rest of the ingredients. The miso and bread round out the flavors and turn it into a creamy soup.

SERVES 4

Heat a large soup pot or Dutch oven over medium-high heat. Add the olive oil and carrots and cook until they begin to caramelize, 7 to 10 minutes. Keep them in a single layer, if possible, so all pieces are in contact with the bottom of the pan and can brown. Add the onion, garlic, and salt and cook until the carrots are lightly blackened around the edges, about 5 minutes.

Add the bread pieces and miso, stir, and cook for 30 seconds. Add the stock and bring to a simmer. Cover the pot, reduce the heat to medium-low, and cook for 20 minutes.

Puree the hot soup in batches in a blender or use an immersion blender. Add a bit more stock or water if the soup feels too thick. Stir in the lime juice.

To serve, ladle the soup into bowls and top with toasted pieces of bread, toasted sesame seeds, a pinch of harissa powder, and a small drizzle of sesame oil.

Mediterranean Artichoke and Spinach Omelet Sandwiches

FOR THE OLIVE TAPENADE

1 cup (140 g) pitted Kalamata olives

1 garlic clove, peeled

2 tablespoons finely chopped fresh parsley

2 tablespoons extra-virgin olive oil

1 tablespoon capers, drained and rinsed

1 tablespoon fresh lemon juice

1 teaspoon Dijon mustard

1 teaspoon finely chopped preserved lemon or finely grated lemon zest

FOR THE SPINACH OMELET

4 large eggs

1 teaspoon kosher salt

2 tablespoons extra-virgin olive oil

1 cup (50 g) fresh spinach

FOR THE SANDWICHES

2 Mini Whole-Grain Walnut Baguettes (page 172), sliced in half crosswise and toasted

¼ cup (125 g) Almond Aioli (page 372)

8 marinated artichoke quarters

Handful of fresh dill fronds

Bocadillo de tortilla francesa was one of my favorite snacks when I was growing up. A simple one-egg omelet is made with a touch of olive oil and salt and stuffed inside a crusty baguette. To this day, it is one of my favorite breakfasts, and if I didn't have to cook for the rest of my family, I would be happy eating it for dinner nearly every night. This recipe elevates that idea with the addition of spinach, artichokes, olive tapenade, and almond aioli. I like to make it with the mini walnut baguettes listed here, but the Sourdough Salted Miso Baguettes (page 81) would work as well.

MAKES 2 SANDWICHES

Make the olive tapenade. In a food processor, combine the olives, garlic, parsley, olive oil, capers, lemon juice, mustard, and preserved lemon and pulse until it forms a chunky paste. Store in an airtight container in the refrigerator for up to 7 days.

Make the spinach omelet. In a medium bowl, beat together the eggs and salt. Heat a 10-inch (25 cm) nonstick or well-seasoned cast-iron pan over medium-high heat. Add the olive oil and spinach and cook until the spinach is wilted, about 1 minute. Add the eggs and swirl them around with a wooden spoon. Cook for 30 seconds, then lift one end of the omelet and fold it in half. Flip the omelet and cook for 30 seconds. Slide it onto a plate and cut the omelet in half.

Assemble the sandwiches. Spread a generous amount of the olive tapenade on one half of a baguette and the almond aioli on the other. Place half of the omelet on the olive tapenade. Top with marinated artichokes and dill, then cover with the other half of the baguette. Repeat and assemble the second sandwich with the remaining ingredients. Serve immediately.

Melty Beet and Sauerkraut Reubens

Thinly sliced beets are coated in a pickling spice blend, then roasted until tender. Serve them on marble rye-style bread with sauerkraut, melty Swiss cheese, and creamy dressing and you won't miss the meat.

MAKES 4 SANDWICHES

FOR THE BEET PASTRAMI

4 medium (1 pound/455 g) red beets, peeled

2 tablespoons extra-virgin olive oil

1 tablespoon light brown sugar

1½ teaspoons (6 g) kosher salt

1 teaspoon mustard powder

1 teaspoon ground coriander

½ teaspoon garlic powder

½ teaspoon onion powder

½ teaspoon smoked paprika

⅛ teaspoon ground cloves

FOR THE DRESSING

½ cup (125 g) mayonnaise or Almond Aioli (page 372)

2 tablespoons ketchup

1 tablespoon finely minced shallot

1 teaspoon Worcestershire sauce

1 teaspoon smoked paprika

FOR THE SANDWICHES

4 tablespoons (55 g) unsalted butter or vegan butter

8 slices Marble Rye-Style Loaf (page 162)

4 to 8 slices Swiss cheese or vegan cheese

2 cups (280 g) sauerkraut

2 dill pickles, sliced lengthwise

Preheat the oven to 375°F (190°C).

Make the beet pastrami. Use a mandoline to cut the beets into very thin slices; they should be paper thin and bendable. Place the beet slices in a large bowl. Drizzle the beets with the olive oil.

In a medium bowl, stir together the brown sugar, salt, mustard powder, coriander, garlic powder, onion powder, paprika, and cloves. Add the spices to the bowl with the beets and massage together so the spices are evenly distributed. Line a sheet pan with parchment paper and spread the beet slices on it. It's okay if some slices overlap, but try spreading them out as much as possible. You might need a second sheet pan if it seems overcrowded.

Bake the beets until they are cooked but still have a bite, 13 to 15 minutes. Do not overcook them or they will become crispy. Set aside.

Make the dressing. In a medium bowl, whisk together the mayonnaise, ketchup, shallot, Worcestershire sauce, and paprika. Set aside.

Assemble the sandwiches. Heat a large cast-iron pan over medium-high heat. Spread ½ tablespoon of the butter on one side of each slice of bread. Place 4 slices of bread (or fewer if your pan isn't big enough) in the pan butter-side down. Toast one side and flip over to toast the other. Spread a tablespoon of the dressing on the bread slices, top with one-quarter of the beet pastrami, 1 or 2 slices of cheese, ½ cup (70 g) sauerkraut, and some pickles. Spread some dressing on the unbuttered side of the other slices of bread and flip them dressing-side down onto the pickles, so the buttered sides are face up. Cover the pan with a lid and cook for 2 minutes, until the bread is toasted on the bottom. Flip the sandwiches over and cook until the cheese is melted, about 2 minutes. Serve immediately, while hot.

Honeyed Pears on Chunky Peanut Butter Toast

I am not one for sweet breakfast, but this toast with salty chunky peanut butter and honeyed buttery pears hits the spot. You can use store-bought chunky peanut butter, but here you can see how easy it is to make it yourself.

SERVES 4

FOR THE PEANUT BUTTER

2 cups (300 g) raw peanuts

1 tablespoon maple syrup or honey

2 to 3 teaspoons peanut oil

1 teaspoon kosher salt

FOR THE HONEYED PEARS

2 tablespoons unsalted butter or vegan butter

2 firm-ripe medium Bosc pears, peeled, quartered, and cored

2 tablespoons honey

1 to 2 tablespoons fresh lemon juice

2 thyme sprigs

Pinch of kosher salt

TO SERVE

4 slices Nordic-Style Seed Bread (page 66), toasted

Freshly ground black pepper (optional)

Preheat the oven to 350°F (180°C).

Make the peanut butter. Place the peanuts on a sheet pan and roast them until they are toasted and smell nutty, 7 to 10 minutes, shaking the pan halfway through. Let them cool for 15 minutes.

Measure out ⅓ cup (50 g) of the peanuts and pulse in a food processor several times until you have very small pieces (but don't pulverize them). Transfer to a bowl and set aside. Add the remaining peanuts to the food processor and blend them for a minute until they are chunky. Scrape the sides and continue processing until you have a smooth paste. Add the maple syrup, peanut oil, and salt and process until smooth. If it feels too chunky, you can add a few drops of warm water. Fold in the reserved peanut pieces and transfer to a jar.

Make the honeyed pears. Warm a medium sauté pan over medium heat. Add the butter and swirl it around. Arrange the pears in the pan, cut-side down, and drizzle with the honey and lemon juice and add the thyme sprigs and salt. As the pears cook, they will release juices that will mix with the butter and honey. Spoon these juices and baste the pears with them as you go. Don't let the honey burn, so reduce the heat if necessary. Cook the pears until tender but not falling apart, about 5 minutes.

Serve. Spread the peanut butter over the toasted bread and top with the pears and the pan juices. Sprinkle with a pinch of black pepper, if desired.

Charred Broccolini and Marinated Artichokes with Romesco on Ciabatta

One of my favorite summertime snacks is a thick piece of toasted ciabatta with a good layer of romesco and sliced tomatoes on top. This sandwich has that same ethos behind it, but with a few more elements like charred broccolini for a little smokiness, marinated artichokes for acidity, and melted cheese for extra creaminess.

MAKES 4 SANDWICHES

FOR THE BROCCOLINI

2 tablespoons extra-virgin olive oil

1 pound (455 g) broccolini, tough ends trimmed, stalks halved if thick

½ teaspoon kosher salt

2 tablespoons water

FOR THE SANDWICHES

4 Sourdough Ciabatta Rolls (page 93)

½ cup (125 g) Romesco Sauce (recipe follows)

8 whole marinated artichoke hearts, halved

½ medium cucumber, thinly sliced

4 ounces (115 g) provolone, fresh mozzarella, or vegan mozzarella-style cheese

Preheat the oven to 425°F (220°C).

Char the broccolini. Heat a large cast-iron pan over medium-high heat. Add the olive oil and enough broccolini to fill the pan in a single layer. You might have to cook it in 2 batches if it doesn't all fit. Season with the salt. Cook, undisturbed, until the broccolini has charred on one side, about 5 minutes. Flip and char on the other side for 2 minutes. Add the water, cover the pan, and continue cooking until the broccolini is tender, 2 to 3 minutes.

Assemble the sandwiches. Slice the ciabatta rolls in half. Spread the romesco sauce on both sides. Top each ciabatta half with 4 artichoke halves, some cucumber slices, charred broccolini, and provolone. Top with the other ciabatta half. Place the sandwiches on a sheet pan and place in the oven for 5 to 10 minutes to melt the cheese. Serve immediately.

Romesco Sauce

MAKES ABOUT 1 CUP (250 G)

FOR THE ROMESCO SAUCE

1 garlic clove, peeled

½ cup (60 g) sliced almonds

2 large pieces jarred roasted red bell pepper

2 tablespoons tomato sauce

2 tablespoons red wine vinegar

1 tablespoon finely chopped fresh parsley

1 teaspoon Spanish pimentón de la Vera or smoked paprika

½ teaspoon fine sea salt

¼ teaspoon cayenne pepper

½ cup (115 g) olive oil

In a food processor, combine the garlic and almonds and pulse until the almonds are finely ground, about 2 minutes. Add the roasted peppers, tomato sauce, vinegar, parsley, pimentón, salt, and cayenne and process until smooth, about 1 minute. Scrape the sides of the bowl, then with the machine running, steadily drizzle in the olive oil. This makes more sauce than you will need for this recipe. Transfer the remaining romesco to a jar and refrigerate for up to 1 week.

Pan-Fried Butter Beans on Romesco Toast

If you have romesco on hand, this sandwich is a breeze to pull together. Open a can of butter beans, cook them with garlic and chili until crispy, and serve on toast with romesco. So simple and so nutritious.

SERVES 4

FOR THE PAN-FRIED BUTTER BEANS

3 tablespoons extra-virgin olive oil

2 garlic cloves, smashed and peeled

4 thyme sprigs

One 15-ounce (425 g) can butter beans or cannellini beans, drained, rinsed, and patted dry

½ teaspoon kosher salt

⅛ teaspoon red pepper flakes

FOR ASSEMBLY

½ cup (125 g) Romesco Sauce (page 385)

4 slices Seeded Whole-Grain Teff Sourdough Boule (page 66) or any other hearty bread, toasted

Handful of baby arugula or microgreens (optional)

Handful of fresh dill fronds (optional)

Extra-virgin olive oil, for drizzling

Freshly ground black pepper

Pan-fry the butter beans. Heat a medium sauté pan over medium-low heat. Add the olive oil, garlic, and thyme and cook, swirling the pan around, until the garlic and thyme infuse the oil and the garlic begins to caramelize slightly, 1 to 2 minutes. Add the butter beans, salt, and pepper flakes. Stir and cook until the beans are slightly golden and crispy, 5 to 7 minutes. You can discard the garlic and thyme, although I like to keep them.

Assemble the toasts. Spread a generous layer of the romesco on the toasted bread. Top with the pan-fried butter beans, some greens, the dill (if using), a drizzle of olive oil, and a pinch of black pepper. Serve immediately.

FOR THE TOMATO CONFIT

- 1 pound (455 g) cherry tomatoes, halved
- ½ cup (100 g) extra-virgin olive oil
- Pinch of saffron (about 25 threads)
- 1 teaspoon fresh oregano leaves
- 1 teaspoon kosher salt
- ½ teaspoon freshly ground black pepper

FOR THE EGGPLANT

- 1 eggplant (1½ pounds/680 g), sliced into rounds ½ inch (1.3 cm) thick
- 6 tablespoons (75 g) extra-virgin olive oil
- 2 teaspoons za'atar
- 1½ teaspoons kosher salt
- 1 teaspoon freshly ground black pepper

FOR ASSEMBLY

- 6 Pillowy Pita (page 272), halved crosswise into pockets
- 1 cup (250 g) roasted cauliflower hummus (see page 367)
- ½ cup (125 g) Almond Aioli (page 372)
- Large handful of microgreens or sprouts (optional)

Charred Eggplant and Saffron Tomato Confit Stuffed Pita

When you keep a refrigerator full of condiments, sauces, and spreads, you can use them at any moment to add layers of flavor to a sandwich. The roasted cauliflower hummus, Almond Aioli, and this saffron tomato confit are great examples of this. Keep the leftovers in the fridge and they can elevate another recipe. The charred eggplant takes on a smoky flavor that is beautiful next to the bright tomato confit. This sandwich takes some of my favorite components and puts them together in a single bite.

SERVES 6

Make the tomato confit. Heat a medium sauté pan over medium heat and add the tomatoes, olive oil, saffron, oregano, salt, and pepper. Stir the mixture and when the oil starts to sizzle, reduce the heat to medium-low and simmer, stirring every 10 minutes, until the tomatoes are soft, about 30 minutes. Remove the pan from the heat and let the tomatoes cool in the pan. (The confit can be made up to 3 days in advance and kept in a mason jar in the refrigerator.)

Char the eggplant. Brush the eggplant slices with the olive oil and sprinkle with the za'atar, salt, and pepper. Heat a grill pan or cast-iron pan over high heat. Add the eggplant slices in a single layer, reduce the heat to medium-high, and cook until charred, 3 to 4 minutes. Flip the slices and grill until the other side is charred and tender, 3 to 4 minutes. You can leave the slices as they are or coarsely chop them.

Assemble the pita. Warm the pita lightly on the hot pan for a few seconds. Spread the hummus on one side of the split pita halves and the aioli on the other. Fill with the tomato confit and charred eggplant and top with the microgreens, if using. Serve immediately.

Resources

FLOURS

Anthony's Goods
anthonysgoods.com

Arrowhead Mills
arrowheadmills.com

Authentic Foods
authenticfoods.com

Big Bold Health
bigboldhealth.com

Bob's Red Mill
bobsredmill.com

PSYLLIUM

Frontier Co-Op
frontiercoop.com

Himalaya Wellness
himalayausa.com

Terrasoul
terrasoul.com

DUTCH OVENS

Challenger Breadware
challengerbreadware.com

Lodge
lodgecastiron.com

Smithey Ironware
smithey.com

Staub
zwilling.com

LOAF PANS

Chicago Metallic
cmbakeware.com

Nordic Ware
nordicware.com

USA Pan
usapan.com

STAND MIXER

KitchenAid
kitchenaid.com

OTHER TOOLS AND INGREDIENTS

BakeDeco (panettone molds)
bakedeco.com

King Arthur Baking Company (bread knife)
kingarthurbaking.com

Miele (oven range)
mieleusa.com

Preserved (food-grade lye)
preservedgoods.com

Wire Monkey (lame)
wiremonkey.com

Acknowledgments

This book was made possible because of so many generous friends, colleagues, but most important, all of you readers who have supported my work, bought my books, participated in my classes, and encouraged me to keep developing recipes. I see you.

Thank you to my editor Judy Pray for giving me time and helping me shape this book. Thank you to the rest of the Artisan team. Judy Linden, my agent of fifteen years, thank you for opening my horizons.

Thank you to my dear friend Dorothée Brand for the most beautiful portraits. Naomi Devlin, thank you for answering some of the in-depth sourdough starter questions. Sharyn Sowell for all the hours you spent cheering me on and meticulously testing nearly all the recipes in the book. Thank you to all the recipe testers who generously gave me time and much appreciated feedback: Allegra D'Agostini, Jacque Altman, Hilary Bovay, Ingrid Emery, Samantha Gainsburg, Carley Knobloch, Carrie Krueger, Chris Park, Kate Roseiro Marks, Sheila Vyas, and Elyse Lankford.

Thank you Dan Souza, Kenji López-Alt, Liz Prueitt, Maurizio Leo, and Zoë François for your endorsements and kind words about this book and for being a huge inspiration in my baking and cookbook writing journey.

Thank you to my family in the Basque Country: Amatxu, Aitatxu, Jokin, Jon. Eskerrik asko. And to the Ayarza clan for giving me the one skill that has allowed me to be creative in life. To my family, in Seattle or wherever we may end up, Chad, Jontxu, Mirentxu. You give my life purpose and meaning.

Index

Note: Italic page numbers indicate photos.

Q

R

S

The Author

Aran Goyoaga is a professionally trained chef, cookbook author, food stylist, and photographer. Aran was born and raised in the Basque Country in northern Spain, where her maternal grandparents owned a pastry shop and her paternal grandparents lived off the land. Aran is a three-time James Beard Award finalist. She lives in Seattle with her husband and two children.